SO-AXJ-643

Concise English Handbook

Third Edition

James W. Kirkland
East Carolina University

Collett B. Dilworth, Jr.
East Carolina University

D. C. Heath and Company
Lexington, Massachusetts   Toronto

Address editorial correspondence to:

D. C. Heath and Company
125 Spring Street
Lexington, MA 02173

For Paula and Jeremi

Acquisitions Editor: Paul A. Smith
Developmental Editor: Linda M. Bieze
Production Editor: Andrea Cava
Designer: Judith Miller
Production Coordinator: Charles Dutton
Permissions Editor: Margaret Roll

Acknowledgments: Article on pp. 478–484 from "Guiding Students Through Research Papers" by Bruce Tone in *Journal of Reading.*

Copyright © 1994 by D. C. Heath and Company.

Previous editions copyright © 1990, 1985 by D. C. Heath and Company.

All rights reserved. No part of this publication may be reproduced or transmitted in any form or by any means, electronic or mechanical, including photocopy, recording, or any information storage or retrieval system, without permission in writing from the publisher.

Published simultaneously in Canada.

Printed in the United States of America.

International Standard Book Number: 0-669-29708-9 (Student Edition)
International Standard Book Number: 0-669-29709-7 (Instructor's Edition)

Library of Congress Catalog Number: 93-70374

10   9   8   7   6   5   4   3

To the Instructor

The *Concise English Handbook,* Third Edition, is based on the principle that writing is a purposeful process involving discovery, precision in thought and language, and sensitivity to audience.

The *Handbook* offers succinct guidance in the processes of writing and in the features of edited American English. It is more than a grammar book although it does treat grammatical topics; it is more than simply a compendium of "rules" although it does survey the conventions of edited American English. Instead, this is a manual emphasizing how writers think and how writing affects readers. For example, the text not only defines and illustrates types of modifiers, it also discusses the contexts in which writers use modifiers and identifies the effects they have on readers; it not only defines and illustrates common writing errors, it discusses why writers make such errors and identifies their undesirable effects on readers.

The book's organization reflects the essential task confronting writers. Writing occurs in a context that influences the writer throughout the process, from conception of subject to choice of particular words. The *Handbook,* therefore, first addresses the process as a whole and then examines crucial aspects such as determining purpose and perspective, generating ideas, and arranging material. The focus then narrows to the particulars of structuring sentences, choosing the most appropriate words, and punctuating. We introduce sentence errors in a separate section because we believe that only after students understand the nature of the writing process can they intelligently identify and correct sentence errors in the context of their own writing.

This arrangement permits students to read the chapters sequentially, thus gaining a systematic orientation to the processes and technicalities of composition. Chapters 1–7 and 10–18 are especially helpful in explaining writing methods and stylistic options. Chapters 8 and 9 offer background in basic grammatical terminology, terminology useful in thinking about the English sentence. Other topics in the book include spelling, writing for special purposes, and writing the research paper.

The *Handbook* has also been designed for use as a reference. Students may refer to the chart inside the front cover to locate the major topics, which are numbered and organized in eight main parts. The pages in each part are marked with colored tabs visible on the page edges when the book is closed; so, using the labels on the back cover, students can quickly locate each part and the topic numbers within it.

In addition, the *Concise English Handbook,* Third Edition, provides succinct definitions of terms; clear supporting examples, including drafts of student writing; exercises designed to help students understand and practice the principles discussed in each chapter; and a detailed research section based on the MLA parenthetical documentation style.

The third edition includes the following additions and revisions.

- A new chapter providing an overview of the punctuation system
- An expanded section on computer use in composition and research
- An expanded and revised chapter on arranging and drafting
- Fuller treatment of critical thinking
- New exercises on nonsexist language
- A new, fully annotated student research paper based on MLA documentation style
- Thirty percent more exercises in Parts II–V

Acknowledgments

Ten years ago, the first edition of the *Concise English Handbook* was published. Many people have helped us prepare and revise the book during these years. We express special appreciation to Craig Kirkland for his assistance in composing new exercises for the third edition. We are also most grateful to Paul Smith and Linda Bieze of D. C. Heath for their guidance and encouragement, to Andrea Cava for production editing, and to Judith Miller for design.

We thank our many students who provided their writing as examples in the text, especially Lisa Baumann, Marty Cherry, Charlotte Crews, Lisa Edwards, Ashley Hinkle, Lisa Anne Oughton, Chan Starling, and Bob Owens.

We are indebted to the scholars and teachers who reviewed this text in manuscript and gave us invaluable advice: Lynn Beene, The University of New Mexico; Thomas G. Beverage, Coastal Carolina Community College; Barbara R. Carson, University of Georgia; Linda J. Daigle, Houston Community College; Robert Dees, Orange Coast College; Kathleen Fitzgerald, The University of Utah; James Helvey, Davidson County Community College; Tim D. P. Lally, University of South Alabama; Kathleen Latimer, Central State University; Lee Ann Leeson, Pepperdine University; Joseph Lostracco, Austin Community College; Helen H. Mackay, Elon College; Elaine M. Miller, Seton Hall University; Terry Miller, Indian River Community College; Elizabeth C. Mitchell, Ocean County College; Arthur A. Molitierno, Wright State University; John V. Pastoor, Montcalm Community College; Allen Ramsey, Central Missouri State University; Alice B. Royer, Pennsylvania State University; Gail Rung, Black Hawk College; Thomas N. Salter, Eastern

Connecticut State College; Laurel A. Smith, Vincennes University; Brooks Thorlaksson, California State University, Chico; Evelyn B. Thornton, Texas Southern University; Samuel Watson, Jr., The University of North Carolina at Charlotte; William H. Wiatt, Indiana University; William F. Woods, Wichita State University; and Stephen F. Wozniak, Palomar College.

To the Student

The main goals of the *Concise English Handbook*, Third Edition, are to help you become a better writer and to help you find rewards in better writing. Thus, the book treats features of the writing process and elements of sentences and paragraphs not as mechanical parts to be assembled according to rigid formulas, but as options at the disposal of your creativity. As you refine your ability to exercise these options, you will find your consciousness developing in ways unique to writers.

Contents

II Structuring Sentences

III   Writing with Precision and Control

V Avoiding Common Sentence Errors

VI   Eliminating Spelling Problems

VII   Writing for Special Purposes

1 · Introduction

1a Literacy

Writing, as we use the term in this book, is more than an encoding of speech sounds; it is an act of literacy. Literate people spend important parts of their lives making meaning by reading and writing because, among all the ways of communicating, written texts are uniquely efficient and powerful. For example, consider the text of a note intercepted one Friday by the teacher of a high school English class:

All tonight I know my hands will be rough handling other players and / footballs. This will ~~still~~ be important to our school. All our friends will be pulling for me and for every player. but what ever I touch all game I will really be trying to touch your heart.

    We might dismiss this note as adolescent emoting unless we examine the writing in its context. The writer, a defensive lineman, had a particular audience of one in mind: his girlfriend. And he had a particular objective in mind: to communicate his feelings for her. The note was not meant to be read by anyone else, so the teacher later forwarded it without comment to the young woman. But clearly the young man wanted the message to be read, not heard. He had used writing to compose a special thought based on a figurative contrast particularly meaningful to him. The thought was that his efforts on the football field that night, while important to the entire school, would also be intended especially for his girlfriend. The figurative contrast is between physically manhandling other football players and psychologically touching her affections. The writer took some care to revise his work by deleting, adding, and substituting words to make his message more accurate and less redundant.

Obviously his proofreading overlooked errors in capitalization, spelling, and punctuation. Nevertheless, the note demonstrates the essential virtue of written composition: It joined the boy and the girl, the writer and the reader, as a community of meaning-makers through a medium that offers an unmatched blend of convenience and power.

The full benefits of reading and writing, however, occur only for those who adopt the spirit of literacy. This spirit directs people to be alert to life and its possibilities. It encourages them to seek new ways of living and to share new experiences, new feelings, new knowledge, and new ways of thinking about problems. Without this spirit, reading and writing are useful only in maintaining records; with this spirit, reading and writing can foster the growth of consciousness for a lifetime.

1b The practical good of composition

Such benefits are rarely appreciated by people who have either not had or not taken the opportunity to enjoy the fruits of literacy. Students who view writing as merely the imitation of incomprehensible models wonder bitterly why schools require the formal practice of writing. As we have suggested, the basic objective of composition in the curriculum is to help students acquire and strengthen the spirit of literacy. For people without the spirit, practical reasons for developing composition skills are unconvincing. Motivated people, however, are encouraged by the specific practical rationale that writing can help increase the power to think.

When, as a writer, you observe yourself and the world, you are compelled to try to achieve such tasks as these: demonstrating which phenomena are related, establishing what something is, showing how or why something functions, proving the merit of a belief, predicting what will happen, and creating an impression of what took place. This effort helps you to originate thoughts and feelings and give them an enduring presence. Writing to explain or argue or share your feelings helps you to select the crucial features of experience, to manipulate them intellectually, and, as a result, to reach conclusions and insights. For example, the high school football player quoted earlier selected aspects of his experience, linked them, made predictions about them, and thus clarified and perhaps strengthened how he felt.

Of course, the social rationale for the study and practice of composition is that it makes for good communication. For a democracy to exist, its citizens must undertake thoughtful, careful discourse, and literate discourse is the means for our most thoughtful, most careful communication in language. The lack of an ability to communicate literately handicaps citizens trying to inform themselves on how best to govern, and if they lose the abilities of self-government, they will lose self-government as well as the rights that go with it. Composition persists throughout the school curriculum, therefore, because citizens in general and educators in particular are convinced that it can help foster the flexible strength of mind required for a full, productive life—the type of life that enriches the individual and our democracy.

1c The writing process

We have defined writing as an act of literacy. This act is commonly understood as a process involving the functions outlined below.

1. *Inventing and planning.*   As good writers begin their work, they spend time thinking about the task ahead of them. They get an image of their audience and of the reasons they are addressing this audience. They decide on their topic and on how broadly they will treat it. They search their own knowledge and attitudes for relevant information, and they may consult external sources, such as libraries and other knowledgeable people. They make tentative plans for the way their writing will be organized, and they tentatively adopt a "voice," or an attitude toward their topic and audience.

2. *Drafting.*   Initially guided by their plans, writers begin putting words on paper or on the screen of a word processor. They do so, however, ever ready to reassume the prewriting perspective and rethink their intentions. As they write, ideas occur and unanticipated patterns emerge. Good writers are also guided by material they have already written. Prior material determines options for the writing yet to come because it is an avenue of meaning already under construction.

Often writers will take a break from their work, not only to rest but also to give the subconscious a chance to work on problems that have obstructed composition. You have probably enjoyed benefits from such periods of "latency" when, after forgetting about a knotty problem for a while, the solution has suddenly popped into your head.

3. *Revising.*   "To revise" means "to see again." As good writers finish drafting, they mentally step back from their work and consider the text as if they were reading it for the first time from the audience's perspective. Their revision lets them improve the text by substituting, adding, deleting, or

moving words, sentences, and paragraphs. Sometimes a writer conceives something that belongs in the essay but does not fit with prior material. Then the prior text must be rewritten to accommodate the new idea; the avenue of meaning must be reconstructed in a new direction.

4. *Editing*. In preparing the final draft, good writers shift their primary concern from the ideas, organization, and flavor of the composition to the mechanics of spelling, usage, and grammar. While they will also have been concerned with these things during composing and revising, they proofread the final working draft with special care to note any language errors, and after the final copy is ready, they proofread it to note any typographical errors or careless omissions.

1d Qualities of effective writing

When thinking about the qualities of composition, you will find it helpful to consider three features: invention, arrangement, and style. *Invention* concerns the writer's ideas. Are they well developed and logical? Is the thesis significant? Are generalizations supported by specifics? Are narrative events worth reporting, and are descriptive details well selected? *Arrangement* concerns the organization of the composition. Do the parts (the sentences and paragraphs, the ideas and images) interrelate so that each part helps every other to give the reader a coherent understanding? *Style* concerns the way words work together in the sentences. Are the best words put in the best places? Are the conventions of written standard English observed? The quality of a composition depends on all of these features. Disorganization or confused language can obscure the most brilliant insights, while even rigorous coherence and close observation of standard grammar cannot save a paper that lacks significance.

This concise handbook is organized to help guide you in the writing process. Part **I** analyzes the process, Part **II** describes the basic language resources at your disposal; Part **III** advises you on using those resources effectively; Part **IV** describes rules of punctuation and manuscript mechanics; Parts **V** and **VI** treat the most common word and sentence errors made by writers; Part **VII** advises you on writing in certain specialized circumstances; and Part **VIII** takes you through the process of writing the research paper.

I

Composing the Essay

2 · Determining Purpose and Perspective

2a Decide on your reasons for writing.

Our reasons for writing influence fundamentally what and how we write. When we adopt an aim for writing and begin the process, we conceive a special mental environment occupied by a writer, a reader, a subject matter, and an evolving piece of writing. Different aims require us to focus differently on these four elements. For example, when you write to share personal experience, you see yourself and your audience quite differently from the ways you do when you write to argue a point. In the first case, you usually assume a trusting relationship with the reader; you write believing you are the person most qualified to relate your own experience, and you achieve your aim if the reader sees and feels what you did. In the second case, you assume a competitive stance and you are willing to enlist greater authorities than yourself to support your argument, for you can achieve your aim only by winning the reader to your position at the expense of those who disagree with you.

Readers also assume certain attitudes and expectations, which are based on the kinds of aims they see in a piece of writing. When these expectations are disappointed, readers may get confused or frustrated. For example, someone approaching an essay expecting to learn about modern urban architecture would be frustrated if half-way through, the author turned the essay into a bitter personal reminiscence about rivalries with other architects. How well readers receive a text, therefore, depends in part on how well the writer has established a supportive environment for the reader. The diagram on page 9 shows how shifting emphases among the four elements influence the kinds of writing this book explores.

Continuum of Writing Environments*

Type of Writing	(Argumentative)		(Critical)	
	Persuasive	Expository	Expressive	Literary
Writer's Primary Concern	with reader	with subject	with writer	with text
Writer's Role	(debater) inducer	teacher	(critic) confider	artist
Reader's Role	skeptic	student	confidant	imaginative participant

*This chart is adapted from scholarship by Roman Jakobsen and James Kinneavy.

1. *Persuading.* As a persuasive writer, you aim to get your reader to act in a certain way—to vote for someone, to buy a product, to participate in an activity, or to adopt a new behavior. You enter the persuasive environment by clarifying an objective, and from then on your writing should be guided by an understanding of the way your audience and your objective relate. What kind of people are you trying to persuade? What are their values, fears, hopes, needs? How can you fit your subject to their needs? What details will best convince your audience of your sincerity? Note how one roommate attempts to persuade another in this excerpt from a letter sent during Christmas break.

Since we didn't see each other much during December, I want to take this chance to share something that has been on my mind lately. At the first of this semester, we kept our dorm room in fairly good order. Recently though we've been so busy with studies and dates that we've neglected the place. Now the dirty and clean clothes, empty cans and bottles, old newspapers, food-smeared plates, books, and miscellaneous junk are so thick that it's hard to get in and out of the room, much less to live in it. You've been complaining about not being able to bring up a date and about not even being able to study at your desk. Obviously we need to clean the room from top to bottom and restart our old habit of straightening up a mess as soon as we make it. With our home base back in order, surely everything else at school will make a little more sense. The day we return in January, let's light into the place before the old sloppy status quo begins to seem inevitable.

2. *Explaining.*   As an expository writer, you aim to inform your readers about something new to them. Such writing does oblige you to attend to the nature of your audience: What do they already know? What are their interests? But as an expositor, you must be primarily guided by your subject matter. Like a good teacher, you must first come to understand your subject before you can efficiently convey the information your audience deserves. What are the facts? How much do you need to write about the subject to do it justice? As a rule, exposition requires a style that reflects enough of the writer's personality for the reader to feel comfortable, but not so much that the writer's personality supplants the subject matter at the center of the reader's attention. Note the approach one student took toward the subject of kinds of roommates in a column for a student newspaper.

The Best Kind of Roommate

Freshmen beginning their residence in a dormitory may anticipate having one of three types of roommates. The invisible roommate reveals his presence as often as twice a month. His few possessions lie unarranged from August to December. During rare appearances, he always seems on his way somewhere else. The ever-present roommate, on the other hand, is only out of the room when he might be of help. He gives no opportunity for solitude. Even when he is not talking, he makes his presence known with barely audible shuffling, tapping, sighing. The most desirable type of roommate is the good friend. He knows when his roommate needs solitude and is able to let his roommate know when he himself needs to be alone. He listens well, gives help when it is needed, and welcomes help when he needs it. The new freshman will find that the best way to get a good friend as a roommate is to be a good friend himself.

3. *Defending arguable propositions.*   Argument is a type of writing which, like exposition, is meant to inform, yet like

persuasion, is meant to influence. Unlike persuasion, argument is more concerned with beliefs than with behaviors; unlike exposition, argument strives more to establish that one proposition is preferable to certain others than to explain the nature of a given reality. Argument is the most intellectually demanding of the kinds of writing because it assumes active opposition. In the face of opposing arguments, we must not only support our position with strong evidence and logic, but we must also defeat the evidence and logic supporting contrary positions. Note how the writer of the following passage confronts a point of view she finds invalid.

The only worthwhile benefits a person can gain from college are intellectual because these are the only benefits higher education is specifically set up to provide. My roommate, though, believes the opposite. She confesses to having no interest in any subject matter in any course in college. Still she thinks the money and time she is spending in college are an investment that will guarantee her future prosperity. She does not see that underemployment and employment out of field are the college graduate's real prospects. If, instead of spending $40,000 to get a degree, she would invest it in a savings institution, by age 64 she would have earned an amount over twice the difference between what the typical high school graduate and the typical college graduate earn in a career. Since, therefore, the only real benefits she can get in college are intellectual and since she has turned her back on these, she is wasting her time and money.

4. *Sharing personal experience.* The aim of expressive writing is to share one's own nature with a reader. Naturally, expressive writers must assume they can trust their audiences to respect the personal information they offer. Because readers of expressive prose approach the text in order to see things as the author sees them (at least temporarily), the content and style of the writing should be influenced primarily by the writer's self-understanding. Your own feelings, values, hopes, fears, and behaviors are the bases of expression, so your best expressive writing will honestly embody your personality. Consider the thoughts one student shares in the passage below.

Unlike most residents of Jones Dorm, I have an attractive view from my room's window. It opens on the thick, deep woods behind the tennis courts. If I stand just a few inches away from the window, I can see only the woods. I am not sure why, but I can stand there looking into the trees for an entire dusk. I'm not interested in spending any time actually in the woods, although I have explored them. I just like being removed from them while I look and think my way into them. Maybe what I'm really doing is looking deep into a quiet, cool place inside myself.

5. *Analyzing critically.* Criticism in formal writing is not a verbal assault of negative comments. To approach a subject critically, we must be prepared to apply criteria and to think imaginatively about possibilities. Criticism establishes both merits and defects. It asks, "What if . . . " about a subject. It systematically compares and contrasts parts and wholes. Like exposition, it seeks to explain given realities, but like expressive writing, it serves as a vehicle for the writer's values. Like an expositor, the critic assumes the role of teacher, but like a confidant, the critic commends to readers his or her way of sizing up the world. The stance assumed by a writer of successful critical analysis can range from impersonal to intimate. Often the most effective critical style compromises between the objectivity of exposition and the personableness of expressive writing. In any case, readers of criticism put a premium on the trustworthiness of the writer and the logical consistency with which the writer applies criteria to the subject. Note in the passage below how the writer applies the criteria of comfort, community spirit, and freedom to assess his dormitory.

Jones Dormitory

On the whole Jones is a pretty good dormitory. It is fairly comfortable, it is not too big, and it is administered well. The rooms are designed so that two roommates have enough space to set things up to suit individual tastes without imposing on each other. The desk chairs are mobile, adjustable, and form fitting, and the beds actually seem to have been made with human beings, not pythons, in mind.

A minor problem is the single ceiling light that leaves most of the room in shadow. Jones has only about eighty residents, so we can all get to know each other. We tend to feel a bond to the group as a kind of institution like a club or even a family. Barton Dorm, on the other hand, is so big that students feel more allegiance to the floor they are on than they do to the dorm as a whole. Our esprit in Jones is encouraged by a mature, caring group of resident counselors. They are not only available for us to go to them with our problems, they go out of their way to find out our problems before things get out of control. They make sure we have a hand in establishing dorm rules, so we feel responsible for the building. None of these good aspects, though, changes the fact that Jones is still a dorm—a place for compact, supervised living—and not an apartment building. The freedom and comparative luxury of apartment living will, I'm afraid, have claimed just about every sophomore now in the dorm by next fall. But if you are a freshman or a budget minded student of any class, and you are looking for a small, comfortable, well-run dorm, then Jones is for you.

6. *Expressing artistically.* Writers of literature strive to create works of art. To do so they naturally draw on experience with external reality, knowledge of themselves, and an image of an audience. More powerful than in other environments, though, are conventions that make a piece of writing a poem, short story, or drama. Note how the student-author of the passage below has used the poetic conventions of line separation and condensed, suggestive language to render an imaginative perception of his roommate.

Roommate

Crusty eyelids stifle a yawn;
Feet steep in fuzzy slippers;
a mouth sags open at the television;
I wave a dim 'bye on my
fast way to the light.

We have seen that certain aims of writing grant you the roles of persuader, debater, teacher, critic, confider, and artist. You should understand, however, that while one of the aims discussed in this chapter may characterize a piece of writing in general, it would not necessarily characterize every sentence and paragraph within the piece. To say, for example, an essay is on the whole expository does not mean it necessarily lacks expressive, literary, or persuasive elements. Note that the expository paragraph on page 10 indirectly conveys much expressive information about the writer's attitudes toward roommates; the most vivid part of the persuasive paragraph on pages 9–10 is the expository description of the room; and the critical paragraph on pages 12–13 could have a persuasive effect on the kind of student mentioned in the last sentence. Still, all these pieces suggest that their authors understood the main obligations their roles conferred.

Just as writers have obligations, so do readers. The continuum on page 9 indicates that as the role of readers changes from skeptic to imaginative participant, increasing responsibility is placed on them to bring information and experience to the text. For example, the reader of a persuasive essay has a right to expect that the writer will give all the information and will clarify all the logic required to understand the text. After all, the writer is obligated to persuade, but the reader is not at all obligated to be persuaded. The reader of a poem, however, has a right to expect only that the poet has used language creatively to render an imaginative experience, one that the reader may or may not have the sensitivity and experience to understand. Sometimes a poem will reward a lifetime of study. This is not to say that readers can leave analytic thinking up to persuaders but cannot trust literary writers to make sense. In fact, readers of persuasions and arguments must be constantly on guard against possible manipulation by writers, while readers of expressive and literary texts willingly put themselves, at least for a while, in writers' hands so they may be borne away from the here-and-now to worlds of the writers' own making.

2b Adopt an appropriate persona.

Whatever your general role, the specific personality you reveal to your readers also has a great deal to do with how well they receive your message. When you write, you create a "persona," or a kind of character who embodies the identity your readers get to know. The persona of a piece of writing is communicated by the **tone** and **stance** taken by the writer. The tone reflects how the author feels about the subject. An objective tone communicates an open mind; an urgent tone communicates emotional commitment; an ironic or satirical tone can suggest disgust; and a whimsical or humorous tone conveys amusement. Stance reflects the author's attitude toward the audience. It may be described in such terms as friendly, aloof, detached, sympathetic, engaged, antagonistic, personal, or impersonal. We may describe the example of persuasion on pages 9–10 as serious, even urgent in tone, but friendly in stance. The expository paragraph on page 10 suggests the author has approached the topic with a combination of objectivity and amusement; his stance is impersonal but not aloof.

You can focus on your relationship to a particular subject and audience first by establishing the aim of your writing, and then by exploring such questions as the ones below:

1. Does the audience know more, as much, or less than I do about the subject?
2. Would expressing my attitude toward the subject advance my aim, or would doing so confuse or unduly divert the audience?
3. Should I establish a personal or a detached relationship with my readers?
4. Would my feelings on the subject be significant and interesting to my audience?
5. If I have an argumentative or persuasive aim, how can I best establish a rapport with my audience? (If I were a

member of this audience, what kind of persona would be most convincing, given the object of the argument or persuasion?)

Exercise

Read each passage below; identify it as persuasive, argumentative, expository, or expressive; and answer the following questions: What is the writer's purpose? Who is the intended audience? What is the writer's tone?

1. Animals are the responsibility of society because we are nature's caretakers. But we often buy a pet without realizing the responsibility that comes with it. One of the most important of these responsibilities is to have our pets spayed or neutered if we do not intend to keep their offspring.

2. Strategic deterence is based on a simple idea: neither side will attack the other because an inevitable counterattack would devastate the side that launched first. Effective deterence, therefore, requires each side to know that the other's weaponry is strong enough to survive an attack and still accomplish its destructive mission.

3. I lived adventures every summer of my childhood. My friends and I would trek though the rolling, wooded hills around our homes in search of monsters, hidden treasure, or the simple but dark unknown. At five, I could run through the forest alone, touch snakes, startle rabbits, climb trees, and wade in black glop.

4. Sexual harassment is a topic that deserves everyone's attention. For years, women have been frightened and con-

fused about this problem. But does society consider sexual harassment a serious problem? I feel that the answer is no. For although there are agencies that handle sexual harassment complaints and courts that hear sexual harassment cases, many people continue to tolerate harassers.

3 · Thinking and Writing

3a Understand the writing task.

Usually circumstances dictate the purpose for writing. You owe a thank-you letter or you must submit an accident report or coworkers need a memo from you explaining a policy. When, however, you are directed to write something, as usually happens in college, your purpose may not be as clear. If you have any doubts about the objective of such writing tasks, look carefully at the language of whatever guidelines or instructions you have been given and, if necessary, ask questions to find out what is expected of you. Words such as "narrate" and "describe," for example, often indicate an expressive aim. Directives such as "analyze," "review," and "critique" typically signal an evaluative purpose. The word "explain" signifies an expository or informative aim. And terms such as "defend or attack," "agree or disagree," are an invitation to argue or persuade. (For a full discussion of the writer's aims, see Chapter 2.) These purposes are by no means mutually exclusive, of course. An essay supporting gun control, for example, might have the primary aim of persuading readers to adopt the writer's position, but it might attempt to achieve this goal by explaining current laws, narrating stories about accidental shooting deaths and brutal murders, and describing in graphic detail the results of such violence.

Understanding your purpose in writing will also help to clarify what you are writing about. The subjects for most forms of academic and professional writing fall into three broad types. Some are assigned (e.g., "Explain Freud's theory of the id, the ego, and the superego"). Others are open but limited in scope (e.g., "Write an essay in which you defend or attack some aspect of US foreign policy"). Still others are open and unlimited, allowing the writer complete freedom of choice (e.g., "Write a research paper on whatever subject interests you"). As you think through your choices, keep in mind how long an essay your audience expects. Limit your subject to fit the required scope of your paper, then inventory what you already know about the subject and consider how you might gain more knowledge.

As you contemplate your subject and purpose, keep in mind also the audience for whom your words are intended. Sometimes you will be able to identify this audience only in very general terms, as Joyce Carol Oates does when she says that her writing is intended for "some understanding and sympathetic readers." On other occasions, you may be able to identify the audience more precisely but still do not know enough about your readers to decide what their expectations are or how to meet them. This is a problem that you have already confronted if you have taken one of the Advanced Placement exams administered by Educational Testing Service or done any other kind of writing that has been evaluated by an anonymous team of readers. Often, however, you will be writing for a known audience—some individual or group whose preferences and biases you are already familiar with. In any case, try to picture your audience as a group of real people, and keep this picture mentally handy throughout your writing.

3b Develop strategies for getting started.

One of the crucial questions that every writer must answer is, "How should I begin?" The answer does not always come easily. Even highly skilled authors sometimes find themselves staring in frustration at a blank piece of paper or making one false start after another, so it is not surprising that inexperienced writers often have the same difficulties when they attempt to begin writing. Reasons vary, but several common ones are evident in the following excerpts from the journals of three students who were attempting to describe how they had written a placement essay on the subject, "Discuss the advantages or disadvantages of being the age you are now."

In writing the paper last Tuesday I really had trouble getting started. First I had to organize my thoughts, which was pretty hard to do since my mind wasn't on writing, but on how my feet were hurting from walking to the English building.

When I first saw the topic for the placement essay, I thought I would have little trouble developing it. I started writing immediately, but after a few sentences I found it more and more difficult to get across my feelings. I found it hard to write what I felt because I wasn't sure if the person who would grade it would understand what I meant.

When the topic was given to me, I read it over and over. I realized I was going to have to begin writing immediately if I was ever going to finish. The ideas did not come as readily as I had expected. My heart kept beating with nervousness as I watched everyone else write and write and write.

Distractions (either physical or mental), uncertainties about audience reaction, anxiety induced by the pressure of a deadline—these were serious concerns for this group of writers. For them and for other writers in the same predicament, one solution is to use a strategy for invention, such as the one employed by another student in the same class.

In composing the placement essay in class the other day, I first jotted down the major ideas and feelings I perceived after reading the question. I generally like to brainstorm for a few minutes before I actually start writing. Once I had written down these notes and ideas, I sorted them into categories so I could later formulate paragraphs. This process included first a general separation of thoughts (i.e., advantages opposed to disadvantages) and then I narrowed down further so that I had an adequate number of ideas under each category. I don't like to write an actual outline, but rather I jot down notes and then organize them into related groups.

In the remainder of this chapter, we will examine more specifically some of the techniques skilled writers use to generate ideas and reason logically.

3c Generate free associations.

There are three main techniques for exploiting free association:

1. *Brainstorming*—a process in which the writer lists ideas, impressions, or facts pertaining to the subject as they come to mind, without regard for sequence or coherence.

2. *Freewriting*—in which the objective is to write for a specified amount of time without stopping or lifting pen from paper, allowing words to flow freely onto the page in a stream-of-consciousness style.

3. *Tree diagramming*—a more structured form of free association in which the writer starts with a single idea or image and branches out into increasingly more specific clusters of related elements.

The examples below indicate more specifically how these strategies can aid the writer. All three were composed by the same student, who was experimenting with different ways to begin an expressive essay about her childhood experiences in Alaska.

Brainstorming

soft, soggy moss
green fades to gray fades to golden brown to blue
little berries scattered—salmonberries and cranberries
uneven ground, but like walking on a mattress
can see almost 200 miles to range
nippy bite to air, but still relatively warm
soft colors and soft feel to air and soft, almost misty look to
    the whole place
occasionally clump of willows—but they seem to fade back to
    flatness
lots of water, the river to one side, small ponds and puddles
    everywhere

Freewriting

Moss and soft and sitting on it and have a damp spot sink slowly
into your jeans and get up but not really dare to sit down again a different way so another damp spot starts forming and eat berries the
cranberries taste sour and creamy—not creamy, mealy but the
salmonberries shock sour and tart yes tart and are an orange sick
color like fish eggs but taste good in ice cream and blackberries, no
not blackberries but raspberries I don't know but they taste the best
and the sky is whitish grey and the horizon isn't here it just fades
back and back even the mountains don't stop the horizon it just
never quite meets the tundra goes on forever forever don't stop to
think, think, think of water forming in small pools and trickling out
to nothing and there are puddles everywhere . . .

Tree Diagramming

3d Keep and use a journal.

During a normal day new ideas, connections, and emotions come regularly but soon fade from our awareness. By keeping a journal we can informally note these thoughts and use them later to stimulate formal composition. Some professional writers report that keeping a journal not only provides them with a record of observations but also causes them to pay closer attention to life and thereby gain insights they would otherwise miss. Journals also provide a safe place to explore and experiment with thoughts. Novelist and essayist Virginia Woolf stated that journal writing "loosens the ligaments. Never mind the misses and stumbles . . . I can trace some increase of ease in my professional writing which I attribute to my casual half hours after tea." Note how one college student used journal entries to look beyond the surface of experience.

One of the guitarists in the band was dressed in the same outrageous punk style as the others, but his posture spoke more than his clothes. He stood, back arched, chin in the air, eyes glazed, moving very little the whole night. He played as he was supposed to, but he never fooled around on stage with the other musicians. He was not of their spirit, so to speak. I sympathized. Sometimes I feel I'm in a group of friends, but not of them. How much do we fool ourselves about where we belong?

What a fabulous sky! Pure, clear winter blue. If you think about it, the sky really ends at the top of the ground, not somewhere overhead. On a clear day like today, it seems like we are walking around in the sky.

As a writer's journal accumulates such entries, it can become a helpful resource whenever deadlines loom and ideas lag. Sometimes even a brief entry can spark inspiration. For example, the paragraph on "Jones Dormitory" on pages 12–13 was developed from the following passage in the author's journal:

What a great guy Robert is. He really doesn't have to concern himself with stupid freshman no-solution problems.

Dying relatives, cruel girlfriends, uncaring parents, impossible chemistry courses, failed sex, successful sex, safe and unsafe sex. . . .

No one would worry that he wasn't earning his resident adviser's room & board if he did nothing more than keep the lid on Thursday nights around here. Really the whole dorm is unusual because of the esprit here. Most guys somehow feel that this is more than just a place to lay their heads.

Given an assignment to evaluate a place, the author read through his journal and found this entry suggestive. At first he concentrated on the staff of resident advisers and the range of problems that crop up in the dormitory. But the notion of "esprit" shared throughout the dorm grew in his mind, and he developed the thesis that the whole environment, physical as well as social, was responsible for the way students felt.

3e Use classical techniques of invention.

In ancient Greece and Rome, scholars carefully analyzed the types of thinking their rhetoric required. They so thoroughly classified ways to discover rhetorical points that today writers still find the traditional categories of invention helpful. Although the classical formulas were designed primarily to develop arguments, modern writers use them to discover expository and expressive insights as well. Each inventional category has a set of simple questions from which writers may choose as they inquire systematically into their subject. As the answers develop, so does the content of the essay. The questions outlined below are adapted from rhetorical analyses by Aristotle, Cicero, and Quintilian.

1. Definition—What is my topic?
   a. What is its kind?

Censorship is the suppression of ideas in speech or writing.

3
e

b. What are its parts?

The ingredients of censorship are fear and aggression: fear of alien values supplanting one's own and aggression toward people with different beliefs.

c. How does it work?

Censorship is expressed in various ways: legal action against writers and filmmakers, boycotts against advertisers who sponsor controversial programs, and organized efforts to ban "objectionable" works from schools and libraries.

d. What are some examples of it?

Book and record burnings in communities all over the country. Passage of stringent antipornography laws in various states.

2. Comparison—What does my topic resemble, and from what does it differ?
   a. To what is it analogous?

Censorship is like a slow-working poison.

   b. How is it different in kind from a related topic?

When a teacher selects a book for students to read, that is not censorship; when a librarian removes a book from a shelf to keep it from students, that is censorship. Selection is a constructive act; censorship is a destructive act.

3. Causal relationship—Is my topic a cause or an effect?
   a. What does it cause?

Censorship causes fear and distrust.

   b. What causes it?

Censorship results from a dogmatic belief in the truth of one's own beliefs and the falsity of everyone else's.

4. Past and future circumstance—What is the past or future of my topic?

a. What happened?

Censors have become increasingly vocal and successful during the past decade.

b. What is possible?

Censors might become so powerful that writers and filmmakers would no longer deal with controversial issues.

c. What is probable?

Censorship will become more prevalent, but the Constitutional guarantee of freedom of expression and the strength of our democratic traditions will ensure that our basic rights are preserved.

5. Testimony—What do others say about my topic?
   a. What do authorities on my topic say about it?

John Stuart Mill says that "the peculiar evil of silencing the expression of an opinion is that it is robbing the human race, posterity, as well as the existing generation—those who dissent from the opinion, still more than those who hold it."

b. What is public opinion?

Opinion polls show that the vast majority of Americans are opposed in principle to censorship.

c. What is the statistical evidence?

In one state, the percentage of formal protest about secondary school textbooks rose by over 50% in a single year.

These strategies for invention provide starting points for thinking, not completed lines of thought. Statements that define, compare, propose a cause or a possibility, or cite other people's notions all require explanation to demonstrate their validity. The analogy between censorship and poison, for example, might inspire the writer to brainstorm about particular similarities and then to organize the details by making a tree diagram. Even if the analogy itself did not appear in the finished essay, the ideas generated by the image of censorship as a form of poison would have influenced the paper's development.

3f Ask the reporter's questions about your topic.

A fourth strategy is that used by newspaper reporters: asking and answering the questions **who, what, when, where, why,** and **how.** Notice how in the following example the writer uses these questions to focus his thinking. The issue with which she is concerned is a proposed 50% increase in student activity fees to finance construction of a new student center.

Who	made this recommendation? Who are its supporters? Who opposes it? Who has the authority to cancel or reduce the amount of the proposed increases?
What	are the specific provisions of the policy? What are the alternatives to it?
When	was this policy adopted? When will it be implemented? When will the people affected by it have an opportunity to voice their opinion?
Where	is the present student center located? Where will the new facility be built? (A related question would be, which location is more convenient for the majority of students?)
Why	is there a need for a new student center? Why is such a large increase in fees necessary?
How	will the proposed facility differ from the present one? How will the new center benefit currently enrolled students? How will low-income students be affected by the higher fees needed to finance the new center?

3g Use valid logic.

However you derive a proposition, you should examine the quality of its logic. Traditionally, scholars identify two types of logic: inductive and deductive. To *induce* is to reach a generalization after considering a number of specific instances.

For example, when you were a child you probably induced that when things glowed, they tended to get hot. To *deduce* is to reach a conclusion after considering two premises. For example, a child might deduce that since his parents get mad at him when he breaks things and since he has just broken a vase, then his parents will surely be angry when they discover the misdeed.

In daily life, induction and deduction are so integrated in our thinking that we do not distinguish separate processes. In fact, the reason two processes are identified at all is to analyze logic, not to generate it. For example, the child worried about having broken a vase will not stop to think that his first premise (that his parents get mad when he breaks things) is an induction gained from past observations; he will simply find himself realizing that he is going to be in trouble. For another example, you might induce from observations of yourself and classmates that when people repeatedly fail in efforts to learn something, they lose interest and give up. Then using that generalization as a first premise, you might proceed to deduce that since a particular friend is failing to learn German (the second premise), he will soon stop studying it (the conclusion). None of these steps, however, will seem apparent as you draw your conclusion.

What analysis can do for your logic is to reveal errors and guide you in correcting them. For example, a major pitfall awaiting writers is the temptation to generalize from facts and examples that are biased. This error usually results from what is called the *hasty generalization*, which occurs when a person leaps to a conclusion after having witnessed just one or two instances. We can trace the origins of an invalid induction in the conclusion one student writer reached, that "Republicans are all selfish." To reach this conclusion the person must have considered only a few individuals who happened to be both Republican and, in the generalizer's eyes, selfish; they are obviously not representative of all members of the party.

3
g

Formal deduction has been practiced since the time of the ancient Greeks. The pattern it follows is called the "syllogism" and consists of three steps: (1) a first ("major") premise is considered; (2) a second ("minor") premise is considered; (3) a conclusion based on the premises is reached. An example is given below:

First Premise: Only students of high moral character should run for office in the Student Government Association.
Second Premise: Carla is not a person with high moral character.
Conclusion: Carla should not run for office in the SGA.

For a formal deduction to reach the truth, both premises must be true, and the conclusion must follow inevitably from the two premises. If we grant that morality is essential for SGA candidates and that Carla is immoral, then we cannot escape the conclusion of the syllogism above. If, however, we find either that immoral students are as qualified as anyone to serve in student government *or* that Carla does have high moral character, then the conclusion is not necessarily true and we must discount the logic. Of course, the value of this particular syllogism depends also on our understanding of the term "high moral character." If the definitions of the terms of the premises are not clear, then a deduction lacks meaning.

A deduction's premises may be true, yet the conclusion offered may not logically follow. Consider the syllogism below:

First Premise: Many people who smoke care little about their health.
Second Premise: Mike smokes.
Conclusion: Mike cares little about his health.

If we grant that smokers tend to be careless about their health and if the evidence leaves no doubt that Mike is a smoker, we might feel comfortable with this conclusion. But if not all smokers (just "many") are careless, how do we know that Mike is not one of the smokers who do care about their health? Given only these premises, we do not know, and we might be misjudging Mike with faulty, unfair logic. You should be alert to your exercise of logic, especially when revising. Reasoning in discourse is rarely obvious, so finding and validating your own logic requires a special sensitivity. For example, the two deductions we interpreted as syllogisms actually appeared as the sentences below:

1. No one that immoral [referring to Carla] has any business running for office in our student government.
2. A two-pack-a-day man [referring to Mike] doesn't give a hoot for his health.

We naturally make such statements when we are trying to conclude something sensible from our experience. Much of your writing in college and your future career will be part of an effort to make sense of such things as facts, results, behaviors, policies, and objectives. Deducing is one of our most powerful tools in this effort, yet because of its power, even the presence of a false deduction lends apparent strength to an essay. So seductive is the natural process of deducing that faulty deductions can lead us to believe we are making sense even as we make nonsense.

One of the most common deductive tactics is to link propositions with the terms "if" and "then." For example, you might propose, "If typical college students are given the chance, then they will cheat academically." This statement invites us to scrutinize its key terms: Who are "typical college students," what is academic cheating, and what constitutes a "chance" to cheat? The statement also invites us to cite evidence to support it: What has happened in colleges that would lead to this conclusion? Finally, it invites comparison with its negation: "If typical college students are given the chance, then they will *not* cheat academically." While this pattern will help you see the logic or illogic of a chain of thought, it is not foolproof. Just because an "if . . . then" statement sounds right on initial examination does not mean it is valid. You must insist that its key terms be meaningful and that it stand up when compared to contradictory statements. The proposition about cheating, for example, may be fatally flawed because of its vague term, "typical college students"; such a proposition can have no meaning if the meaning of any of its terms cannot be established.

Below are some informal guidelines to follow in assessing your logic.

1. Watch for common signals of deduction: "Therefore," "if . . . then," "because," "thus," "so." Trace the reasoning of the conclusions which contain such terms.
2. Consider the meanings of the key words in your logical conclusions, especially the nouns and adjectives. Do these meanings accurately reflect reality? Is your understanding of the meanings accepted by your audience?
3. Look for sentences that state principles. Do they depend on assumptions you and your audience should accept? What kind of support do you provide for them?
4. After identifying statements derived from your logic, challenge them objectively. Assume the role of a hostile reader and pick at the definitions and conclusions. How do your statements hold up? How might they be strengthened?

3h Practice critical thinking.

Logic helps us tell whether our reasoning is valid, but simply being logical will not necessarily ensure the ultimate truth, morality, or usefulness of our propositions. To gain confidence in the truth and worth of our ideas, we must exercise "critical thinking."

When we think critically, we assume a special attitude that encourages us to be skeptical, reflective, and knowledgeable as well as logical. A skeptical person questions what others take for granted, especially when only weak evidence supports assumptions. Of course we wouldn't get anywhere if we spent all our time doubting everything. A productive doubt allows us to have confidence in our beliefs while we remain alert to circumstances that do not make complete sense. At crucial times, healthy skepticism leads us to question our assumptions in the faith that if the assumptions are confirmed, they are strengthened, and if they are proven false, we would be better off abandoning them.

But we must not be hasty in dealing with suspicious conclusions. Once we identify a problem, we should spend the time to define unclear terms and to examine contradictions, facts, and possibilities for their significance. Critical thinkers not only open their minds to alternative ideas, they also investigate the merit of these ideas. They not only identify unexamined assumptions, they think through the implications of contrary beliefs and predict the effects of solutions. Critical thinkers also monitor their own level of knowledge when they engage a topic. They learn to recognize when they are out of their element and thus require more inquiry to gain enough information to reflect and reason cogently. When they do lack sufficient knowledge to make a judgment, they ask questions of colleagues, consult published sources, and research in other ways.

We can note a writer's critical thinking in the paragraphs quoted on page 61. In his essay "Being Prepared in Suburbia," Roger Verhulst critically examines the proposition that guns are fundamentally evil devices. His reflections lead him to note that "whenever a gun was put to effective use . . . something broke." From this premise and from the unstated premise that habitually breaking things is bad, he deduces that it is "absurd to go through life breaking things" with a gun.

Later in the essay, however, he describes the effects of acquiring a Crossman Power Master BB repeater pump gun (for teaching target practice to Cub Scouts). When he fires the weapon, he finds a powerful pleasure in the experience, a pleasure that worries him. His reflections guide him to an explanation: "The gun extended my potential range of influence to everyone within sight; I could alter the world around me simply by pulling the trigger. I felt as omnipotent as Zeus." He uses his new knowledge about guns to skeptically reexamine his values. In the end, he renews his original antigun values but concludes that because of the sense of power people gain from owning guns, he does "not have much hope that private ownership of deadly weapons will be at all regulated or controlled in the foreseeable future."

3i Avoid logical fallacies.

One of the greatest benefits critical thinking offers is the disclosure of logical fallacies. Taking a second, doubting look at your conclusions or at those of others can reveal deceptive points that appear logical but that really do not follow from reasonable lines of thought. Below are some of the most common fallacies.

1. The *post-hoc* ("after that") fallacy consists of proposing that because one event happens after another, the first event caused the second. We are tempted by the *post-hoc* fallacy because effects always follow causes; but we should resist being hasty in ascribing cause, since precedence itself is not proof. For example, we would be wrong to conclude that because the crime rate has decreased after the imposition of the death penalty, the death penalty has caused the decrease. The new rate might be the result of hidden causes, such as a decrease in the proportion of the population which is in the crime-prone ages of sixteen to twenty-eight.

2. We commit the *ad-hominem* ("to the man") fallacy when we focus on the person who holds a belief rather than

on the belief itself: "Because Darwin was agnostic, his ideas on the origins of life have no value." Theories are true or false regardless of who advances them.

3. The frequent occurrence of the *ad-hominem* fallacy suggests how powerfully we are affected by associations. Writers gain appeal when they convey the impression that they are of upright moral character. Readers are more convinced of an argument if its proponent seems to be a good, honest person. Conversely, if a writer seems selfish, egocentric, or otherwise corrupt, readers may reject his or her ideas regardless of merit. We sometimes assume, therefore, that a person or an idea is validated just by association with something good or is invalidated just by association with something bad. An example of *guilt (virtue) by association* is to dismiss respect for authority "because it is a fascist value which can only result in the exploitation of people who hold it." It is true that exploitative totalitarian regimes of all kinds, including fascist Germany of the 1930s and '40s, touted respect for authority as a great virtue. Still not even the most democratic society can function unless at least tentative deference is granted to responsible leaders. In itself respect for authority is not bad; its context renders it healthy or harmful.

4. A statement is *begging the question* when it avoids giving information that the writer seems to promise. For example, a writer might explain a careless act as follows: "She forgot to bring the food basket to the picnic because her memory is so bad." Such an explanation actually states that something is because it is. The explanation "begs" the question, "Yes, but why?" In a more subtle form of this fallacy, a *questionable term* is used: "Abortion is murder, because it is the killing of babies." The term "baby" begs the question, "Is a fetus a baby?"

5. When two propositions which do not relate as premises are nevertheless used in a deduction, the conclusion is called a *non sequitur* (a Latin phrase meaning "it does

not follow"). For example, a writer might offer this argument: "Since student government is not benefiting our college and since only fifteen percent of the students vote in campus elections, the quality of student government will improve only when all students are required to vote." This writer has given no reason to conclude that a low percentage of voters is related to effectiveness of student government; it does not follow, therefore, that requiring students to vote will improve student government.

6. A *false choice* offers the reader only two alternatives when there are actually more: "We must either accept the demands of terrorists or ignore them altogether." Such a proposition ignores other tactics, such as negotiating to save hostages' lives.

7. A writer can sometimes *rely on ignorance* to reach conclusions. To insist on a proposition contradicted by facts is to demonstrate *invincible ignorance*. For example, some people persist in arguing that smoking is not bad for their health despite overwhelming evidence to the contrary. To *argue from ignorance* is to conclude that a proposition is false because it lacks proof. For example, some argue that the theory of evolution is disproved because scientists cannot agree on how it occurs. Such a position depends on a lack of complete knowledge, not on the general merit of the theory in question.

8. When we come up against a strong argument, we may be tempted to attack it only at its weakest point, so we set up a *straw man* to knock down. In opposing antismoking legislation, a pro-tobacco interest group published advertisements that attacked antismoking groups for being intolerant of people with different tastes; the antismokers, according to the pro-tobacco group, were creating barriers between people by sponsoring legislation to segregate smokers from nonsmokers. Obviously it is much easier to attack antismokers on the trivial grounds that they inhibit interpersonal relations than

to attack them on the much more significant grounds that they err in trying to protect public health.

9. If you claim that an action will cause a snowballing chain of bad effects, and you give no evidence that these effects will actually follow the action, then you lead your audience to a fallacious *slippery slope*. The argument that a woman's place is in the home has been supported by the following slippery slope: As more mothers enter the workplace, more children are bereft of the nurturance that only mothers can give; as these children grow up with minimal parenting, their values will be stunted and the future generations will become increasingly immoral and unloving; before long our society will be so degenerated that it won't be able to stand up to hostile totalitarian systems and we will lose our democratic way of life. Such an emotional argument diverts us from noting that it offers no support for the assumption that working mothers and day-care facilities cannot give children the nurturance they need—very possibly they can.

Exercise

Identify the fallacies below as *post hoc, ad hominem,* guilt (virtue) by association, begging the question, *non sequitur,* false choice, reliance on ignorance, straw man, or slippery slope.

1. You should ignore Marvin's candidacy for student body president because he's in a fraternity.

2. Every time I wear those red socks to a basketball game, our team wins; so you may be sure I will wear them to the championship game.

3. America: Love it or leave it.

4. Once certain people succeed in outlawing abortion, they will then outlaw all forms of contraception, and soon they will be dictating the nature of sexual morality in general.

5. We should oppose environmentalists' efforts to restrict offshore drilling because they argue the drills ruin our view of the ocean; our economy is more important than the beauty of a stretch of ocean.

6. Although studies of acid rain have demonstrated its adverse environmental effects, I see no need for antipollution legislation at this time.

7. That candidate cannot have it both ways: Either he is for the Equal Rights Amendment or he is against women's rights.

8. Student achievement began its decline after the Supreme Court ruled against officially sanctioned prayer in the public schools. Reinstituting formal prayer in the schools will, therefore, reverse academic decline.

9. We should elect someone to Congress who is not a professional politician because the professional politicians got us in the mess we are in.

10. People are puzzled by modern art because they cannot figure out what it means.

11. We can reject any policy advocated by tree huggers in the Sierra Club.

4 · Arranging and Drafting

4a Plan your composition.

After you've determined why and for whom you are writing (Chapter **2**) and after you've reflected on your topic by brainstorming, freewriting, tree diagramming, or other means (Chapter **3**), you will be ready to make some tentative decisions about arrangement. At this point in the composing process, your main objectives should be to find a pattern in the material you have accumulated, formulate a tentative thesis, and arrange details in some meaningful sequence. Then, when you have a good idea about the shape your composition will take, you should be well prepared to begin drafting.

Remember, though, that discovering ideas, organizing them, and revising them are deeply interrelated. When we analyze the writing process, we separate its aspects artificially. So you should consider the following procedures for determining arrangement and for drafting not as stages that you pass through once, but as activities that you will repeat throughout your writing.

1. *Determining a tentative thesis and pattern.* A thesis is a single sentence that expresses the point you want to make about your subject. This sentence might be a persuasive appeal: "We should clean our dorm room because the mess is making it hard for us to continue our education." It might state a proposition requiring argumentative defense: "The main benefit of a college education is intellectual, not monetary." It might make an expository statement: "There are three types of roommates." Or it might express an impression: "The view from my window makes me feel relaxed and reflective." If the thesis is to aid you in planning and structur-

ing your essay, you should be able to answer "yes" to the following questions:

1. Does the thesis sentence deal with only one subject?
2. Is it expressed in a complete sentence?
3. Is the point it makes consistent with the evidence I've accumulated?
4. Does it indicate how the subject has been limited and how it will be developed?

A negative answer to any of these questions means that you need to rewrite the thesis or accumulate additional data to support it. Even if the statement you've formulated meets all these criteria, you may have to revise it later to reflect the changes that occur as you draft and revise.

Sometimes in the early stages of composition, the details you think of will form a pattern. For example, the student writing about her experiences in Alaska (page 21) used a tree diagram to generate ideas and found that her details fell into four main categories. You may find that the pattern suggests a thesis. Whatever the sequence of your early ideas, as you proceed in your later planning you should keep in mind your understanding of the main idea of your composition.

2. *Discovering more material.* Guided by the thesis and your earlier thinking, draw systematically on your own knowledge, logic, and memories—and possibly on external sources—for relevant points. You can also reuse the tactics for invention suggested in Chapter **3**. Write your thoughts as they come, sometimes noting ideas in phrases, sometimes developing several sentences that trace a whole line of thought.

3. *Deciding on an overall pattern.* As you accumulate enough information to get a good idea of how your thesis will be developed, look for a pattern in your details, a way for your materials to cohere. At this point you might simply confirm a pattern you discerned earlier. Sometimes one of the

standard patterns discussed in **4c** will be appropriate. Other times the material will require you to modify or combine the standard patterns or to devise a unique organization. The decisions below illustrate the kinds of judgments made at this stage.

"I will organize my paper to trace effects and causes; I will describe effects first and suggest certain causes."

"My material fits under three main points, which I will arrange in order of increasing importance."

"My impressions and attitudes seem to fall naturally in a contrasting pattern: those before I met Susan and those afterward."

4. *Relating specific points to the overall pattern.* Now is the time to cluster your specific points under the sections of your pattern. For example, you might at this stage separate your specific effects and causes, or you might cluster the details of what you felt before and what you felt after a crucial event.

5. *Filling content voids and eliminating irrelevant material.* After you cluster your points, you may find that the emerging coherence suggests new ideas and reveals that some old ideas do not belong. Consider each point for how pertinent it is, for how efficiently it helps develop your essay, and for how specific it needs to be. Discard marginally pertinent items, redundant items, and items too vague or general for your thesis. Then judge if your planned composition promises to address your subject completely enough, given your purpose and thesis. If it does not, you will need to develop more material.

6. *Arranging the particulars in a sequence.* Now you should be able to develop an outline that orders the particulars you sorted in the previous stage. You might do this in a formal outline that puts major and subordinate points in order (as for an essay that classifies types of child abuse), or you might simply list particulars in a planned sequence (as for a narrative that traces a personal experience). Techniques for formal outlining are given in **4b.**

4 b

Exercise 1

Number the steps given below so they will follow the order of the six-stage process for determining arrangement:

You decide on a comparison pattern for your essay.

You list in sequence the major points about cars and subordinate the supporting details in order under each major point.

You determine the major points and their relevant details.

You review in general your past experience with cars, your area of interest, and you realize how much auto styles and buyer attitudes have changed in the last dozen years. You decide to show in your essay how the public's attitude has shifted from a desire for large, powerful cars to a desire for small, efficient, economical cars.

You decide you have less content than your purpose requires, so you add a major point and some details.

In the library you consult auto magazines published during the last dozen years, looking for particular changes in car designs and specifications. You use this information to supplement your own observations and memories.

4b Prepare an outline.

A formal outline may help you plan the sequence in which you will discuss your points throughout your composition and establish subordinate and coordinate relationships among these points.

An outline shows by indentation how points are subordinated. Outlining convention requires that at each level of indentation there must be at least two entries. The conventional numeration and indentation are given below.

Outline Numbering Conventions

I.
   A.
      1.
         a.
            1)
            2)
         b.
      2.
   B.
II.

4
b

This scheme shows main point **I** divided into two sub-points, **A** and **B;** point **A** is subdivided into **1** and **2; 1** is subdivided into **a** and **b;** and **a** is subdivided into **1)** and **2).**

Be consistent in the way you state the points in your outline. In a topic outline, every heading should be a word or phrase. In a sentence outline, every numbered or lettered heading should be a complete sentence.

Emphasize the coordinate relationship of the main headings and that of the items within each subgroup by stating them in the same grammatical form. For example, if point **I** is a noun, the other Roman numeral headings should also be nouns; if the **A** term in one subgroup is a prepositional phrase, the other capital letter headings in that group should also be prepositional phrases, and so on.

Taking into account the previous information on determining pattern, examine the following example of the entire planning procedure used by a freshman composition student whose purpose was to explain what he believed was wrong with his university's system for dropping and adding courses.

First he listed all points he felt to be relevant to his topic:

1. Frequent computer errors in schedules
2. Impersonality of the whole system

3. Small, cluttered, uncomfortable facilities
4. Physical discomfort due to weather conditions
5. Too many forms to fill out
6. Long lines outside and inside building
7. Anxiety about getting necessary courses and hours
8. Uninformed people at drop and add tables
9. People who ignored students' questions
10. People who were rude to students
11. A few courteous people
12. Not enough people to handle the volume of students needing to drop or add courses

The student then examined all the items more closely, searching for a cluster of related points. What he discovered was that most of the information he had written down (everything except items 1, 2, and 12) could be classified under three broad categories: inefficient procedures, inadequate facilities, and unsatisfactory personnel. After considering these clusters of specific points, he added several more specifics and eliminated some.

Next he developed the following topic outline:

Confusion on Campus: The State College Drop/Add System

Thesis: There are three main problems with the drop/add system at State College: the procedures for dropping and adding courses are inefficient, the facilities are inadequate, and the registration staff are, for the most part, incapable of meeting students' needs.

  I. Inefficient procedures
    A. Too many forms to have signed by professors
    B. Too many different lines to stand in
    C. Too few staff members to process change forms
 II. Inadequate facilities
    A. Inadequate shelter in the area where students wait in line
    B. Poor conditions in the room where drop/add is held
      1. Inadequate space
      2. Inadequate ventilation
      3. Inadequate cooling system

III. Unsatisfactory personnel
   A. Staff members ignorant of necessary information
   B. Staff members indifferent to student questions
   C. Staff members rude to students

The student might have decided to write a sentence outline, in which case each entry would be a complete sentence. Such an outline would give him a chance to plan his content more thoroughly.

   I. Inefficient procedures prolong registration.
      A. There are too many forms to fill out.
      B. There are too many different lines to stand in.
      C. Too few staff members are available to process change forms.
   II. The facilities are not large enough.
      A. Long lines of students must stand outside.
         1. In warm weather students swelter.
         2. In cold weather students freeze.
      B. The gym does not accommodate all the people.
         1. People are jammed together from wall to wall.
         2. The lack of ventilation is suffocating.
         3. The air conditioning cannot cope with the heat.
   III. The personnel can't provide adequate service.
      A. Staff members give students incorrect information.
      B. Staff members ignore students' questions.
      C. When staff members do respond, they are rude.

Despite their apparent rigidity, these conventions offer considerable flexibility. For an in-class writing assignment, you might prepare a one-level outline (Roman numeral headings only). For a short out-of-class paper, a two-level outline (Roman numeral headings plus capital letter headings) might be more helpful. And for longer, more complex projects such as research papers, a three- or four-level outline might better serve your purposes. You can also vary the number of main headings and subheadings in accordance with your organizational aims and the scope of your paper. Perhaps the most important point to keep in mind when preparing an outline is that it can be changed at any time during the composing process to accommodate new information or insights.

Exercise 2

Arrange the list of topics below in the outline format indicated.

Misbehavior in Our National Parks
Deliberately defacing natural objects
Littering
Interfering with animals
Knocking on exhibit windows
Vandalizing
Throwing trash from vehicles
Behaving destructively
Leaving trash in campsites
Carelessly abusing facilities and environment
Deliberately wrecking park facilities
Throwing food scraps into cages

   I.
      A.
      B.
  II.
      A.
      B.
         1.
         2.
 III.
      A.
      B.

4c Consider adopting a standard pattern.

Sometimes writers choose to develop their ideas within a traditional pattern of organization. Such patterns can help focus your search for content and can help you achieve coherence throughout your paper. Blindly following a pattern, however, can handicap you by restraining you from discovering features of your subject that do not fit. You should, therefore, consider the seven patterns outlined below not as rigid molds into which you pour content, but as recipes that you adapt according to your particular resources and objectives.

1. *Procedure.* The most clear-cut pattern is the specification of the steps in a procedure such as giving a set of directions or tracing a process. Your task is to identify in sequence all steps that make up that procedure. A complex procedure may have clusters of related steps, and you should make these larger stages clear. For example, directions on how to fish for trout with artificial flies might organize all the skills into five main categories: how to prepare the equipment, how to negotiate a stream, how to cast the fly, how to set the hook, and how to net the fish. Here are other important points to consider.

   a. If the objective is not clear from the title of your composition, orient your reader by briefly describing the objective or result of the procedure.
   b. Define any terms and identify any parts the reader may not be familiar with.
   c. To trace the procedure, simply begin with the first step and lead the reader through each subsequent step, using transitional words (**next, second,** etc.) to help the reader keep track.
   d. To conclude, you might describe how the result of a successful procedure looks or works.

Often an audience for a procedure will require only the content mentioned in *c* above. In such cases, simply begin the paper with the first step and end with the last step.

2. *Report and narrative.* A *report* tells what happened first, what followed, and what happened last. The journalist's six questions (see **3f**) can often serve as a guide: tell **who** did **what; when, where,** and **how** it was done; and, if the reasons are significant, **why** it was done.

4
c

Narrative refers to an account that portrays people (or other creatures) coping with a problem. In this sense, *narrative* and *story* are synonymous. Although "story" suggests literary fiction and drama, nonfiction narratives are useful in all kinds of composition, for true stories can persuade, instruct, and reveal expressively with great power.

To be complete a narrative must have at least one *episode,* which is an account structured in the five stages outlined below:

    a. *Setting*—Readers need some sense of place and time in order to envision an episode.

    b. *Complication*—Something must happen to upset the equilibrium of the setting. The complication creates a problem or conflict.

    c. *Psychological response*—Readers must be able to empathize with the response that the episode's characters have to the complication.

    d. *Attempt to cope*—The characters act (mentally or physically) to solve the problem or end the conflict.

    e. *Results*—There must be an outcome to the attempt.

You can see these stages at work by experimenting with the account below. When you have read it, you will likely find that it fails as a story:

The Visitor

One morning when a farmer named Brown was harvesting in the south forty and Mrs. Brown was canning vegetables, there came a knock at their farmhouse door. Mrs. Brown opened the door and was shocked and distressed to see Mr. Smith standing there. He asked to see Mr. Brown. Mrs. Brown, struggling to keep her composure, replied that her husband was not on the farm and that she didn't know when he would be back. Mr. Smith said that he was sorry and that he would return that afternoon.

As soon as he left, Mrs. Brown dashed out the back door and over the fields to her husband. When she reported that Mr. Smith had just been asking for him, the farmer was more shocked and distressed than his wife. At her recommendation, he decided to run away and hide at his brother's house in the town of Blue Springs. So he rushed back to the farmhouse, packed a few things, and left immediately.

That afternoon, Mr. Smith returned and once again asked Mrs. Brown if he might see her husband. She replied that he had left the farm for an extended journey.

Mr. Smith said, "I'm sorry to hear that because I have an appointment with him this evening in Blue Springs."*

This passage does not make sense as a narrative because we cannot tell why the couple react as they do, and we cannot discern a result at the end. If we change one word, however, the story will suddenly pop into focus: instead of *Mr. Smith*, read *Mr. Death*. Now the people's motives and the result are clear, and we can understand the account as a narrative.

3. *Description.*   Describing a person, place, or thing requires you to select only those details that will most efficiently create an impression. The four patterns below can help you organize an impression as well as guide you in selecting details.

> a. Details may be treated in the order in which they are noted by an observer. The observer either passes through a scene or witnesses details as they appear. The perspective is like that of someone walking down a street or watching things happen in a restaurant.
>
> b. Details may be treated in their order in space. The observer might describe from left to right, from top to bottom, from front to back, or in some other spatial progression.
>
> c. The prominence of a feature can determine its order. The observer might begin with the most outstanding detail and progress to the least noticeable

*Collett B. Dilworth, "Structuralism, Stories and English Teaching," *English Journal* 72 (January 1983): 82.

yet still significant detail, or the writer might reverse this order.

d. A detail's significance, in light of the writer's purpose, can also govern arrangement. The observer
picks and orders only those details that will give a
specific impression. The same used car might be
described in terms of its dented fenders and worn
tires or conversely in terms of its polished paint
and clean interior. Of course, the significance of a
detail should always be a consideration for the descriptive writer whatever the pattern.

4. *Comparison.* Your topic may concern two subjects
alike in some ways but different in others. Your purpose in
comparing such subjects may be simply to inform your audience of their similarities and differences. It could also be to
show how one thing is superior to another or to explain
something unfamiliar in terms of something familiar.

To organize a comparison, determine common areas of
similarities and differences. If, for example, you were comparing two political candidates, you would want to treat each
in terms of the same general points. If you discuss the economic proposals, the outlook on foreign policy, and the connections to special interests of one candidate, you should discuss these same points for the other.

There are two traditional patterns for organizing comparisons. In one pattern, you discuss all selected points of comparison for one subject and then all points for the other.

I. Political candidate Jessica Fenster
   A. Economic proposals
   B. Outlook on foreign policy
   C. Connections to special interests
II. Political candidate Phillip Bloom
   A. Economic proposals
   B. Outlook on foreign policy
   C. Connections to special interests

In the other pattern, you discuss each point of comparison in turn:

I. Economic proposals
  A. Jessica Fenster
  B. Phillip Bloom
II. Outlook on foreign policy
  A. Jessica Fenster
  B. Phillip Bloom
III. Connections to special interests
  A. Jessica Fenster
  B. Phillip Bloom

Note that the first pattern focuses on the candidates, whereas the second focuses on the issues. Choose your pattern according to which aspects of your content you wish to emphasize.

5. *Classification.*   Classifying particulars into general categories is a type of thinking essential for making sense of the world. We would have little to talk or think about if we lacked concepts such as **vegetable** and **animal, rural** and **urban, truth** and **falsehood.** Your purpose in classifying is, therefore, to give your readers a new tool for organizing experience. You do so by arranging phenomena according to important shared characteristics.

A classification should be based on a single meaningful principle. A paper on kinds of advertisements would lack a single principle if it discussed the following categories: funny ads, ads for household products, and television ads. Such a paper would be based on a single principle if it classified ads according to their humor and seriousness or according to the type of product or according to the type of medium, but not a combination of these. A paper on television ads that lacked a meaningful classification would be one that grouped them according to length: long, medium, and short. Unless there are substantive differences related to length of time, such an essay could offer little useful information.

Just as your classes should be coherent and meaningful, they should also be mutually exclusive and complete; that is, they should not overlap and should not exclude elements that belong in the classification system. For example, a classification of the media used in political campaigns as electronic, print, and mail is overlapping because mailed materials are a form of print media; the system is also incomplete because it omits personal campaign appearances.

Once your classification system is clear, the pattern of organization for your paper will be obvious. The body of your paper will fall naturally into sections, each treating one of your main classes. The order of your classes should follow some logic such as size (largest to smallest) or importance.

The example paragraph on page 10 illustrates classification.

6. *Persuasion.*   Almost any rhetorical form can be turned to persuasive purposes. Certainly in the appropriate contexts, narration, description, comparison, and classification can move people to action. There are also patterns specifically designed for persuasion, and one is outlined below.

    a. *Background of the problem*—Trace the history of the present problem. This step can implicitly suggest that if a problem can come into existence, it can go out of existence.

    b. *Portrayal of a need*—Describe the problem objectively but vividly. You should convince your audience that conditions are not what they should be.

    c. *Portrayal of solution*—Specify what must be done to improve conditions. Stress the feasibility and reasonableness of the recommended course of action.

    d. *Visualization*—Describe what conditions will be like after the solution. This description should draw the audience away from the current state toward the improved state.

e. *Call to action*—Conclude with a recommendation on how to begin addressing the problem. Stress the practicality and feasibility of this first step.

The example paragraph on pages 9–10 illustrates this persuasive pattern.

7. *Argument.* In composition, "argument" does not mean the type of contention occurring when two people in disagreement raise their voices and speak at the same time. Argument is a type of discourse that makes and supports propositions in the light of at least one other contrary proposition. Its objective is to demonstrate that a thesis inevitably follows from a line of logic, and perhaps to convince readers that a thesis represents a superior morality. Argument and the logic that supports it constitute venerable fields of study; since ancient times, scholars have described and recommended argumentative tactics. The pattern below is a simplified outline of an arrangement advocated in ancient Greece and Rome and still respected by modern scholars.

a. *Introduction*—Establish an appropriate stance and tone to draw the reader intellectually and perhaps emotionally into the issue. The stance, for example, could be earnest or indignant, and the tone serious or satirical. Introductory devices include illustrating a problem with a narrative, a description, or a statement of a paradox.

b. *Background*—State the facts behind the issue. The **who, what, when, where, how, why** approach of the reporter is often useful at this point.

c. *The writer's argument*—Trace a line of reasoning to show that a particular proposition is valid. All your wisdom, logic, and moral sense may be brought to bear. The strategies for invention and the rules of logic outlined in Chapter **3** are all useful in developing an argument.

4
c

    d. *Refutation*—At some point, summarize the oppos-
       ing argument objectively and analyze it critically.
       The objective here is to reveal illogic or immorality
       in the opposing argument.
    e. *Conclusion*—Conclude by clinching your argument.
       An effective tactic is to briefly review the opposing
       theses and highlight the point-for-point superiority
       of your argument. At the end of an argument the
       reader should feel invited to join a company of en-
       lightened people in opposition to error.

The example paragraph on page 11 illustrates this argumentative pattern.

Exercise 3

1. Answer these three questions for each of the thesis statements that follow.
   a. Is the thesis adequately limited in scope?
   b. What suggestions, if any, do you have for improving
      the thesis statement?
   c. If you read this sentence in the introduction to an
      essay, which of the standard patterns discussed in **4c**
      would you expect the writer to use?

   1) The differences between my high school English teacher and
      my college English teacher are dramatic.
   2) Everyone needs a chance to grow and develop at an early age
      in order to become independent later.
   3) The first time I ever drove a standard shift car, I was lucky to
      survive.
   4) In the first thirty minutes before a play begins, many actors,
      actresses, producers, and stage crew members experience
      nervousness that often becomes plain old fear.
   5) Censoring student newspapers is bad.

2. Study the following list of ideas that a student jotted
   down while doing a brainstorming exercise for his com-

position class and answer these questions:

a. What is the thesis suggested by this list?
b. Which items, if any, should be deleted from the original list because they are irrelevant to the thesis?
c. Considering the thesis and the remaining items, number the items in the order you would expect the writer to treat them in an essay.

Being a smoker in the '90s is a constant frustration.
At some point every smoker makes a determined effort to stop.
One usually starts smoking by following the example of other smokers, usually older peers.
There are new laws and regulations banning smoking.
Nonsmokers ostracize you.
How one becomes a smoker . . . the stages.
You overcome the early unpleasantness of smoking by determining to succeed in acquiring a new enjoyment.
You realize you are hooked on nicotine and think you can't stop.
You either become a more confirmed smoker or you succeed in quitting.

5 · Writing Effective Paragraphs

5a Understand the function of paragraphs.

One of the simplest but most important conventions of written discourse is the indentation that marks the boundaries between paragraphs. Without the aid of this typographical indicator, readers would face much the same problem they would encounter if there were no spaces between words or no periods between sentences.

Notice, for example, how difficult it is to read the sentence below.

Revengeisakindofwildjustice.

When the words are separated, however, their meaning and the meaning of the sentence as a whole become immediately comprehensible.

Revenge is a kind of wild justice.

Francis Bacon

Likewise, a group of sentences without terminal punctuation and capital letters to signal the beginning of each new sentence would be a confusing jumble of words, as in the following example:

A mohawk of metallic blonde hair adorned Perry's egg-shaped head dangling bravely from his left ear was a silver safety pin in sharp contrast to his unruly hairdo and pierced ear, Perry wore a khaki green army jacket with matching trousers his shoes were a pair of old combat boots that clumped loudly, warning the public to stand at attention dark, horn-rimmed sunglasses sat perched on his pointed ears, even in the darkest of rooms.

Student essay, "Perry the Punker"

If you were to read this paragraph as it was actually written—with periods after **head, pin, trousers,** and **attention**—you would have no difficulty following the author's line of thought or distinguishing one physical detail from the next. This writer was also conscious of the need to subdivide her entire essay into comprehensible units of meaning. Had she not done so, her readers would have been faced with the task of deciphering her intentions from the long, unbroken passage below.

Perry the Punker

Sliding into my desk, I noticed a strange aroma filling my nostrils. I turned to discover its source, an alien-looking creature slouched in the desk next to mine. In an attempt to make conversation, I asked the person his name. "Perry" was the cold, clipped reply. It was obvious from the clothes he wore, the way he smelled, and his strange behavior that Perry was not an ordinary boy. A mohawk of metallic blonde hair adorned Perry's egg-shaped head. Dangling bravely from his left ear was a silver safety pin. In sharp contrast to his unruly hairdo and pierced ear, Perry wore a khaki green army jacket with matching trousers. His shoes were a pair of old combat boots that clumped loudly, warning the public to stand at attention. Dark, horn-rimmed sunglasses sat perched on his pointed ears, even in the darkest of rooms. Perry emitted an aroma of burnt cheese. I discovered his father owned the local pizzeria, where he worked as a delivery boy. Sometimes the odor was so strong I was forced to hold my breath at specific intervals. This was a difficult task, so I avoided sitting next to him whenever possible. One rainy night, my mother decided to order out for supper. Unfortunately, she called the pizza place where Perry worked. Within minutes, our doorbell was ringing. I flung open the door to find Perry dripping all over our "pan special." My heart sank as mother invited him inside. He grabbed the money from her hand and bolted out the door into the pouring rain. Slowly shutting the door, my mother remarked that strange boys should not deliver pizzas. Whenever I smell the pungent odor of burnt mozzarella, it always reminds me of Perry. I wonder if he is still peddling pizza. I doubt it. He probably is living on a gorgeous estate in California and designing costumes for punk rock bands.

Exercise 1

1. After reading "Perry the Punker," mark the point at which you think each new paragraph should begin.
2. Then consider the sentences enclosed within these boundaries and explain why they constitute a paragraph.

Of course, writers should do more than arbitrarily mark boundaries in their prose. The material within those boundaries must be unified, coherent, and complete. And the paragraph as a whole must be clearly and logically related to other paragraphs in the same essay.

5b Compose unified paragraphs.

A paragraph is unified if all its parts contribute to the development of its controlling idea or impression. There are two ways to achieve this result in your own writing.

1. State the main point explicitly in a *topic sentence* and add sentences to qualify, explain, illustrate, or in some other way develop it. In this pattern, the topic sentence usually comes at the beginning of the paragraph.

In the spring the sea is filled with migrating fishes, some of them bound for the mouths of great rivers, which they will ascend to deposit their spawn. Such are the spring-run chinooks coming in from the deep Pacific feeding grounds to breast the rolling flood of the Columbia, the shad moving in to the Chesapeake and the Hudson and the Connecticut, the alewives seeking a hundred coastal streams of New England, the salmon feeling their way to the Penobscot and the Kennebec. For months or years these fish have known only the vast spaces of the ocean. Now the spring sea and the maturing of their own bodies lead them back to the rivers of their birth.

Rachel Carson

A topic sentence, however, can also be used in other positions. Note how Loren Eiseley builds up to his topic statement in the final sentence of this paragraph.

Some years ago the old elevated railway in Philadelphia was torn down and replaced by a subway system. This ancient El with its barnlike stations containing nut-vending machines and scattered food scraps had, for generations, been the favorite feeding ground of flocks of pigeons, generally one flock to a station along the route of the El. Hundreds of pigeons were dependent upon the system. They flapped in and out of its stanchions and steel work or gathered in watchful little audiences about the feet of anyone who rattled the peanut-vending machines. They even watched people who jingled change in their hands, and prospected for food under the feet of the crowds who gathered between trains. **Probably very few among the waiting people who tossed a crumb to an eager pigeon realized that this El was like a food-bearing river, and that the life which**

haunted its banks was dependent upon the running of the trains with their human freight.

2. Omit the topic sentence and communicate the unifying idea or impression implicitly through word choice, sentence structure, and sentence relationships.

In the passage below, N. Scott Momaday conveys a sense of vastness and mystery through a series of powerful visual images. Note that the opening sentence sets the scene and focuses attention on the houses, but it does not introduce an explicit controlling idea.

> Houses are like sentinels in the plain, old keepers of the weather watch. There, in a very little while, wood takes on the appearance of great age. All colors wear soon away in the winds and rain, and then the wood is burned gray and the grain appears and the nails turn red with rust. The windowpanes are black and opaque; you imagine there is nothing within, and indeed there are many ghosts, bones given up to the land. They stand here and there against the sky, and you approach them for a longer time than you expect. They belong in the distance; it is their domain.

5c Compose coherent paragraphs.

A paragraph is coherent when each sentence is clearly related to the next. Conversely, a paragraph lacks coherence if it moves unpredictably from one point to another. There are many ways to achieve coherence within a paragraph, but the seven strategies discussed below are among the most effective.

1. *Sequence in time or space.* A technique used extensively in narrative and descriptive writing, this pattern is usually characterized by explicit time markers (**then, later,** etc.) or a movement from one visual reference point to the next.

> Never shall I forget the Christmas dances at Taos, twilight, snow, the darkness coming over the great wintry mountains and the

lonely pueblo, **then** suddenly, again, the dark calling to dark, the deep Indian cluster—singing around the drum, wild and awful, **suddenly** rousing on the last dusk as the procession starts. And **then** the bon-fires leaping suddenly in pure spurts of high flame, columns of sudden flame forming an alley for the procession.

D. H. Lawrence

2. *Logical order*.   In this kind of relationship, which is especially common in persuasive or argumentative discourse, one sentence is a proposition and the next is a conclusion or result. Observe that the second sentence in the following passage serves this purpose even though there is no explicit transition word, such as **therefore.**

The Surgeon General has established that breathing smoke from other people's cigarettes is at least as unhealthy as actually smoking. Surely no one can object if we ban cigarette smoking in our classrooms.

3. *Amplification*.   In this pattern, one sentence clarifies an earlier one by defining, qualifying, or illustrating it.

Those who believe in the idea of freedom and in the idea of democracy also believe that the truth will set you free, that to have knowledge is to have the chance to understand, perhaps even to cope. **By truth I mean actuality or objective matters capable of discovery.**

Ramsey Clark

The large mammalian brain is the most complicated thing, for its size, known to us. **The human brain weighs three pounds, but in that three pounds are ten billion neurons and a hundred billion smaller cells.**

Isaac Asimov

4. *Accumulation*.   In this method, one sentence introduces an idea or example similar to that of a preceding sentence. Usually the sentences provide evidence that accumulates to support a topic sentence. This kind of relationship is sometimes signaled by a transition word such as **likewise, also, and, moreover,** or a similar connective.

Even when I was a fairly precocious young man the nothingness of the hopes and strivings which chase most men restlessly through life came to my consciousness with considerable vitality. **Moreover,** I soon discovered the cruelty of the chase, which in those years was much more carefully covered up by hypocrisy and glittering words than is the case today.

Albert Einstein

5. *Contrast.*   Another strategy for achieving coherence is to contrast the idea of one sentence with that of another.

Of course, it would be a mistake to suppose that there is more blind acceptance of brutal practices in organized football than elsewhere. **On the contrary,** a recent Harvard study has approvingly argued that football's characteristics of "impersonal acceptance of inflicted injury," an overriding "organization goal," the "ability to turn oneself on and off" and being, above all, "out to win" are of "inestimable value" to big corporations.

John McMurtry

6. *Repetition.*   In this arrangement, two or more sentences are linked by repetition of key words.

Then, **he** [Charles II] **loved** the theater, **and** it was thanks to his **patronage** that actors and acresses, hitherto a rather derided race, attained proper respectability. **He loved** horses, **and** the great English racing center of Newmarket owed everything to his **patronage.**

Antonia Fraser

Take care that such repetition does not become an irritation to the reader (see **16b**).

7. *Parallelism.*   The passage above is a good example not only of repetition but also of parallelism, the balance achieved by duplicating sentence structures. The sentences that follow are also parallel, but for different reasons. These writers achieve balance by beginning each sentence with the same determiner-adjective-noun pattern and by contrasting such key words as **night—day** and **heavy cover—open spaces.**

The **thick-set leopard,** heavier by 30 pounds, operates in the shadows of the **night,** relying on **heavy cover,** stealth and close-up ambush tactics. The **trim cheetah** is a creature of the **day** who likes **open spaces** and long vistas.

Emily and Ola d'Aulaire

These seven techniques can be used singly or in various combinations to achieve paragraph coherence. In the first example below, the writer relies almost exclusively on amplification. In the second paragraph, the author combines the amplification strategy with repetition and parallel structure.

Euphemisms and palliative phrases are a favorite form of evasive language. "To select out" someone means to dismiss him from a job. People "misspeak" themselves; they never say foolish or deceptive things or (heaven forbid!) lie. Everything from nonsense and propaganda to vicious slanders and incitements to violence is described as "rhetoric." Similarly any falsehood, no matter how malicious, and any indoctrination, no matter how unconscionable, is "consciousness-raising."

Richard Gambino

If I were to describe my dream university, I would have it organize itself around a central trunk of three disciplines: philosophy, the art studio, and the poetry workshop. Philosophy would be asked to return to the teaching of ontology, epistemology, ethics, and logic in order to remedy the shameful deficiencies of the reasoning now common in the fields of academic specialization. Art education would provide the instruments by which to carry out such thinking. Poetry would make language, our principal medium for communicating thought, fit for thinking in images.

Rudolph Arnheim

For additional information on paragraph structure, see Chapter **4.** It discusses seven commonly used patterns for essay development, all of which can be used as well to achieve paragraph coherence.

5d Develop paragraphs adequately.

Judgments about whether a given paragraph is adequately developed always involve subjective considerations because there are no universal conventions governing paragraph length. In fact, most experienced writers consciously vary the length of their paragraphs just as they vary the length and structure of their sentences. One reason for this practice is that uniformity often translates into monotony. Furthermore, paragraphs varying in importance or purpose should vary in length. Consider the following two paragraphs, both of which are drawn from Roger Verhulst's "Being Prepared in Suburbia."

> Gun legislation is dead for another year. As a result, if statistics are any guide, there's every likelihood that a lot of people now living will also be dead before the year is over.

· · ·

> Until last fall, I had never owned any weapon more lethal than a water pistol. I opposed guns as esthetically repugnant, noisy, essentially churlish devices whose only practical purpose was to blast holes of various sizes in entities that would thereby be rendered less functional than they would otherwise have been. I didn't object merely to guns that killed people; I also objected to guns that killed animals, or shattered windows, or plinked away at discarded beer bottles. Whenever a gun was put to effective use, I insisted, something broke; and it seemed absurd to go through life breaking things.

Although these paragraphs differ greatly in length, each paragraph is adequately developed for its purpose. By its very brevity and directness, the first paragraph draws the reader's attention to the startling parallel between dead legislation and dead people, setting the stage for the argument that the essay subsequently develops. The second paragraph is much longer and more detailed because it sums up the author's earlier antigun sentiments and prepares for a later conflict between these attitudes and the allure of gun ownership. You are free to exercise those same kinds of options in your own writing, provided that your decisions are based on an understanding of what each paragraph should accomplish and how much information is needed to satisfy your readers' expectations. Here are some specific suggestions to help you make such judgments:

1. Whenever you write a one- or two-sentence paragraph, check to see if its brevity serves some purpose. If not, you have the option of deleting the paragraph, adding supporting sentences, or combining it with the paragraph(s) next to it (if the paragraphs are related).

2. Put yourself in the position of the reader, and ask yourself whether you would be able to understand the point of each paragraph on the basis of the information it provides. If not, add details, using the strategies discussed in **5c.**

5e Use transitions to achieve coherence between paragraphs.

All of the techniques for achieving coherence within paragraphs can be used to establish the same kinds of relationships between paragraphs. Especially useful for this purpose are transitional words or phrases and repetition of key words or their synonyms.

1. To indicate explicitly how one paragraph is related to another, use an appropriate transitional word or expression. A partial list is given below:

Purpose	*Transition Words*
to list	first, second, next, last
to indicate time sequence	before, previously, now, later, meanwhile, then, afterwards
to establish a spatial relationship	below, above, along, beside beneath, behind, in front
to amplify	that is, in fact, in other words

Purpose	*Transition Words*
to exemplify	for example, for instance
to establish a logical relationship	therefore, consequently, thus, as a result, for
to add information	and, also, too, in addition, furthermore, moreover
to compare	similarly, likewise
to contrast	but, however, on the other hand, conversely, nevertheless, otherwise

2. Another effective means of achieving coherence between paragraphs is to repeat key words or synonyms, as in the following series of paragraphs drawn from the body of a student essay entitled "The Second Street War":

Car by car, mower by mower, we waged a neck-to-neck battle with our new neighbors. Each week my father would add a new gadget to his already adequate lawn and garden supplies. He would then proudly strut out on our front yard and demonstrate its many uses. Within minutes, Mr. Jones would charge out his door with the latest weed eater or hedge groomer. The air filled with machine gun blasts of yard warfare. At the climax of the metallic cantata, Mrs. Jones would appear on the horizon modeling the latest addition to her wardrobe. Her outfit hit my father like a low flying torpedo—below the belt. With wallet in hand, he began a desperate search for my mother.

Although material items were the most obvious prizes in the Second Street War, we battled for superiority in physical fitness as well. Every morning my family assembled on the sidewalk bordering our house. In his most commanding tone, my father hurled exercise instructions into the crisp air. In an effort to even the tug of war, Mr. Jones led his troops on a mile run. Both squads were determined to be the healthiest household on the block. Our den closet became a haven of exercise apparatus. More than once, I was forced to rescue my mother from the clutches of a monstrous muscle toner.

Despite the physical torture we subjected ourselves to, we extended the battle to another front. My parents had never considered joining the posh Country Club until the Joneses moved in. Piano and dance lessons became necessities for my sister and me (we both agreed this was equivalent to life imprisonment in a concentration camp). Dinner parties, bridge and garden clubs, as well as the Daughters of the American Revolution, invaded our living room each week. Not to be outdone, the Joneses held outdoor barbecues, book club galas, and church circle meetings.

Although there are two explicit transition words (**Although** and **Despite**), the continuity we sense in reading this group of paragraphs results mainly from the sustained metaphor of warfare and the varied synonyms for combat used to keep this neighborhood conflict in focus (e.g., **battle, charge, machine gun blasts of yard warfare, troops, squads, conflict**).

Exercise 2

The three paragraphs below have been excerpted from an expository essay that traces the major developments in Madonna's career from 1984 to the present. Read the passage carefully and for each paragraph, answer the questions that follow.

In the two year period of 1989 through 1990, Madonna delivered a seemingly neverending assault of product and publicity in three consecutive waves. She released three albums (*Like a Prayer*, the soundtrack to *Dick Tracy*, and *The Immaculate Collection*), produced two videocassettes (*The Immaculate Collection* and *Justify My Love*), and had a starring role in Warren Beatty's film *Dick Tracy*. Her earnings for this period were said by *Forbes* magazine to be over $16,000,000.00, making her the fourth richest entertainer in America.

When *Like a Prayer* hit record stores in 1989, Madonna was dubbed "Artist of the Year." Gone were the nonsensical party-girl tunes of the early '80s. This release showed true talent, a term that had never before been used to describe Madonna's singing efforts.

The songs were still in the dance genre, but a maturity was evolving within the music. It was time, because as Madonna grew up, so too did her fans.

By this point, Madonna was acutely aware of her influence. She had tested and refined her approach, meticulously designed her own forum from which to educate, and so began to use it all in an effort to promote, among other things, safe sex and the awareness of AIDS. In each copy of *Like a Prayer*, she included a pamphlet which explained the nature of AIDS and how it can be transmitted. She spoke publicly about the disease and gave benefit concerts to raise money for research. In videos for the album, she tackled interracial relationships and freedom of female sexuality. Education was combined with Madonna's stereotypical lewdness, in order to hold viewers' attention, so they might receive the message while still being entertained.

1. Which sentence serves as the topic sentence?

2. Which of the seven strategies discussed in **5c** does the writer use to develop this paragraph?

3. Is the paragraph adequately developed? Why or why not?

5f Write effective introductions and conclusions.

1. *Introductory paragraph.* In most essays, the introduction has two basic functions: to engage readers' interest and to prepare them for what is to follow. Though your decisions about how to accomplish these goals will be influenced to some extent by the purpose for which you are writing (see Chapter **2**), the specific methods you use are almost unlimited. In an essay based on an experience involving some memorable person, for example, you might begin, as the

author of "Perry the Punker" does, with a story that captures the essence of that person's character. Or, you might choose instead to describe the setting that serves as a backdrop for a story that will be told later in the essay.

> In the summer of 1960 my family emigrated to the United States, fleeing the tyrant Trujillo. In New York we found a small apartment with a Catholic school nearby, taught by the Sisters of Charity, hefty women in long black gowns and bonnets that made them look like peculiar dolls in mourning. I liked them a lot, especially my grandmotherly fifth grade teacher, Sister Zoe.
>
> Julia Alvarez

If neither of these approaches seems appropriate for your purposes, you might begin with a generalization and then narrow the focus to the particular person or situation you are writing about, following the amplification arrangement discussed on page 58.

These choices don't begin to exhaust the possibilities. You might state an explicit thesis at the beginning of the introduction, as Roger Verhulst does in the short paragraph on gun control cited on page 61, or save the thesis statement for the end of the paragraph, as the author of "Perry the Punker" does. On the other hand, you might omit the thesis statement altogether, relying instead on description or narration alone, as N. Scott Momaday does in the sample paragraph on page 57. Still other options are to use a question-answer format or to pose a problem and follow with a solution.

> How do you celebrate the 25th anniversary of James Bond's explosive assault on the movies? First you launch a search for a new Bond to replace the urbane but long-in-the-tooth Roger Moore, who turned in his license to quip after seven Bond flicks. Then you float enough rumors to create the biggest casting fuss since the search for Scarlett O'Hara. At the last minute, you announce a dark-horse victor—a rugged English stage and film actor whom most Americans haven't quite heard of. And when you finally unveil him as the fourth James Bond, following in the catlike footsteps of Sean Con-

nery, George Lazenby and Moore, he turns out to be a magnificent throwback. Far from the high-tech cartoon character that the recent Bond had become, the new guy is intense, macho and almost believable—just the man to lure back the nostalgia buffs who'd left James Bond to the kids.
Cathleen McGuigan

The Institute for Creation Research and the Creation Research Society, with the support of the Moral Majority and similar religio-political groups, have been waging a nationwide campaign to require the teaching of creationism alongside evolution in public school biology classes. Last year, Florida's Hillsborough County School Board voted in favor of such a requirement. This was a regrettable decision, one that will cost a lot in time, energy, and taxpayers' dollars, not to mention student confusion, before it is inevitably reversed. It does reveal how prevalent are popular misconceptions about religion and science. But it obscures the real concerns at the heart of the fundamentalist attack on contemporary culture, and so delays any rational attempts to resolve the deeper issues.
Anne Marie Brennan

2. *Concluding paragraph.* The ending of an essay is in some respects like the beginning because the last paragraph usually redirects the reader's attention to the issues introduced in the first paragraph. The conclusion should not simply repeat what has already been said, however; rather, it should lead the reader to some revelation or insight that provides a strong sense of closure.

Like introductory paragraphs, conclusions may take a variety of forms. If you have written your essay in the form of an extended narrative, you might close with an incident that dramatizes the meaning or significance of preceding events. In "Once More to the Lake," E. B. White tells of returning with his son to a camp in Maine where his family had spent many vacations in his youth. The essay ends with the author's realization of his own mortality.

When the others went swimming, my son said he was going in, too. He pulled his dripping trunks from the line where they had hung all through the shower and wrung them out. Languidly, and with no thought of going in, I watched him, his hard little body, skinny and bare, saw him wince slightly as he pulled up around his vitals the small, soggy, icy garment. As he buckled the swollen belt, suddenly my groin felt the chill of death.

If, on the other hand, your aim is to evaluate, you might prefer to conclude in a different way, restating the criteria on which you have based your judgments or reemphasizing the judgments themselves. In an editorial attacking the grossly misleading stories found in tabloids, *Discover* magazine concludes by reinforcing the criterion of objectivity in reporting.

The tabloids often disagree with each other. In reporting that a previously unknown cosmonaut named Tanya had been violated by aliens in space during a secret mission in the 1960s, the *Examiner* assured its readers that both the recent flight of Sally Ride and the 1982 mission of cosmonaut Svetlana Savitskaya had been "incident free." Not according to the *Sun*. In what should be the biggest scoop of the year, that paper claims that Savitskaya conceived a baby while on board Salyut 7. It actually goes on to quote her: "The conception was a physical act performed solely for the sake of science." That is more than can be said for the bizarre conceptions of the American weekly tabloids.

Another common method of structuring conclusions— one that is especially appropriate to expository and argumentative writing—is to summarize the points developed throughout the essay and to generalize from them. Note how Bruce Catton ends his essay on the Civil War leaders Grant and Lee.

Lastly, and perhaps greatest of all, there was the ability, at the end, to turn quickly from war to peace once the fighting was over. Out of the way these two men behaved at Appomattox came the possibility of a peace of reconciliation. It was a possibility not wholly realized, in the years to come, but which did, in the end, help the two sections to become one nation again . . . after a war whose bitterness might have seemed to make such a reunion wholly impossible. No part of either man's life became him more than the part he played in this brief meeting in the McLean house at Appomattox. Their behavior there put all succeeding generations of Americans in their debt. Two great Americans, Grant and Lee—very different, yet under everything very much alike. Their encounter at Appomattox was one of the great moments of American history.

A fourth approach is to use the data accumulated in the body of the essay to project future conditions. Edward Abbey employs this strategy in his essay "The Damnation of a Canyon" to win support for his argument that the Glen Canyon Dam should be dismantled and the Colorado River allowed to resume its free-flowing course.

This will no doubt expose a drear and hideous scene: immense mud flats and whole plateaus of sodden garbage strewn with dead trees, sunken boats, the skeletons of long-forgotten, decomposing water-skiers. But to those who find the prospect too appalling, I say give nature a little time. In five years, at most in ten, the sun and wind and storms will cleanse and sterilize the repellent mess. The inevitable floods will soon remove all that does not belong within the canyons. Fresh green willow, box elder and redbud will reappear; and the ancient drowned cottonwoods (noble monuments to themselves) will be replaced by young of their own kind. With the renewal of plant life will come the insects, the birds, the lizards and snakes, the mammals. Within a generation—thirty years—I predict the river and canyons will bear a decent resemblance to their former selves. Within the lifetime of our children Glen Canyon and the living river, heart of the canyonlands, will be restored to us. The wilderness will again belong to God, the people and the wild things that call it home.

Exercise 3

Below are the introductory and concluding paragraphs of the student essay "The Second Street War" on pages 63–64. Read them, relate them to the body of the essay, and answer the questions that follow.

Introductory paragraph

I shall never forget the day the Second Street War started. It was a cold, moist, summer morning. A halo of fog delicately floated above our neighborhood. My sister and I were sitting on our front porch arguing, our favorite pastime. Out of the corner of my eye, I spotted a yellow moving van coming down our street. It pulled into the driveway directly opposite ours. Three enormous men in dirty jumpsuits began unloading its contents. My sister and I forgot our disagreement and stared wide-eyed at the exquisite furniture being carried into the house. A sleek automobile of sparkling burgundy stopped at the curb. I heard a loud gasp behind me and turned to see my mother, who was ghost-white and trembling. "Would you just look at that!" she exclaimed through quivering lips. This phrase was the cannon blast that initiated the financial, physical, and social see-saw of "keeping up with the Joneses."

Concluding paragraph

It was in the middle of two of these simultaneous gatherings that the atomic bomb exploded. Declaring our abstention from the status-seeking games our parents played, Jeremy Jones and I announced our engagement. Our wedding was not only a union of two persons but of two families. I am proud to say Jeremy and I own a solar-heated A-frame home, much nicer than my sister's shabby abode, and my two lovely daughters are enrolled in Madame Goule's secondary ballet class. And, would you just look at that—we have some new neighbors!

1. Which of the introductory tactics discussed in this chapter does the writer use?

2. How does the writer achieve unity and coherence in the concluding paragraph?

6 · Revising

6a Understand the nature of revision.

We've all occasionally wished to go back in time to change something we've said—to make a completely different statement or to say something in a slightly different way or even to remain silent. This feeling derives from a natural urge to communicate; we're distressed when we haven't said what we meant or when others misunderstand us. Revision—which means "to see again"—gives us a chance to exploit this urge, to shape and reshape communication so that when our readers receive it, they will understand it as we wish. Unless we revise, we lose this chance.

Realizing this fact, experienced writers continually reevaluate their work in the light of their original intentions and improve the text in the following ways:

1. by adding words, sentences, and paragraphs when the information is incomplete
2. by deleting material when they discover it to be false, inappropriate, or needlessly repetitive
3. by substituting new words for old when simple deletion leaves gaps in content
4. by reordering words, sentences, or phrases when such changes are necessary to improve coherence.

Exercising good judgment in making such changes requires a special ability called writer's empathy, which allows you to identify with your readers and to imagine how your words would affect them. Assuming this perspective will give you the detachment needed to evaluate the effects of revision within the context of the entire essay—to see how each change affects what has already been written and influences whatever writing is yet to come.

This approach to revision most clearly distinguishes experienced writers from inexperienced ones. Experienced writers, Nancy Sommers tells us, first ask themselves, '"What does my essay as a *whole* need for form, balance, rhythm, or communication?' Details are added, dropped, substituted, or reordered according to their sense of what the essay needs for emphasis and proportion. This sense, however, is constantly in flux as ideas are developed and modified; it is constantly 're-viewed' in relation to the parts."

Changes such as these can affect a piece of writing on three levels: the whole essay, the paragraph, and the sentence. Changes that affect the whole essay include altering a sequence of sentences or paragraphs, changing a key definition, adding sentences to increase support for a thesis, or even rewriting a thesis statement to reflect discoveries made during drafting. Paragraph-level changes involve adding or rephrasing a topic sentence, reordering sentences within the paragraph, inserting transitional words or phrases, or deleting irrelevant material. Sentence-level revisions focus on the grammatical form or spelling of specific words, the placement of punctuation marks, or the clarity of individual sentences.

6b Revise in light of your developing aims.

We can see the results of this comprehensive approach to revision in the following excerpt from the first draft of an essay called "Sailing Simple," which was written for a college class but later published in a popular sailing magazine:

1. There is no need to make sailing a complicated activity. My first instinct/response after buying a little cruising boat was to make lists . . . of all the things that had to be repaired, replaced, and added on in order for me to have her properly equipped for fall cruising and frostbite racing.

2. The engine didn't work, the stove came apart in my hand the first time I tried to light it, the deck leaked, and the drain valve-stem wrung off when I tried to clear the sink. There's no radio, chart, or safety gear aboard. The battery is dead, and my guess is that none of the lights work anyway. The rig is so loose that the spreaders flop around when power boats go past. The compass globe is so yellowed from 12 years in the sun that I can't read the card. And I'm not about to try the head, since it has a long crack in it that's already been patched with bathtub sealer.

3. The boat is . . . basic. Basically old and threadbare. The only things the previous owners didn't stip off were the stuff that didn't work or was outdated. So, what's to do but set about getting the boat properly set up and equipped.

4. I went sailing instead. Instead of backing out of the slip with the outboard, I just untied the dock lines and pushed her out. Instead of the stove and sink, I ate cold food of paper plates. Instead of charting my courses and following the compass, I just sailed a general direction dictated by the wind. Instead of the head, I used the rail. There was no weather forecast without a radio, and no way to call anybody. So I took what the weather dished out as it came, and talked to myself instead of chattering to friends.

5. I was out by myself, singlehandling, so I had a challenge in those frequent moments when 5 or 6 hands were needed in 3 different places at once to handle the tiller and lines. I began to experiment and explore the values of simplicity by playing at making do and doing without.

In his personal assessment of this draft, the writer complained that "the flow wasn't there. It seemed jerky and confused. There was no cohesion to the ideas and thoughts." Having identified these problems, he attempted to resolve them in several ways. To improve overall coherence, he reordered paragraphs, moving the third paragraph to a position between the first and second, and added the transitional word "so" at the beginning of the fourth paragraph. With these changes, he was able to "just relax and tell the story," as he puts it, describing in a new chronological sequence how he made lists of needed repairs; attempted to equip the boat for sailing; became frustrated in his efforts to repair the broken stove, valves, and the like; and finally "went sailing instead." To improve the piece's coherence and clarity, he made a number of other changes by adding, deleting, or substituting words. He added the words "last month" to indicate when he had purchased the boat. He deleted two unnecessary phrases in what is now paragraph 3 and for the same reason cut the first of the two references to weather in the fourth paragraph. And he rewrote a number of sentences, replacing the general phrase "wouldn't work" at the beginning of the present paragraph 2 with the more precise "wouldn't start," condensing six words into two at the beginning of the fifth paragraph, and making similar substitutions throughout the draft. Later, after making other substantive changes in the remaining pages of this draft and doing several additional rewrites, he edited the manuscript to correct errors such as the misspelling of the word "strip" in paragraph 3.

6c Apply specific rewriting strategies.

1. Examine your current revision practices to determine whether you are taking full advantage of the options available to you. Among the issues you might consider in this self-assessment are the ones addressed in the following questions:

- When writing an essay, what percentage of your time do you usually devote to revision?
- Do you revise as you draft, or do you think of revision as a separate process?
- How many drafts do you usually write for an essay assigned in a composition class?

6
c

- Which of the four types of revision discussed earlier in this chapter do you regularly use? Which do you consider most important?
- When you revise, what do you concentrate on first: content? organization? sentence flow? grammatical errors? punctuation?
- Do you focus on a different problem in each draft, or do you make various kinds of changes in each?
- Do you feel that you've been successful with the revision strategies you're now using? If not, which of the techniques discussed in this chapter would you consider adopting?

2. When given the opportunity to rewrite an essay, make a commitment to take it through multiple drafts, using all of the previously discussed techniques: addition, deletion, substitution, and reordering.

3. Identify the distinctive traits of the kind of writing you intend to do and keep these in mind as you revise. For example, in revising a summary of someone else's writing, you would want to be sure that you had explained objectively the author's main points rather than making subjective judgments about them as you would in an evaluative essay.

4. If you revise as you draft, either in your head or on paper, don't abandon that approach if you've been successful with it. But don't become preoccupied with editorial revisions during the early stages of the composing process—especially if you have trouble getting started or find yourself constantly interrupting your flow of thought to check for misspellings, punctuation problems, or grammatical errors. Instead, think of your initial efforts as exploratory drafts intended to help you discover content, find a focus, determine arrangement, and in various other ways provide an impetus for the more structured and polished drafts to come.

5. As you compose, stop periodically to examine your work from your readers' perspective, asking yourself ques-

tions such as these:

- Have the subject and purpose of this piece of writing been clearly expressed?
- Is the subject sufficiently limited for an essay of this scope?
- Is the subject consistently and thoroughly developed?
- Is there some recognizable pattern of organization?

6. As you make essay-level revisions, consider also how you might strengthen and refine individual paragraphs. Here are some questions to guide you:

- Does this piece of writing have an introduction that engages readers' attention and enables them to predict what is to follow?
- Does each paragraph in the body of the essay contribute to the central idea or impression that is intended to unify the work?
- Are the sentences in each paragraph arranged in a predictable sequence?
- Is each paragraph clearly related to the ones preceding and following it?
- Is there a conclusion which unifies the essay by fulfilling the expectations raised in the introduction?

7. List any stylistic faults you are aware of in your writing (see Part **III**):

- Do you tend to repeat some of the same words over and over again rather than varying your word choice?
- Are you sometimes satisfied with a general word or a familiar conversational expression when you could find a more precise one by drawing upon your observations and recollections or by consulting a dictionary or thesaurus?
- Are the majority of your sentences similar in length and structure?

• Do you overuse the passive voice, expletive constructions such as "It is" and "There are," forms of the verb
"be," and nominals?

6d Apply specific proofreading and editing strategies.

By the time you have answered the preceding questions and
rewritten the text accordingly, you will be ready to devote
your full attention to matters of style and correctness. To do
so, you must assume a different role from the one you
adopted when inventing, arranging, drafting, and rewriting—the role of proofreader and editor.

As a proofreader, your task is to identify your tendencies
for error and to be alert for such problems, as well as for careless errors and typographical mistakes. As an editor, your
main responsibilities are to correct errors in grammar, punctuation, mechanics, and spelling.

Among the proofreading and editing strategies you
might consider adopting are the ones discussed below.

1. Make a list of the errors you are most likely to make,
using these questions as a guide:

• What kinds of words are you most likely to misspell
(see Chapter **48**)?
• Which punctuation marks do you consistently use correctly, and which are you less confident about (see Part
IV)?
• What kinds of grammatical errors do you tend to make:
fragments? subject-verb disagreement? comma splices
(see Part **V**)?
• What mechanical conventions (capitalization, hyphen-
ation, syllable division, etc.) cause you the most problems (see Part **IV**)?

2. Read your manuscript line by line, looking first for obvious careless or typographical errors such as the inadvertent omission, addition, or reversal of letters within a word.

3. When you have finished, reread the text with the same attentiveness and objectivity, concentrating this time on the tendencies for error you identified in #1 above. Each time you discover a possible error, either correct it before proceeding further or—if you are not sure what changes to make—circle the words or sentences that warrant closer scrutiny so that you can reconsider them later. To check for spelling errors, for example, you might first circle all the words you do not ordinarily see in print, as well as all the more common words you have a tendency to misspell, and then look them up in a dictionary. (Another method available to writers who compose on a word processor is to use one of the spelling checker programs that have been designed for this purpose.)

4. Before making final corrections, read your manuscript aloud, noting any words, phrases, or sentences that force you to slow down or stop. At each of these junctures, check to see if the interruption in the flow of words signals an error in grammar or punctuation, omitted words, confused sentence structure, or some other kind of problem. You might even want to tape-record your reading so that you can play it back at your leisure, as many times as you wish. Or you might try a slightly different approach and ask a friend to read instead so that you can distance yourself far enough from what you have written to judge it with the same degree of objectivity as your audience will.

Exercise

On page 80 is the first draft of an argumentative essay written by a student in a college composition class in response to the following assignment.

Choose a subject about which you feel strongly and write an essay of 3–5 typed pages in which you argue the superiority of your point of view. Your purpose in this piece of writing is to convince your readers (in this instance, the other members of the class) to reject opposing points of view and to adopt yours. Your specific tasks are to: (1) define the nature and scope of the problem you are addressing, (2) state your response to that problem in a thesis statement, (3) anticipate opposing arguments and demonstrate why your readers should reject them, (4) support your own case with facts, definitions, personal observations and experiences, interviews, and other sources of information, (5) systematically arrange supporting logic and evidence, (6) offer conclusions/solutions that follow logically from the arguments developed throughout the essay, (7) carefully examine the completed draft to determine whether any words, sentences, or paragraphs need to be added, deleted, replaced, or reordered, and (8) proofread and edit the manuscript to correct errors in punctuation, spelling, and grammar.

Read the essay very carefully and on a separate sheet of paper, comment on how well the writer has accomplished each of the eight tasks identified above. Indicate the strengths of the essay and the areas in which revisions are needed.

Drug Testing

Many people oppose random drug testing in the workplace because it is a violation of their rights to privacy and Constitutional rights to pursue life, liberty, and happiness. Well, if people are not doing drugs, then why else would they oppose to being tested for drugs? The same people who oppose drug testing would probably be the first ones to sue their employers if an accident happened at work under drug related circumstances. They would stand up and accuse their employers of not taking necessary precautions to protect them from druggies and addicts.

Many of the people who want their rights protected are the ones who are the first to cry out in protest when an issue such as mandatory drug testing arises. I don't think these people realize that in order to protect their rights to not be harmed by other people, someone's rights to privacy have to be violated. Personally, I do not believe that drug testing is a great violation of privacy considering that a little precaution could save the country a lot of money and save a person a lot of pain and grief.

I think a lot of the privacy judgement should be left up to the employer. If he thinks that a job requires that its operators be "clean," then he should require drug testing. If the employees refuse to be tested, then they should not complain or sue their employer when an accident occurs or they should be fired. The government requires drug testing in all of its positions and is rightly justified by doing so. Drug problems result in absences from the workplace and reduced productivity. It can save vast amounts of tax dollars by eliminating the drug users and hiring efficient workers to fill the vacancies. I'm sure that one great employee will perform much better than two that have drug problems.

Drug testing can also help those that are using drugs. If it can be identified that a person has a drug problem through testing, then perhaps that person can be reached and helped before it is too late for that person to turn back.

Overall, I think that drug testing is not a violation of privacy, but an attempt to protect the workers in their work environment and to protect the employers from inefficiency in their firms.

7 · Using Word Processors

Word processing is a means of using a computer to prepare typewritten text. Word-processing programs enable a personal computer to behave almost like a magic typewriter. As you enter your thoughts from a keyboard, the letters you type appear on a screen. If you want to change anything about your text, a few strokes can erase the old and enter the new, move part of your text from one place in the paper to another, or correct misspelled words throughout the paper. After you have the paper just the way you want it, a few keystrokes send the text to a printer where the whole paper is printed with each page numbered automatically.

You might begin a new essay by developing some ideas with the help of an "outliner," a program often available with word processors for entering and arranging text in outline form. Or you might begin by freewriting with the word processor. You can keep your freewriting as a separate file or place it at the beginning or end of the essay for easy reference. If you want to keep your initial notations and freewriting always at the end of the essay, just enter several blank lines above the notes and return to your developing essay. The cursor will automatically push the notes ahead and out of sight until you want to skip down to consult or delete them.

As you enter text you will want to change things. You might mistype a letter, think of a better word than the one you just entered, or decide you need another sentence early in the paragraph you have just finished. In such cases, you simply use the "arrow keys" or mouse to move your cursor to the place where changes should be made. With your cursor at an unwanted word, you enter the one- or two-key command to delete the word, and it disappears, its space automatically filled by the following words. If you want to add a word or words to a sentence, you position the cursor in the appropriate space and type the words, and the following text will automatically move over to make room. If you want to delete the whole line, give the appropriate one- or two-key command, and away goes the line, its space filled by the following text.

Sometimes you want to move one or more sentences or paragraphs from one place to another. In this case, position your cursor at the first letter of the text you want to move and enter the command to mark the beginning of a "block" of text; then move your cursor to the end of the text you want to move and enter the command to mark the end of the block. Finally, position the cursor at the point in your essay where you want the block moved and enter the command to "move block." Immediately, the text is rearranged just as you want. You can also use block commands to delete whole sentences and paragraphs. When you are through writing at least for a while, you end your word-processing session by entering the command to "save" the file to your disk; then you may turn off the computer, your text preserved for later work or long-term storage.

Some programs are designed to analyze the style, grammar, punctuation, and capitalization of your writing. After entering text using your word processor, you can use such a program to examine your essay for incorrect punctuation and spelling, for awkward or long-winded phrases, for questionable word choice, for overuse of passive voice, and for numerous other grammatical and stylistic problems. These programs will not only highlight potential problems, they will also suggest revisions. If you use such a program, however, you should beware of slavishly following its advice. Sometimes the stylistic features it calls into question are actually fine for your specific writing task.

The program *Grammatik* is one of the earliest developed of these grammar and style checkers and can demonstrate the benefits it offers. The text and illustration on page 84, taken from the *Grammatik User's Guide,* describe the program's function as it just begins to proofread a piece of writing. The illustration shows that the program has found a homonym problem: The writer has entered "it's" instead of "its." The program shows the error in its context and suggests a way to correct it. All the writer has to do is move the computer cursor to the "Replace/Next" rectangle and press the "Enter" key. The program will replace "it's" with "its" and continue with its analysis until it finds another problem.

Page from the *Grammatik User's Guide*

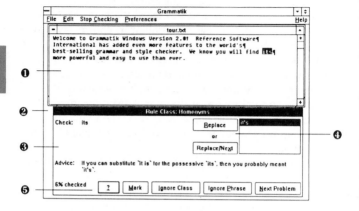

Figure 5-3 Grammatik's Edit and Advice windows

The numbered items in Figure 5-3 are described as follows:

❶ Edit window - displays the current writing problem highlighted in the context of the sentence.

❷ Rule class - displays the rule class for the current problem.

❸ Advice window - identifies the writing problem and gives advice and options for correcting it.

❹ Replace options - displays one or more suggested corrections to replace the problem word or phrase. It is only displayed if the problem has a replace option.

❺ Command buttons - options for responding to the problem.

Programs such as *Grammatik* can also summarize your document's characteristics. For example, one table gives an indication of your composition's school reading level (for example, seventh-grade reading level), the percent of predicates in the passive voice, the average sentence length, the average word length, and the average paragraph length, all of which indicate the document's readability.

7

Obviously, the most striking benefit of word processing is the ease and depth of revision it makes possible. There is, however, one feature that can be disadvantageous. The screen of the video display shows only part of a page of text. While you may "scroll" from line to line and page to page of your file, you will only have visible the same number of lines at a time, and this limited view of an essay can discourage writers from perceiving and revising the essay as a whole. The solution is to enter commands for the printer to print out a draft copy of your essay. With a printed copy, you can view the essay as a relatively coherent whole and indicate additions, deletions, and text movements on the printed pages to guide your final revisions with the word processor. At this stage there is no substitute for the old-fashioned pencil.

Below are listed some operations common to popular word processors. Before you select a program for your own use, you might examine its documentation to see how easy it is to invoke these operations.

Text Formatting

Left justification The lines of text are automatically aligned down the left side of the page.

Right justification The words at the right side of the page may be aligned by automatically inserting spaces between words to stretch all lines to even length.

Center justification A line of text may be automatically centered on the page.

Proportional spacing   The spaces between letters are varied according to their size; for example, "l" takes less space than "m."

Adjustable left and right margins   The margins of text may be set at whatever point on the page you wish and may be altered within documents.

Adjustable top and bottom margins   Space at the top and bottom of the page is variable.

Variable tab settings   Tabs may be put anywhere on a line.

Double line spacing   Lines may be automatically double spaced, as is standard for manuscripts.

Triple line spacing   Lines may be automatically triple spaced.

10 characters per inch   Pica type size is available.

12 characters per inch   Elite type size is available.

17 characters per inch   Compressed type size is available.

Letter enhancement features   The following features are available and shown on screen when invoked: underline, bold print (thicker, darker letters), italics, strikethrough (letters with lines struck through them to show reader what is deleted), and small capitals (capital letters the size of lowercase letters).

Hard page breaks   A line on the video display screen automatically indicates when text has filled a page.

Conditional page breaks   The writer can create page endings anywhere in the text.

Automatic page numbering   Each page is automatically numbered at a desired location.

Headers   At the top of each page a standard set of words will be automatically printed.

Footers   At the bottom of each page a standard set of words will be automatically printed. Page numbers can be incorporated into headers and footers.

Command Indications

Menus   The choice of commands available to the writer is listed on the screen, so there is no need to memorize commands.

Bypass menus   If the writer does not need a menu, it can be eliminated to make room for more text on the screen, and it can be temporarily called back when needed.

Command line   This is a mode in which you can give the computer commands to perform functions outside the word-processing program without having to close your work within the program.

Function keys   The "F1" through "F10" keys on a computer keyboard serve as shortcuts to multikey commands. As many as 30 additional complex commands can be shortened by combining the "shift," "alternate," "command," and "control" keys with the function keys.

Ruler line   Displayed at the top of the page is a line showing the width of the margins and the position of tab settings. The ruler line can be suppressed to make room for an additional line of text.

Status line   This is a line that shows the page number, the name of the file being processed, the number of the line the cursor occupies on a page, and the number of the column the cursor occupies on a line.

Text Entry and Editing

Deleting   Characters, words, lines, and marked blocks of text can be deleted.

Undelete capability   A command can cancel a previous deletion.

Blocking capabilities   Writer-determined portions of text can be marked as blocks to be deleted, copied to other places in the text, or moved from one place to another.

Search and replace   Words can be found anywhere within the text and the cursor moved to them automatically. Words can be automatically changed as the writer specifies (particularly helpful when a word has been misspelled or misused throughout an essay).

Cursor movement   Commands are available to move the cursor to the end or beginning of a word, line, sentence, paragraph, screen, or entire file.

Automatic paragraph alignment   When additions and deletions are made, the text within a paragraph automatically rejustifies.

Word Help

Spelling checker   This is a dictionary of English words in the program to which the program can compare the words in your essay. The dictionary should have at least 50,000 words. Most dictionaries permit the writer to add words.

Thesaurus   This provides a set of synonyms for each word in the dictionary that the writer can call up for consideration. Some thesauruses provide antonyms too.

WYSIWYG   "What you see is what you get" means that the display screen shows just what the printed page will look like.

II

Structuring Sentences

8 · Understanding the Parts of Speech

8a The parts of speech

Consider the words below:

and	excitedly	into	stadium	wow	colorful
football	push	watch	crowd	huge	shuffle	we

Each word by itself can suggest to a reader one or more meanings. **Watch** might be a device for telling time or the act of observing; **into** means from the outside to the inside; **and** suggests the coordination of one thing with another.

To communicate, we arrange words so that each word gains meaning from its place in the group while lending to the group its most appropriate meaning. But only certain types of words go together. **Excitedly stadium** and **push colorful** do not make sense while **colorful crowd** and **football stadium** do.

Obviously there are only certain ways to group words meaningfully in English. For example, you will recognize **colorful crowd** and **football stadium** to be the same type of group as **huge watch.** And you will recognize **we shuffle** and **the crowd pushes** to be the same type of group as **we watch.**

Note that when **watch** comes after **colorful,** it means something different than when it comes after **we,** and it serves a different purpose. After **colorful, watch** serves as the name of something; after **we,** it serves to express an action. Before **stadium, football** serves as a describer; after **colorful,** it serves as a name. Traditionally we recognize eight different purposes words can serve, and these purposes we identify with the *parts of speech.* If we rearrange the 13 words listed at the opening of this chapter and add two determiners, **the** and **a,** we find all eight parts of speech at work. The numbers key these words to each part discussed on the following pages.

3   1   4   2   1   7   1   5   6   4
We watch the colorful crowd shuffle and push excitedly into a huge

   4   2   8
football stadium. Wow!

1. Verb   5. Adverb
2. Noun   6. Preposition
3. Pronoun   7. Conjunction
4. Adjective   8. Interjection

8b Verbs

The *verb* is the heart of the sentence. Most verbs tell what happens (**sleep, fly, decide, become**); others express a state of existence (**be, seem, taste**). And certain verbs may be used with other verbs (**have** gone, **is** going). A verb requires a *subject*, which identifies what or who is acting, occurring, existing, or receiving an action. Some verbs also take an *object*, which tells what or who is acted upon. (See **9a** for a full discussion of the verb's role in the sentence.)

The winter **birds** (subject) **sang** (verb of action) all morning.

Their **feeder** (subject) **was** (verb of existence) full.

They (subject) **ate** (verb of action) **every seed** (object) by afternoon.

1. *Regular verbs.* Verbs assume different forms, called *inflections*, to give certain kinds of information in addition to a basic meaning. Three of those forms are the *principal parts:* the *infinitive*, the *past tense*, and the *past participle*. *Regular verbs* all inflect the principal parts the same way. The infinitive is the basic form which undergoes the inflections. It is the form used just after **to** and is the same form used with **I, we, you,** and **they** when the verb expresses something occurring in the present.

We want **to believe** all our leaders.

I **believe** that politician.

We use a verb's infinitive when we refer to it as a word.

The verb **lie** is rarely used in face-to-face debate.

The infinitive is the form used for listing a verb in a dictionary.

The *past tense* form indicates that the happening or existence is in the past. Regular verbs form the past tense by adding **-d** or **-ed** to the infinitive.

Last year I **believed** that politician, but she **disappointed** me.

The *past participle* form for regular verbs is the same as the past tense form. We indicate an occurrence in the past with the past participle by using **have, has,** or **had** before it.

I **have supported** that politician before, but I am reluctant to support her now.

Past participles can also be used to help describe nouns or pronouns.

Ms. Barton is an **elected** official.

Two other inflections are formed by the addition of **-ing** and **-s** or **-es** to the infinitive. The *present participle* is the **-ing** form. Used with a form of **be**, it can indicate ongoing occurrences; used alone it can modify nouns or pronouns.

I **am preparing** a political campaign. [an ongoing action]

She lends a **helping hand** to the needy. [modifying a noun]

Whenever we express an occurrence in the present with a singular noun (**8c**) or third person pronoun (**8d**) as subject, we add **-s** or **-es** to the verb.

Her **manager holds** the purse strings of her campaign. [singular noun as subject]

He **argues** with her about her extravagant travel budget. [third person singular personal pronoun as subject]

Everyone **believes** that politician now. [singular indefinite pronoun as subject]

 2. *Irregular verbs.* Some English verbs do not form their past tense or past participle in the regular way. There are four patterns typical of these *irregular verbs:* (1) changing a vowel instead of adding **-ed;** (2) adding an **-n** instead of **-ed;** (3) changing only one form from the infinitive; and (4) not changing the infinitive for either past tense or past participle.

	Infinitive	Past Tense	Past Participle
(1) vowel change	ring	rang	rung
(2) addition of **-n**	arise	arose	arisen
(3) one change	find	found	found
(4) no change	let	let	let

Below is a list of common irregular verbs:

Infinitive	Past Tense	Past Participle
be	was	been
bite	bit	bitten
blow	blew	blown
break	broke	broken
build	built	built
choose	chose	chosen
come	came	come
deal	dealt	dealt
dig	dug	dug
dive	dived, dove	dived
do	did	done
draw	drew	drawn
drink	drank	drunk
drive	drove	driven
fly	flew	flown

Infinitive	*Past Tense*	*Past Participle*
freeze	froze	frozen
get	got	gotten
give	gave	given
go	went	gone
have	had	had
know	knew	known
lay (place *or* put)	laid	laid
lead	led	led
lend	lent	lent
lie (recline)	lay	lain
lose	lost	lost
ride	rode	ridden
rise	rose	risen
run	ran	run
see	saw	seen
set	set	set
shine (give light)	shone	shone
shine (polish)	shined	shined
sing	sang	sung
sink	sank, sunk	sunk
sit	sat	sat
steal	stole	stolen
sting	stung	stung
swim	swam	swum
swing	swung	swung
take	took	taken
think	thought	thought
throw	threw	thrown
wear	wore	worn
write	wrote	written

8 b

3. *Helping verbs.* Certain verbs are used with other verbs as *helping* or *auxiliary* words to communicate such information as time, type of statement, and the singular or plural nature of the subject. Common auxiliaries are **be, have, do.**

The students **have** finished their work but the period **has** not ended. [**Have** and **has** help to indicate a sequence in time as well as the plurality and singularity of the subjects, **students** and **period.**]

Did she give us an assignment? [**Did** helps to indicate a question as well as past time.]

A number of auxiliaries indicate the *mode* of an occurrence and so are called *modal* auxiliaries. *Mode* refers to such indications as ability (**can, could**), possibility (**may, might**), and necessity, duty or willingness (**must, ought, shall, should, would**).

All the pupils in the third grade class **could** do the work, but only a few **would** do it without a threat.

4. *Linking verbs.* *Linking verbs* relate a subject to a word or words that help identify or describe the subject (see **9b**). The way linking verbs serve a clause is similar to the way an equal sign (=) serves an equation. The most common linking verb is **be.** Others are **seem** and verbs referring to the senses (**taste, smell,** etc.).

The artist **was** a vegetarian.

Those mountains **seem** distant.

The pizza **smells** delicious.

5. *Tense.* A verb's *tense* communicates time of occurrence. There are three major types of tenses: the *simple tenses,* the *perfect tenses,* and the *progressive tenses.* The simple tenses are the present (using the infinitive form), the past (using the past tense form), and the future (using the infinitive form plus **shall** or **will**).

	Regular	*Irregular*
Present	She asks	She rings
Past	She asked	She rang
Future	She will ask	She will ring

The *perfect tenses* communicate a comparison of times; they express an occurrence at a time before some other time. They are formed with the auxiliary **have** and the *past participle*.

Present Perfect	She has asked	She has rung	[before the present]
Past Perfect	She had asked	She had rung	[before some past time]
Future Perfect	She will have asked	She will have rung	[before some future time]

The *progressive tenses* communicate a continuing occurrence at a particular time. They are formed with the present participle and the auxiliaries **be** and **have.**

Present	She is asking	She is ringing
Past	She was asking	She was ringing
Future	She will be asking	She will be ringing
Present Perfect	She has been asking	She has been ringing
Past Perfect	She had been asking	She had been ringing
Future Perfect	She will have been asking	She will have been ringing

The usage of **shall** and **will** has changed in this century. Formerly, **shall** was used with the first person (I, we shall) and **will** was used with the second and third persons (you, she, they will). Today **will** has replaced **shall** (I, we will) except in the most formal contexts. To indicate resoluteness or obligation, **shall** may be used with second and third persons.

He shall not make that mistake again.

To ask a first person question requesting an opinion, **shall** is sometimes used.

Shall we continue to tolerate these conditions?

6. *Mood.* The *mood* of a verb communicates certain things about the writer's thinking. The *indicative mood* is almost always the mood of normal discourse, for it helps indicate that the speaker is expressing impressions, facts, or beliefs; and it is the form verbs take in questions. All the sentences used as examples so far in this chapter have verbs in the indicative mood.

Sally **asks** about you every time I see her. [fact or exaggeration]

Does Sally ever **ask** about me? [question]

Sally **needs** more time away from her books. [opinion]

The *imperative mood* is used in giving commands. The imperative verb form is no different from the indicative form used with **you,** but in a command, the subject **you** is omitted.

Ask Billy to the party before someone else does. [**You** as subject of **ask** is deleted.]

Stop! [**You** as subject is deleted.]

The *subjunctive mood* is uncommon even in formal discourse. When used, it helps communicate that the writer is expressing something contrary to fact or that the writer is expressing a request, suggestion, or requirement. Certain verbs followed by **that** require the subjunctive: among these verbs are **ask, insist, recommend, require, request, suggest, urge, wish.** Most of these verbs, whatever their tense, take only the *present subjunctive,* which is the form used with **you** in the present tense.

I recommend [or recommended] that she **reevaluate** her goals from time to time.

The plant manager insisted that each supervisor **keep** a daily record of production.

Wish is an exception because it can take the *past subjunctive.*

The past subjunctive takes the same form as the past tense.

I wish that she **reevaluated** her goals from time to time.

The plant manager wished that each supervisor **kept** accurate records.

The subjunctive form of **be** is **were** when the verb is in an **if** construction or when it helps express a wish.

If Mary **were** free on the weekends, she would be able to finish writing her novel.

Mary wishes I **were** happier.

In certain constructions, the subjunctive of **be** is **be.**

I require that you **be** on time.

Be it resolved that we will oppose the President's policy.

7. *Voice.* A verb's *voice* is the form it takes to help communicate whether the subject acts or is itself acted upon. The *active voice* makes the subject the actor.

Neil Jones **sold** most of the houses in this development.

The *passive voice* shows that the subject is acted upon.

Most of the houses in this development **were sold** by Neil Jones.

(Active and passive voices are treated more fully in **9c** and **18.**)

Exercise 1

Circle the main verbs in each of the following sentences, and underline any auxiliary verbs.

1. The mishap would have been a disaster if not for the

   gymnast's quick recovery.

2. Despite repeated efforts, the frantic parents could find no trace of their missing child.

3. The ceremonies will be starting in an hour.

4. Irritated about my poor performance on the first calculus test, I vowed to study harder for the second exam.

5. The Alumni Director will soon announce several large donations to the university library.

8c Nouns

Nouns are the naming words in English. Whenever we wish to speak of a phenomenon, we can usually choose a noun to represent it. If the phenomenon is new to our culture, we may have to invent a word. **Ship, night,** and **mother** are relatively old nouns in English; **proton, Nevada,** and **astronaut** are relatively new nouns.

Like other parts of speech, nouns are identifiable by their special relationships with other words:

1. *Noun determiners.* Nouns take the special noun-marking *determiners* (also called *articles*) **the** and **a** or **an** immediately before them. **The** and **a/an** always signal the reader that a noun will soon follow:

the stadium, **a** crowd, **an** astronaut

2. *Noun positions.* Nouns occupy only certain positions, such as sentence subject and complement, or phrase object (see Chapter **9**).

subject   complement
Ostriches are flightless **birds.**

3. *Noun form changes.* Nouns change their form to convey plurality and possession. Most singular nouns can be made plural by adding a suffix, usually **-s** or **-es:** several crowd**s,** three astronaut**s,** dozen**s** of dish**es.** Note that some nouns are irregular: two child**ren,** several phenomen**a.** Nouns not ending in **-s** add **-'s** to show possession: the crowd**'s** anger, the children**'s** courage, the horse**'s** bridle. Singular nouns ending in **-s** add **-'s:** Mars**'s** orbit, Bill Jones**'s** money. Regular plural nouns add only an apostrophe to show possession: the astronauts**'** food, the United Nations**'** future. (Chapter **31** further explains the apostrophe.)

Words that name general classes (**ship, crowd, anger**) are called *common nouns.* Words that name specific places or people or that act as titles are called *proper nouns* and are capitalized: **Nevada** (place), **Bill Smith** (person), **The Beatles** (title). Some nouns are also said to be *concrete* or *abstract.* We can touch what concrete nouns name: **water, car, skyscraper.** We can only think about what abstract nouns name: **justice, foolishness, democracy.** Three types of nouns refer to quantities. A *collective noun* names a group: **orchestra, pile, committee.** A *count noun* names something that can be counted: **nail, person, inch.** A *mass noun* names something tangible but not usually counted and so not usually found in the plural: **air, water, dirt.**

When a present participle is used as a noun, it is called a *gerund.*

Jogging is a popular recreation.

Lying and **cheating** are violations of the honor code.

Exercise 2

Circle the nouns in the following sentences, and underline any noun determiners.

1. Miles of sea stretched away from the castaways on their tiny isle, making them feel minute and insignificant.

2. The whirlwind romance came to an end when Jan discovered that Mike had three other "steady" girlfriends.

3. The presence of the security chief in the central office indicated to the employees that something was amiss.

4. That painting is not as interesting as its frame.

5. In 1988, the US space program was revived with the launching of the shuttle *Discovery*.

8d Pronouns

Pronouns do not name in the same way as nouns, but they can serve any role in a sentence that a noun can serve. A pronoun usually stands for a noun, and this noun is called the pronoun's *antecedent*. Compare the two sentences below:

As the people hurried into the stadium, the people craned the people's necks anticipating the excitement in store for the people.

As the people hurried into the stadium, they craned their necks anticipating the excitement in store for them.

The first example is difficult to read because the noun **people** draws our attention so often that it diverts us from the sentence's meaning. The revised example is more understandable because appropriate pronouns are substituted for the antecedent **people.**

1. *Personal pronouns.* The pronouns most often used and the ones with the most *inflections* (different forms) are called *personal pronouns.*

Personal pronouns change their form to reflect three things: *number, person,* and *case. Singular* pronouns stand for one individual; *plural* pronouns stand for more than one. *First person* pronouns refer to the writer; *second person* pronouns refer to an individual whom the writer is addressing; *third person* pronouns refer to individuals or things about whom someone is writing.

**8
d**

Personal Pronouns

	Subjective Case	Objective Case	Possessive Case	Possessive Case (noun marker)
First Person				
singular	I	me	mine	my
plural	we	us	ours	our
Second Person				
singular and plural	you	you	yours	your
Third Person				
singular	he	him	his	his
	she	her	hers	her
	it	it	its	its
plural	they	them	theirs	their

The *subjective case* is used when the pronoun is the subject of a clause or phrase or is a complement of a subject:

I have a cat. [subject of clause]

The only victims of the robbery were my sister and **I.** [subject complement]

The *objective case* is used when the pronoun is the object in a clause or phrase.

The cat scratched **me.** [object of verb **scratched**]

I opened a can of food for **her.** [object of preposition **for**]

(Subjects and objects are discussed in **9a** and **9b.**)

Personal pronouns can indicate ownership in the *possessive case* in two ways. As noun markers, they can act like determiners by preceding a noun.

That is **my** cat.

Or they can stand alone.

That cat is **mine.**

The table at left shows that some pronouns do not inflect when others do. For example, **you** has the same form for the subjective and the objective cases. When one pronoun form can serve in more than one role, we must use either the position of the pronoun in the sentence or the context of the statement to tell what the pronoun means.

As **you** know, **I** have high regard for **her.**

Reading the sentence above, we can tell that **you** is the subject of its clause by its position, but we cannot tell whether it is singular or plural without knowing the larger context of the sentence. We know **I** is the subject of the second clause because of its position and its form. (We would not write, "**Me** have high regard for her.") We also know that **I** refers to only one individual, as does **her,** but only the context tells us that **her** is an object and not a possessive preceding a noun (as in, "I have high regard for **her taste**").

In addition to personal pronouns, there are six other traditional classifications according to the role the pronoun serves.

2. *Reflexive and intensive pronouns.* Personal pronouns with **-self** or **-selves** added can be *reflexive* or *intensive*. *Reflexive* pronouns refer to the subject of a clause and indicate that the subject receives the action of the verb.

Bill almost killed **himself.**

An *intensive* pronoun stresses a preceding noun or pronoun by in effect repeating it just for emphasis.

Bill sold his house **himself.**

Note that you can delete an intensive pronoun, and the sentence's essential message will remain; but you cannot delete a reflexive pronoun and preserve the sentence's message.

   3. *Demonstrative pronouns.* A writer using *demonstrative pronouns* (**this, that, these, those**) seems to be gesturing or pointing out something.

Those are the cheapest, and **these** are the most expensive.

   4. *Indefinite pronouns.* Indefinite pronouns (**all, one, each, either, anyone, something, everybody,** etc.) refer to persons or things generally.

In the United States there is more space where **nobody** is than where **anybody** is.
                                                                        Gertrude Stein

   5. *Relative pronouns.* A *relative pronoun* (**who, which, that, whoever, whichever**) relates a word to its antecedent noun or pronoun. Like personal pronouns, the relative pronoun **who** changes form to reflect case: subjective—**who,** possessive—**whose,** objective—**whom. That** does not inflect. **Which** sometimes inflects its possessive as **whose** and sometimes as **of which.**

I know a woman **who** kept over thirty cats. [subject of verb **kept;** antecedent—**woman**]

I know a woman **whose** cats ate over $250.00 worth of food a month. [possessive; antecedent—**woman**]

I know a woman **whom** cats drove crazy. [object of the verb **drove;** antecedent—**woman**]

In the kitchen were four cabinets, the sole use **of which** was to store cat food. [possessive; antecedent—**use**]

6. *Interrogative pronouns. Interrogative pronouns* (**who, which, what**) introduce questions.

Who kept over thirty cats?

Note that a *relative pronoun* relates words after it to a noun before it.

The folklorist interviewed a man **who** claimed to have magical powers [**Who** refers to **man.**]

Interrogative pronouns, on the other hand, represent an unexpressed noun that is requested as an answer.

Who claimed to have magical powers?

7. *Reciprocal pronouns. Reciprocal pronouns* (**each other, one another, one . . . other**) help communicate a give-and-take relationship between two or more creatures or things.

The armies fought **each other** until darkness separated them.

Exercise 3

Circle the pronouns in the following sentences, and draw an arrow to their antecedent nouns if an antecedent is present.

1. As Phyllis watched the children playing, she reflected sadly on the differences between their world of childhood and the world of childhood that had been hers.

2. A fan who had spent the entire game yelling at the umpires injured himself when he dropped a bottle of beer on his big toe.

3. Almost every year, someone claims to have discovered new evidence that confirms the existence of UFOs.

4. Whoever knows enough chemistry to understand the ingredients on a box of cake mix should be able to pass the final exam in Chemistry 1100.

5. Negative campaigning has its detractors, but candidates who refuse to use such tactics risk defeat.

8e Adjectives

Adjectives give information about (modify) nouns and pronouns. Adjectives describe by specifying quality or quantity.

We all stopped work to enjoy the **cool** breeze.

A **few** stragglers limped by.

Like nouns, adjectives can appeal to the senses, as in the first sentence above, or can appeal to abstract thought, as in the second sentence.

Linking verbs can be used to link subjects with modifying adjectives. The adjective in such a pattern is called the *subject complement*; it is also called the *predicate adjective*.

The breeze was **cool.**

Certain *pronouns* are traditionally said to serve as adjectives when they precede a noun. The possessive pronouns (**my, our,** etc.), the demonstrative pronouns (**this, that,** etc.), and certain others (**what, which**) can precede nouns and modify them.

Our work discouraged us. [possessive adjective]

That breeze was cool. [demonstrative adjective]

What breeze are you talking about? [interrogative adjective]

Participles can serve as adjectives.

The **discouraging** work exhausted us. [present participle]

A well-**accomplished** job can make workers proud. [past participle]

Nouns can modify other nouns and thereby function as adjectives.

The **football** field was repaired only one hour before the game.

Certain inflections can transform other parts of speech into adjectives. For example, **-y, -al, -ish,** and **-ous** are *adjectival suffixes:* **health—healthy, nature—natural, self—selfish, fame—famous.**

Note also that certain adjectives can be inflected to be nouns by adding *nominal suffixes:* **good—goodness; stupid—stupidity.**

Certain adjectives are inflected to communicate *comparative* and *superlative degree. Degree* means the extent of the quality communicated by the adjective. The regular comparative suffix is **-er,** and the regular superlative suffix is **-est.**

The breezes are **cooler** today than yesterday. [comparative]

This is the **coolest** day we've had this summer. [superlative]

Some adjectives have irregular inflections for degree: **good, better, best; bad, worse, worst.**

Exercise 4

Circle the adjectives in the following sentences, and draw an arrow to the words they modify.

1. The engine of the stalled car belched forth thick, black

   clouds of noxious fumes, causing traffic in the tunnel to

   come to a complete halt for several hours.

2. The evidence against the political prisoner was fabricated, and the trial itself was a shameful farce.

3. The worst thing about attending a large university is having to stand in long lines to accomplish any official business.

4. Last winter left no visible scars, but the memory of it lay over the people like a dark cloud.

5. In recent years, the accomplishments of many Olympic athletes have been overshadowed by drug scandals and biased judges.

8f Adverbs

Adverbs can modify verbs, adjectives, and other adverbs as well as groups of words. They usually help communicate how, when, where, or to what extent something occurred or existed.

Victoria listened **carefully.** [**Carefully** modifies the verb **listened.**]

Victoria was **carefully** attentive at the concert. [**Carefully** modifies the adjective **attentive.**]

Victoria listened **very** carefully. [**Very** modifies the adverb **carefully.**]

Most adverbs are formed by adding the suffix **-ly** to an adjective, as in sentence #1 above (**careful—carefully**). Note, though, that some adjectives also end in **-ly.**

Victoria was **lovely,** but she did a **cowardly** thing.

Other ways to form adverbs are to add the prefix **a-** to other words (**a**loud, **a**drift, **a**new); to add the suffix **-wise** to certain nouns (length**wise**); to add the suffix **-wards** to certain nouns (back**wards**); to add **some, any, every,** or **no** to certain words (**some**place, **any**way). Several common adverbs are not formed from other words: **always, even, later, now, often, perhaps, seldom, still, then.** Certain other adverbs are called *qualifiers* or *intensifiers:* **very, more, rather.**

Exercise 5

Circle the adverbs in the following sentences, and draw an arrow to the words they modify.

1. The audience laughed uproariously at the wildly absurd antics of the chimps.

2. Professional umpires seldom lose their composure, even before insanely hostile coaches, players, and fans.

3. The orchestra conductor often wondered privately if the musicians would function as well without him as with him.

4. Essay exam questions usually require students to write clearly and to develop ideas fully.

5. Some specialists believe that the steadily rising cost of malpractice insurance will adversely affect the quality of health care in the US.

8g Prepositions

A *preposition* relates a noun, a pronoun, or a group of words acting as a noun to another part of a sentence. The noun or pronoun or word group that follows a preposition is called the *object of the preposition*. The preposition and its object are called a *prepositional phrase*. The relationship that prepositions establish between words is often a matter of sequence in time (**after, until**) or position in space (**in, under**). Common prepositions are listed below:

about	beside	like	till
above	between	near	to
across	beyond	of	toward
after	by	off	under
against	concerning	on	unlike
along	considering	onto	until
amid	despite	out	unto
among	down	outside	up
around	during	over	upon
as	except	past	with
at	for	regarding	within
before	from	round	without
behind	in	since	
below	inside	through	
beneath	into	throughout	

Bob was very nervous when he was **among** strangers. [The noun **strangers** is the object of the preposition **among;** the preposition helps establish the relationship between **he** and **strangers.**]

Several people in the club objected to the discussion **about** who should be denied membership. [The preposition **about** relates its object, **who should be denied membership,** to the word **discussion.**]

Exercise 6

Circle the prepositions in the following sentences, and underline the prepositional phrases.

1. The lawyer was known throughout his career as a man given to theatrics.

2. The scientist studied the photographs sent from the surface of the distant planet by an unmanned probe.

3. The local police chief decided that the case was outside his jurisdiction and called the FBI for assistance.

4. At the end of the dirt road stood a dilapidated frame house.

5. The hurricane swept across the mainland with devastating force.

8h Conjunctions

Conjunctions, like prepositions, relate words and word groups.

1. *Coordinating conjunctions.* *Coordinating conjunctions* link words or word groups of the same type:

and	for	or	yet
but	nor	so	

Martha **and** Philip have little in common. [two nouns linked]

Martha skydives, **but** Philip is afraid of heights. [two independent clauses linked]

Philip must choose whether to jump **or** to watch. [two infinitives linked]

2. *Correlative conjunctions. Correlative conjunctions* are word pairs that link words or word groups of the same type:

both . . . and   neither . . . nor
either . . . or   not . . . but
not only . . . but also

Both Philip **and** Martha play poker but not with each other. [two nouns linked]

They **neither** smile **nor** frown during a game. [two verbs linked]

3. *Subordinating conjunctions. Subordinating conjunctions* link clauses so that one clause is incorporated as a modifying part of another clause. Some common subordinating conjunctions are **although, because, if, unless, while.** (A more extensive list is given in **11b.**)

Martha skydives **although** she is afraid of heights.

The subordinating conjunction **although** makes the clause **she is afraid of heights** subordinate to the clause **Martha skydives.** This *subordinate clause* tells something about the conditions under which Martha does her skydiving. It is actually an adverbial modifier that can be moved within the sentence:

Although Martha is afraid of heights, she skydives.

Note the difference in the ways that coordinating and subordinating conjunctions relate word groups. Coordinating conjunctions are bound between words or word groups of equal significance, so they cannot be moved from their place between the constructions they coordinate. For example, sentence #1 is grammatical, but sentence #2 is not.

Grammatical

1. Martha belongs to several clubs, **but** she hates to attend meetings.

Ungrammatical

2. **But** she hates to attend meetings, Martha belongs to several clubs.

Subordinating conjunctions, on the other hand, precede modifying clauses that can be moved to different places in a sentence. For example, we can grammatically change sentence #3 to sentence #4.

3. Philip waterskis **although** he cannot swim.
4. **Although** he cannot swim, Philip waterskis.

4. *Conjunctive adverbs.* Independent clauses may be linked not only with coordinating conjunctions but also with *conjunctive adverbs.* In linking two independent clauses, a conjunctive adverb modifies the clause following it.

After the speeches, we beat a hasty retreat; **meanwhile,** the audience remained to cheer the speakers. [**Meanwhile** links the two clauses and tells when the audience remained to cheer.]

The flood left ten inches of mud in the hotel. **Nevertheless,** the Optimist Club held its regularly scheduled meeting there.

Note that when conjunctive adverbs occur between two independent clauses they require a semicolon or period immediately before and a comma immediately after.

Common conjunctive adverbs are listed below:

accordingly	furthermore	meanwhile	similarly
also	however	moreover	still
besides	incidentally	nevertheless	then
consequently	instead	now	therefore
finally	likewise	otherwise	thus

These words can also serve as simple adverbs.

She was **finally** gone.

However ugly Fido was, he will remain in our hearts.

Exercise 7

Circle each conjunction in the following sentences, and indicate what kind of conjunction it is.

1. It's up to you to perform this task because you have the proper qualifications.

2. Neither the plaintiff nor the defendant was happy with the court's decision.

3. The kidnapper's father was a reluctant but effective go-between for his son and the multitude of law enforcement officials concerned with the case.

4. Both the National Park Service and private environmental groups supported the controversial wildfire policy.

5. Although both presidential candidates expressed concern over the budget deficit, neither offered a solution to the problem.

8i Interjections

Interjections are expressions that either stand alone or have no grammatical connection with the rest of the sentence in which they appear. They do not work as subjects or verbs or modifiers or words that relate one part of the sentence to another. They are there only to express a writer's exclamation.

Phooey!

Why **in heaven's name** did you do that?

8j Use your understanding of the parts of speech.

Being able to identify the parts of speech is not a skill that in itself will help you write. For your knowledge of the parts of speech to be helpful, you must apply it in analyzing your writing. Consider, for example, the passage below:

1. A dress code in the public schools might result in the prevention of competition among students in their dress, but it would be an inhibition to their way of expressing their personalities.

In this sentence, you will find two verbs (counting **result** and its auxiliary **might** as one), ten nouns (counting the gerund **expressing**), two adjectives (including the adjectival noun **dress**), four pronouns, five prepositions, and one conjunction. Now consider sentence #2, which is synonymous with #1 but which has a different distribution of the parts of speech.

2. A dress code in the public schools might prevent competition among students in the way they dress, but it would inhibit the way they express their personalities.

Sentence #2 has four verbs, six nouns, three pronouns, two adjectives, four prepositions, and one conjunction. Sentence #2 has twice as many verbs, four fewer nouns, and five fewer total words than sentence #1. Most readers would say that sentence #2 is easier to read, yet some readers and writers might find #1 more impressive and might think that a writer who relies on nouns seems somehow wiser than one who relies on verbs. One reason for such a belief may be that the ability to name things is a characteristic of knowledgeable persons, so the more we translate our knowledge into names rather than actions, the wiser we appear. Unfortunately, in doing so, we often make our message harder for our readers to understand. As you can see from this analysis, an understanding of the parts of speech provides a means for thinking constructively about the language we use.

Exercise 8

Change each of the sentences below as directed.

1. Change the tense of the verb from future to future perfect:

   I will talk to their representative Tuesday.

2. Change the tense of the verb from past to present progressive:

   The teachers expected too much from their students.

3. Change the mood of the verb from indicative to imperative. Make any other changes necessary to create a logical and coherent sentence:

   Marsha should help Walt with his homework.

4. Change each noun from singular to plural:

   I told the child to stop throwing the paper everwhere.

5. Change each common noun to a proper noun, deleting noun determiners in the process:

   The sheriff told the gunslinger to get out of the town.

6. Change each second person pronoun to third person. Make any necessary changes in the verb forms:

You are foolish to believe that you can make your fortune

by selling vacuum cleaners door-to-door.

7. Change all modifiers so that the sentence reflects a positive attitude toward the host's remarks:

The insulting remark by our host left us shocked and

disgusted.

8. Change all modifiers so that the sentence reflects an unfavorable attitude toward the fire fighter:

The courageous fire fighter found the appreciative

victims.

9. Change the meaning of the sentence by substituting different conjunctions:

The parents or the children will receive a sandwich and a

drink at intermission.

10. Change each preposition to create a different meaning:

I arrived outside the coliseum before the rock concert had

begun.

9 · Creating Basic Sentences

9a The basic sentence

An English sentence has at least these two parts: a *subject* and a verb or verb phrase, or as we will refer to it here, a *predicate*. The subject names a topic for the sentence, and the predicate either asserts something about that topic or specifies action involving it.

Subject	*Predicate*
Running and jogging	are different.
Ann	rode.
All five interior linemen	couldn't protect the aging quarterback.

In this text, what we call a *basic sentence* consists of a subject and a predicate that cannot be made briefer without destroying the sentence's grammatical nature or its fundamental message. **Running and jogging are different** and **Ann rode** are basic sentences; we cannot delete words from the first without destroying its statement, nor can we delete words from the second without destroying it as a sentence. But **All five interior linemen couldn't protect the aging quarterback** is not basic; we can substitute the word **The** for **All five interior,** and we can delete the word **aging** without destroying the essential subject and predicate: **The linemen couldn't protect the quarterback.**

9b Five basic sentence patterns

Basic sentences occur most frequently in five patterns, each of which has a particular kind of predicate.

1. *Linking verbs* (see **8b**) identify a basic sentence's subject directly with a following noun or adjective in the pattern *noun (or pronoun)—linking verb—noun or adjective*. The word after the linking verb is called the *subject complement* (SC).

    N   LV   N(SC)
1. The boys were pranksters.

    N   LV ADJ(SC)
2. Chelsea seems content.

Sometimes the subject complement is omitted from a basic sentence, but the complement remains understood. For example, in a context questioning the identity of some alleged pranksters ("Who were those pranksters?") sentence #1 might be abbreviated to sentence #3.

3. The boys were. [**the pranksters** omitted but understood]

Note that sentence #1 is the basic sentence from which sentence #4 is derived:

4. **The** frightened **boys were** utterly inept and harmless **pranksters.**

2. A verb is *intransitive* if it does not require a noun or adjective after it to complete its expression of an action. A basic sentence with an *intransitive verb* has the pattern *noun—intransitive verb* (IV).

    N   IV
5. The students doze.

  PN   IV
6. She has gone.

Note that we would not say **The students doze something.** Note also that sentence #5 is the basic sentence from which sentence #7 is developed:

7. **The students,** in the grip of a smothering boredom, **doze** through interminable announcements.

3. *Transitive verbs* require objects to complete the expression of an action. When the predicate of a basic sentence has

a transitive verb in the pattern *noun—transitive verb (TV)—noun,* the noun following the verb is called a *direct object* (DO).

      N   TV   N(DO)

8. The vandals destroyed the books.

     N   TV   N(DO)

9. Jack fooled his sister.

Compare sentences #8 and #9 with sentences #5 and #6. Note that verbs such as **doze** and **go** do not invite the reader to ask "what" or "who" but that verbs like **destroy** and **fool** do invite the reader to ask those questions. Many verbs can be both transitive and intransitive depending on their context: **What is Jack doing? He is painting (IV). What is Jack painting? He is painting (TV) the door (DO).**

    4. When the transitive verb of a basic sentence requires its direct object to have a *complement,* the pattern is *noun—transitive verb—noun—noun or adjective.* The last noun or adjective in this pattern is called the *object complement* (OC), and it is generated with verbs that promise a name or a describer for the direct object.

      N   TV N(DO) N(OC)

10. His sister called Jack a fool.

    PN   TV   PN(DO) ADJ(OC)

11. She considered him inept.

    5. *Certain transitive verbs,* such as **give, send, lend,** and **bring,** specify an act of transference in the pattern *noun—transitive verb—noun—noun.* In this case the noun right after the verb names who or what receives the transfer, and it is called the *indirect object* (IO); the subsequent noun, a direct object, tells what was transferred.

      N   TV   N(IO)   N(DO)

12. May bought her father a car.

    PN   TV   PN(IO)   N(DO)

13. I shall send him the package.

Exercise 1

Circle the subject, write the kind of predicate (transitive, in-transitive, or linking) over the main verb, and underline any complements or direct objects.

1. The discontented gathering quickly became unruly.

2. The discovery of a new type of virus sent shock waves through the medical profession.

3. The front office sent Sheryl a letter of commendation.

4. The heated debate between the art critics continued for hours.

5. The Englishman thought the visiting Texan quite a character.

6. Inefficiency is a growing source of frustration in our legal system.

7. Most rock groups shun costumes.

8. Political theorists disagree about the effects of economic sanctions on terrorist nations.

9. My adviser sometimes gives incorrect information.

10. I am relaxed, open minded, and free spirited.

9c Four alterations to the basic sentence

Basic sentence structures can be changed to meet the special requirements of giving commands and asking questions; and they can be changed to passive and expletive constructions. Those four alterations are described below.

1. *A command* is a sentence with the verb in the present tense and the subject **you** deleted:

Call your sister.

Stop!

2. We can transform a basic sentence into a *question* by moving an auxiliary or linking verb to the first of the sentence: **Were the boys pranksters? Has she gone? Did Jack fool his sister? Shall I send him the package?** Note that questions in this form can be answered *yes* or *no*.

To the beginning of these questions, we can add certain adverbs (**why, when, how**) and so invite extended, detailed answers: **Why did Jack fool his sister? How shall I stay within my budget?** And we can substitute interrogative pronouns for objects and complements, put them at the beginning of questions, and so require objects or complements as answers: **What did the vandals destroy? The vandals destroyed the books** (DO). **What did she consider him? She considered him inept** (OC).

We can also make interrogative pronouns the subjects of questions (see **8d**): **Who kissed the guitar player? What is on the table?**

3. The previous example sentences in this chapter have verbs in the *active voice*. The subjects of these verbs do the behaving or existing proposed in the sentence. In any basic sentence with a direct object, the words may be rearranged and the verb may be converted to the *passive voice* so that the sentence has a subject that receives the action. To express in the

passive voice, we do four things:

    a. Either delete the original subject or put it at the
       end of the sentence with **by** before it.
    b. Transfer the direct object to the subject slot.
    c. Substitute the past participle of the verb in the verb
       slot.
    d. Add a form of *be* as auxiliary to the past participle.

Active   Jack fooled my sister.
                (b)   (d)   (c)   (a)
Passive   My sister was fooled by Jack.

When the active verb is in the present or future tense,
we must add more than one form of **be** before the past
participle.

Active   The vandals are destroying the books.
Passive   The books **are being** destroyed by the vandals.

Active   I will send him the package.
Passive   The package **will be** sent to him. (**By me** is deleted here.)

The passive voice is effective only in certain situations
(see Chapter **18**).

Exercise 2

Change the following sentences from passive voice to active
voice.

1. The integrity of professional sports is being destroyed by
   rampant greed and the resulting adverse fan reaction.

2. The new employees were easily manipulated by the
   office manager.

3. After the controversial ruling in the third inning, the
   game was played under protest by the home team.

4. While the tax auditor stood in the door, she was bitten by our poodle.

5. Because my flight was cancelled by the airline, I had to sleep in the airport lobby.

4. *Expletives* are the words **there** and **it** used not to stand for anything but simply to occupy the position of sentence subject. Compare sentences #1 and #2 with sentences #3 and #4.

1. A book is on the washing machine.
2. An excited fan kissed the guitar player.
3. There is a book on the washing machine.
4. It was an excited fan who kissed the guitar player.

There and **It** are place holders and do not have a meaning of their own. Such expletive constructions can emphasize the fact that a condition exists. In sentence #2, for example, the transitive main verb (**kissed**) focuses our attention on an action; but in sentence #4 the linking main verb (**was**) and the expletive **It** shift our attention from the action to the fact that an action happened. Because they are wordy, expletive constructions are effective in few contexts (see **15e**).

Exercise 3

Eliminate the following expletive constructions and change the sentences to more direct statements.

1. There were thousands of fans greeting the victorious team.

2. It is a wise person who can grasp reality without becoming cynical.

3. There were many people present who disagreed with the conclusions of the board.

4. It is my belief that teachers should not schedule exams for the day before a holiday.

5. There was a gigantic pit bull snarling at me from my neighbor's back yard.

6. The word "not" was given new meaning in the film *Wayne's World*.

7. In a recent dispute with the elections board, citizens seeking access to voting records were required to file written requests.

8. The special needs of part-time students are not always recognized by college administrators.

9. It has been discovered that the Pacific yew tree is a source of taxol, a substance that may cure certain forms of cancer.

10. A recycling plan was recently implemented by the university administration.

Exercise 4

Create sentences according to the following basic patterns, adding modifiers to create interesting and informative sentences.

1. Pronoun—Linking Verb—Noun (Subject Complement)
2. Noun—Intransitive Verb
3. Noun—Transitive Verb—Pronoun (Indirect Object)—Noun (Direct Object)
4. Pronoun—Linking Verb—Adjective (Subject Complement)
5. Noun—Transitive Verb—Pronoun (Direct Object)—Adjective (Object Complement)
6. Noun—Transitive Verb—Noun (Direct Object)
7. Pronoun—Transitive Verb—Pronoun (Direct Object)—Noun (Object Complement)

10 · Modifying with Individual Words and Phrases

10a Words that modify

As we have noted, basic sentences can be expanded by adding appropriate words. In Chapter **9,** we expanded the first sentence below to read as the second sentence.

The boys were pranksters.

The frightened boys were utterly inept and harmless pranksters.

The words added to the first sentence are all *modifiers.* They give additional information about the subject and predicate. We could expand this sentence with modifiers indefinitely.

The foolish, confused, frightened boys were utterly inept and harmless pranksters.

Exercise 1

Circle the one-word modifiers in the following sentences, and draw an arrow from them to the words they modify.

1. Foolishly, the convict attempted a poorly planned and executed escape just one month before his parole hearing.

2. A spokesperson for the petroleum industry arrogantly disclaimed responsibility for the latest oil spill.

3. When faced with the incriminating tapes and photographs, the powerful politician made a fiery speech against her accusers, labeling them "witch hunters."

4. Because a negligent cook left the beans on the stove for several hours, they were stuck to the bottom of the pan.

5. As the leading runner stretched toward the finish, her unscrupulous opponent tripped her.

6. The newspaper headline reads, "Companies can't afford poorly prepared workers."

7. Within a few weeks, I realized that most of my peers disliked reading.

8. In the old abandoned theater, I stood and remembered some of my most stirring moments, including my first kiss.

9. The exact location of the proposed landfill was kept secret by the Board of Commissioners.

10. Financial aid is becoming increasingly difficult for most students to obtain.

10b Placement of modifiers

The usual place for adjectives in an English sentence is just before the noun they modify. Adverbs may or may not be next to the words they modify.

  adj.   adj   adv.
The **inept** and **harmless** pranksters were **soon** discovered by their friends.

Often modifiers can be moved from their usual place so that they receive special emphasis. Note that wherever they are in a sentence, adjectives should be close to the nouns they modify; adverbs are usually more free to be moved throughout the sentence.

  adv.   adj.   adj.
Soon the pranksters, **inept** and **harmless,** were discovered by their friends.

10c Phrases that modify

Three types of phrases may modify nouns: prepositional phrases, participial phrases, and infinitive phrases. Prepositional phrases and infinitive phrases may also serve as adverbs. Other modifiers may pertain to an entire sentence.

1. A *prepositional phrase* is a preposition, its object, and any modifiers the object might have.

Many people **in the United States** celebrate New Year's Day by watching football **on television.** [prepositional adjective phrases modifying **people** and **football**]

The revelers danced **until twelve midnight.** [prepositional adverb phrase modifying **danced**]

2. A *participial phrase* is a present or past participle plus words acting as the participle's subject, complement, or modifier.

Passively celebrating New Year's Day, Glen slept in front of the TV. [present participial adjective phrase modifying **Glen**]

Martha, **discouraged by her husband's stupor,** gazed out the window at the bleak, cold day. [past participial adjective phrase modifying **Martha**]

3. An *infinitive phrase* is an infinitive plus any modifiers and objects.

All the child wanted was a pet **to treat as a friend.** [adjective infinitive phrase modifying **pet**]

To avoid detection, the smugglers disguised themselves as nuns. [adverb infinitive phrase modifying **disguised**]

4. *Sentence modifiers* are words and phrases that modify the entire sentence rather than a word or phrase within the sentence.

Obviously he has lost all sense of reality. [adverb as sentence modifier]

To tell the truth, I'm worried about this election. [infinitive phrase as sentence modifier]

5. An *absolute phrase* is a sentence modifier consisting of a noun or pronoun and a participle.

The big day having arrived, we left in a cloud of exhaust.

Her school work finished, the girl saw no reason not to go to the arcade.

When the participle in an absolute phrase is **being** or **been,** the participle may be omitted.

His mother nowhere in sight, the child toddled weeping through the department store.

Exercise 2

Underline the modifying phrases in the following sentences, and indicate whether they function as adjectives, adverbs, or sentence modifiers.

1. On the far side of the property stretched a tranquil lake.

2. The game having been lost before it started, our team played like broken robots.

3. The climber, clinging to her lifeline, made one last attempt to reach the summit of the peak.

4. Smiling sheepishly, the youngster announced his intention to join the Navy, like his father before him.

5. Having completed my annual report early, I decided to relax for a few hours.

10d Effects of modifying words and phrases

Note how much information the sentence below gives:

The confused, frightened boys were utterly inept and harmless pranksters.

Each adjective with the noun modified carries the same information as a statement, so the phrase **the frightened boys** gives the same information as the clause **The boys were frightened.** In fact, this one sentence has the same information as might be conveyed by seven sentences.

The boys were confused.

The boys were frightened.

The boys were pranksters.

The pranksters were inept.

The pranksters were harmless.

The extent of the ineptness was utter.

The extent of the harmlessness was utter.

Obviously modification is an efficient way to impart meaning, but like all stylistic options it can be abused by over- or underuse or by imprecise use.

Original

The really beautiful, lovely pond lay under the bright, hot sun.

The student who wrote the sentence above justified doing so by claiming she had made the scene more vivid. She later revised the sentence, though, deleting the vague and redundant modifiers **really, beautiful,** and **lovely** and deleting the overly familiar **bright** and **hot.** She substituted specific images of time and place and used a verb that bore considerably more imagery than **lay.**

Revised

Surrounded by low grass banks, the pond shimmered under the August sun.

Modification is like the ingredients in a dish of food: too little, and potential for meaning (or taste) is wasted; too much, and the meaning (taste) is obscured. In fact, a sentence can gain in impact if the writer will delete an adjective or adverb that at first seemed vivid but on reconsideration seems excessive. For example, compare the sentences below.

The foolish, confused, frightened boys were utterly inept and harmless pranksters.

The frightened boys were inept and harmless pranksters.

Comparing the sentences in a context, we might decide in light of preceding sentences that the ideas of confusion and foolishness and the intensifier **utterly** do not provide sufficient new information to warrant their inclusion; therefore, we might judge that even though the second sentence is shorter, it is stronger and helps the reader focus more clearly on the remaining modifiers.

Exercise 3

Expand the following sentences by changing and adding modifying words and phrases.

1. The woman enjoyed the movie.
2. The game was important.
3. After the shower, the sky was beautiful.
4. The locomotive puffed.
5. Poverty affects people.

Exercise 4

Combine each of the following pairs of sentences by making one into a modifying phrase.

1. The road was a popular place to park.
   The road was by the lake.

2. The drive was a long one.
   The drive was to the nearest hospital.

3. The master criminal's scheme was daring.
   The master criminal's scheme was ingenious.
   The master criminal's scheme was to blackmail the United States government.

4. When the bell rang, the boxer collapsed into his corner.
   The boxer was bleeding from cuts above each eye.

5. The tiny infant began to cry.
   The tiny infant was exhausted from being passed around.

Exercise 5

Combine the sentences in the following passage by changing some of them into one-word modifiers or modifying phrases.

Something appeared.
Its appearance was sudden.
Its appearance was mysterious.
It was a spacecraft.
The spacecraft was alien.
The spacecraft had a glint to it.
The glint was metallic.
The spacecraft hovered.
It hovered above the street.
The street was filled with people.
The people were shouting.
The people were pointing.
The spacecraft disappeared.
Its disappearance was sudden.
Its disappearance was mysterious.

11 · Modifying with Clauses

11a Independent and dependent clauses

A *clause* is a group of related words that has a subject and a verb. A clause is *independent* when it can serve as a sentence.

That book offers information on beekeeping.

Bees swarm.

Note that the example sentences in Chapter **9** are all independent clauses. Basic sentences such as these can be expanded by adding modifying words and phrases (see Chapter **10**), other independent clauses (see Chapter **14**), and modifying clauses. Clauses that modify, called *dependent clauses,* cannot serve as sentences; they must always be included in another clause, where they serve as either adjectives or adverbs. There are two types of dependent clauses: *subordinate* clauses and *relative* clauses.

11b Modifying with subordinate clauses

To form a subordinate clause, simply add a subordinating conjunction or a relative pronoun to the beginning of an independent clause.

Certain subordinators can make clauses serve as adverbs expressing relationships such as those given below.

Time: **when, whenever, after, before, since, while, until, as, as long as, once**

Until **you have passed the water safety course,** the recreation department will not hire you.

Place: **where, wherever**

Our neighbors hid their house key *where* **no one could find it.**

Condition: **if, provided, since, unless, whether**

Unless **the rain stops soon,** we will be forced to abandon our homes.

Contrast: **although, even though, as if, though**

Though **I was initially disappointed at being categorized an extremist,** I gradually gained a measure of satisfaction from the label.

Martin Luther King

Reason: **in order that, so, so that, that**

More and more colleges must increase tuition **so that** they can continue to operate.

Cause: **because, since**

I want to climb the mountain **because** it is there.

Clauses introduced by subordinating conjuctions can also serve as adjectives.

The moment **before** dawn breaks is my favorite time of day.

Most frequently, though, subordinate clauses used as adjectives are formed with the relative pronouns **who, which,** and **that.**

On my eighteenth birthday I learned a lesson **that I will never forget.**

An *elliptical clause* is a subordinate clause with certain words deleted.

Those are the shoes **I want.** [The subordinator **that** is deleted.]

If nominated, I will not run. **If elected,** I will not serve. [The subject and the auxiliary verb **I am** are deleted from both clauses.]

William T. Sherman

A common type of elliptical clause occurs in comparisons after the conjunction **than.**

She plays bridge much better **than her husband.** [The verb and the object **plays bridge** have been deleted.]

11c Modifying with relative clauses

When you use a relative pronoun as the subject of a clause, you form a relative clause. Relative clauses usually serve as adjectives.

A fool is a man *who* **never tried an experiment in his life.**

Erasmus Darwin

We got food poisoning in a restaurant *that* **had been rated four stars.**

Exercise 1

In the following sentences, underline the modifying clauses and indicate whether they function as adverbs or adjectives.

11 c

1. Although experts disagree over how long the earth's resources will last, geologists have noted an accelerating decline in the reserves of several vital minerals.

2. Rudolf Nureyev, who was one of the most acclaimed ballet dancers in the world, defected from the Soviet Union when he was twenty-three years old.

3. The film industry's rating code, which has been in effect since 1968, has often been criticized.

4. Unless new sources of financial aid can be found, many students who are now enrolled in college may be forced to drop out of school.

5. When the optometrist forgot her glasses, the patients were distressed.

11d Effects of clauses that modify

Like all modifiers, adjective and adverb clauses enrich sentences by embedding information. But because they have subjects and verbs, they modify with greater emphasis than do phrases and single words. For example, in the King James version of Genesis, Adam says to God, "The woman **whom thou gavest to be with me,** she gave me of the tree, and I did eat." Suppose instead of the adjective clause, **whom thou gavest to be with me,** the text gave a participial phrase, "given to be with me." The "woman" would still be modified, but Adam's attempt to escape guilt would be much less emphatic because he would not be stressing that God created the woman in the first place.

Words that introduce modifying clauses also establish a special coherence among ideas in a sentence. For example, the sentence by Martin Luther King quoted earlier expresses a contrast between two attitudes.

Though I was initially disappointed at being categorized as an extremist, I gradually gained a measure of satisfaction from the label.

If King had wanted to stress equally his initial disappointment and his later satisfaction, he might have made both clauses independent.

I was initially disappointed at being categorized an extremist, but I gradually gained a measure of satisfaction from the label.

Instead he subordinated his first clause to his second, so the sentence builds a momentum that forcefully emphasizes his change in attitude.

Exercise 2

Combine each of the following pairs of sentences by making one sentence a modifying clause.

1. Monica Seles has reached a rare pinnacle in sports. She makes headlines when she loses.

2. Edgar Allan Poe was fascinated with the workings of the human mind. Poe wrote many stories about the conflict between sanity and madness.

3. Charles Darwin's *The Origin of Species* was published in 1859. *The Origin of Species* continues to have a profound influence on scientific and religious thought.

**11
d**

4. Some teachers are skeptical about using computers to teach nontechnical subjects. Computers offer one means of providing individualized instruction.

5. Trifoliate orange is a sharp-edged, fast growing plant. It has been called the "Rambo of the vegetable kingdom."

Exercise 3

Expand the following simple sentences by adding one or more modifying clauses.

1. Television commercials often present women in stereo-typed roles.
2. A tall, shrouded figure emerged from the shadows.
3. *Raiders of the Lost Ark* is one of the most popular films of all time.
4. Buying a stereo system can be a complicated task.

5. Some states require students to pass a competency test in order to graduate from high school.

Exercise 4

Combine the sentences in the following passage by changing some of them into subordinate and relative clauses.

The alarm rang at 6:00 A.M.
I stumbled out of bed.
I tripped over a stack of books.
The books were lying where I had
   left them just four hours earlier.
I walked slowly toward the kitchen.
I bumped into a lamp.
The lamp crashed to the floor.
The noise woke up my cat.
He was angry at being awakened
   so early.
He dug his claws into my leg.
Suddenly I realized the horrible truth.
It was Monday.

12 · Using Nominals and Appositives

12a Nominals

Nominals are words or word groups occurring in positions typically occupied by nouns. Infinitives and infinitive phrases, gerund phrases, prepositional phrases, and subordinate clauses may all be used nominally as subjects, complements, and objects.

To know her is **to love her.** [infinitive phrases as subject and as subject complement]

Running a student store is giving Allison ulcers. [gerund phrase as subject]

Near the exit is the best place to sit during this play. [prepositional phrase as subject]

Volunteers in the fire department understood **that they would have no time to enjoy the holiday.** [subordinate clause as object of verb **understood**]

What we have been makes us **what we are.** [subordinate clauses as subject and objective complement]   T. S. Eliot

12
a

Adjectives can also be nominals.

Bigger is not necessarily **better.** [adjectives as subject and subject complement]

Exercise 1

In the following sentences, underline each nominal and indicate whether the nominal is a subject, object, or complement.

1. "Following that act will be tough," moaned the nervous

   amateur contestant.

2. That the star was glamorous was undebatable; that she

   couldn't act was unimportant.

3. Milt thought that across the state line was too far to ride

   for a drink, so he gave up alcohol.

4. To view the proceedings of a typical court on a typical

day is to witness first hand the inefficiency and inequity

of our system of justice.

5. The child's favorite activity was watching the harvesters

in the fields.

12b Effects of nominals

Nominals provide a means for achieving clear and strong
sentences when the thoughts expressed are complex. Consider the sentence below.

1. The parole board rejected his appeal, but **this** did not seem to
   bother the convict.

This in sentence #1 refers to the whole idea in the clause
immediately preceding it. Pronouns such as **it, such, that,
this,** and **which** can refer to general ideas expressed in
clauses and so are said to have *broad reference.* Broad reference
is often abused, however (see Chapter **43**), and we may narrow such constructions by reducing the clause to a nominal
and eliminating the broad pronoun. For example, the first
clause in sentence #1 can become a subordinate clause nominal replacing **this** as subject.

2. **That the parole board rejected his appeal** did not seem to
   bother the convict.

We can reword #1 in other ways to achieve similar results. In sentence #3, the first clause's verb has been trans-
formed into a noun.

3. The parole board's **rejection** of his appeal did not seem to
   bother the convict.

Of course, the context of the sentence should be your guide in determining the wording. Sentence #1 would be most appropriate if you wanted to stress the parole board's judgment and the convict's response as separate, equal acts. Sentences #2 and #3 stress the convict's response, but sentence #2 keeps the parole board as an active agent whereas #3 reduces the parole board to a modifier of a noun.

Note that when the nominal is a gerund, an infinitive, or a clause, it can not only clarify the focus but also strengthen the sense of action.

4a. The students complained bitterly about the exam, but this did not influence their final grades.
  b. The students' bitter **complaining** about the exam did not influence their final grades.
5a. An endorsement for this candidate is an investment in disaster.
  b. **To endorse** this candidate is **to invest** in disaster.

In the first pair of sentences, the broad reference (**this**) in #4a has been clarified by a gerund (**complaining**) in #4b. In the second pair, an infinitive subject (**to endorse**) followed by an infinitive complement (**to invest**) in #5b conveys a greater sense of action than the noun subject (**endorsement**) and the noun complement (**investment**) in #5a.

Exercise 2

Combine each of the following pairs of sentences by changing one sentence into a nominal.

1. The talk show host had a nightmare that was the worst she could imagine.
   The nightmare was to be locked in a room with William F. Buckley, Jr.; Joan Rivers; and Truman Capote.

2. The students realized something.
   They realized their teacher was not in the mood for jokes.

3. Something made Sue turn pale.
   Sue turned pale when she saw a shadow loom suddenly behind her.

12
c

4. There was a way to go to the isolated city that was best.
   The way was through the mountain pass.

5. It was obvious.
   The new residence hall adviser disliked students.

12c Appositives

An element similar to the nominal is the appositive. *Appositives* rename or further identify the words they follow. Usually an appositive is a noun alone or a noun with modifiers that helps define a preceding noun.

Robert Herrick, **the poet,** had an appreciative eye for pretty women, but he never married.

In the dark pit, we saw a teeming population of gnathobdellida, **leeches with teeth and jaws.**

Appositives can always replace the words they refer to in the sentence.

In the dark pit, we saw a teeming population of **leeches with teeth and jaws.**

Appositives may also define other parts of speech. In the sentence below, the appositive defines the infinitive **to rappel.**

After scaling the cliff, he proceeded to rappel, **to slide down using a double rope.**

12d Effects of appositives

Appositives are similar in function to relative clauses (**11c**).

1. My cousin, **who is a man of dark moods,** has been unable to hold any job for long.

If we have a relative clause with a form of **be** as the main verb, as in sentence #1, and if we are unsatisfied with the length and emphasis of the clause, we can reduce the clause to an appositive; we simply delete the relative pronoun and the verb and use the clause's complement as an appositive.

2. My cousin, **a man of dark moods,** has been unable to hold any job for long.

The subject complement of the relative clause in sentence #1 has been used as an appositive in sentence #2. The effects of this revision are to make the sentence more concise, to give less emphasis to the fact that the cousin has dark moods, and thus to focus on the fact that he cannot hold a job for long.

Exercise 3

Circle the appositives in the following sentences and draw an arrow to the words they rename or help define.

1. The pioneers in this field, Macon and Wickley, claim that

   the implications of their discoveries are astounding.

2. In Spain we witnessed a bullfight, the ritualistic murder of a noble animal.

3. The manager of the store, a woman with strong convictions, refused to go along with the idea of opening for business on Sunday afternoons.

4. The winner of the talent show is my roommate, an excellent blues guitar player.

5. Outland, the fictionalized world created by cartoonist Berke Breathed, is populated by a bizarre assortment of human and animal characters.

Expand the following sentences by adding appositives.

1. The outfielder hit a home run to win the game.
2. The star of the movie flatly refused to perform without a completely closed set.
3. The final exam survival kit contained many useful items.
4. The stalled car blocked the intersection for hours.
5. Under the Christmas tree were several presents.

Exercise 4

Combine the sentences in the following passage by changing some of them into nominals or appositives.

A ship steamed through the night.
The ship was called *The Riptide*.
The ship had a captain.
The captain's name was Peter
    Aronson.
Aronson had two major tasks.
One task was to guide the ship.
One task was to keep the crew's
    morale high.
The captain was a veteran of the sea.
He understood something.
The spirit of the crew was the most
    important thing on a ship.

13 · Modifying Restrictively and Nonrestrictively

13a Restrictive and nonrestrictive modifiers

Restrictive and nonrestrictive modifiers are illustrated below.

1. Karen invited the neighbors who are her friends to the party.
2. Karen invited the neighbors, who are her friends, to the party.

Sentence #1 implies that not all Karen's neighbors are her friends and states that only those among her neighbors who are friends received invitations. Sentence #2 states that all the neighbors are Karen's friends, and they all received invitations. The two sentences describe two quite different circumstances: We can imagine the Karen of sentence #1 to have a personality less outgoing, a social life more restricted, or a neighborhood less friendly than the Karen of sentence #2.

You will note that the only difference between the two sentences is the use of commas to set off the relative clause in sentence #2. Those commas indicate that the relative clause **who are her friends** is a *nonrestrictive* modifier. Nonrestrictive modifiers are always set off by commas (**23e**). The modifier provides extra information, but it is not required to establish the meaning of a preceding noun, in this case **neighbors.** We can delete any nonrestrictive modifier and still preserve the essential meaning of the sentence.

3. Karen invited the neighbors to the party.

Sentence #3 preserves the basic message of sentence #2 but omits the extra information that the neighbors were Karen's friends.

In sentence #1, though, the relative clause is a *restrictive* modifier; it restricts the meaning of a preceding noun, specifying the particular **neighbors** invited. We cannot delete the relative clause from sentence #1 and retain the basic meaning, which is that only certain neighbors were invited by Karen.

When using **that** and **which,** writers usually follow this convention: Restrictive adjective clauses are introduced by **that** and nonrestrictive adjective clauses are introduced by **which.**

The practical joke **that** we played on Jeff has backfired on us all.

The bait and switch, **which** we once played on Jeff, can be a disastrous practical joke.

Sometimes this convention is not appropriate. The use of a second **that** instead of **which** in the sentence below would be repetitive.

That was the car **which** tried to run us down.

Like adjective clauses, adjective phrases can modify restrictively and nonrestrictively.

The men **in the blue suits** made their way to the front of the auditorium. [restrictive prepositional phrase specifying the **men**]

Marie, **with eyes flashing,** led the charge of the irate parents. [nonrestrictive prepositional phrase giving extra information about **Marie**]

Appositives can also be restrictive or nonrestrictive.

Bella Abzug, **former Congresswoman from New York,** sported the most colorful hats on Capitol Hill. [**Former Congresswoman from New York** is an additional identification of Bella Abzug.]

William Shakespeare's play **_King Lear_** has some of the most chilling scenes in all literature. [**_King Lear_** is required to identify the subject **play.**]

13
a

Exercise 1

In the following sentences, underline nonrestrictive modifiers once and restrictive modifiers twice.

1. The swimmer escaped the pull of the current that threatened to sweep him out to sea.

2. At a recent convention, I saw one of my old high school friends, who is now the manager of a large department store.

3. Suzie and Rob, two of the most unpredictable people I have ever met, have just announced that they are going to be married in a bowling alley.

4. Rooftop restaurants, which sometimes revolve 360° in an hour, make me dizzy.

5. The movers who packed my belongings this year were more careful than the ones that my family hired the last time that we moved.

13b Effects of restrictive and nonrestrictive modification

Because restrictive modifiers are essential for the meaning of a noun, they are rarely a matter of stylistic choice. We include them whenever a nominal cannot be fully understood without them. Nonrestrictive modification, however, is always optional. Since choice determines style, good writers remain alert to opportunities for including modifiers that enrich meaning.

My old friend Sally, **who has made a name for herself in educational films in New York,** had dinner in Los Angeles recently with another old friend, **who has made a much bigger name for himself in television.** Settling down over late-night brandies, she was stunned when he turned to her and said, "You know, I can't imagine being married to you. I'd panic and run." "Why?" Sally asked, **hurt that their friendship, which had never even touched on the subject of marriage, seemed suddenly flawed.** "You're a star," he said.

Linda Bird Francke

In the passage above, the first two nonrestrictive adjective clauses expand the reader's knowledge significantly, and their parallel forms help the reader make all this information coherent. Note how much less integrated these ideas are when the nonrestrictive modifiers have been omitted.

My old friend Sally has made a name for herself in educational films in New York. Another old friend has made a much bigger name for himself in television. Recently they had dinner in Los Angeles.

The third nonrestrictive modifier in Francke's passage, **hurt that their friendship . . . seemed suddenly flawed,** is a complex adjectival construction containing within it a fourth nonrestrictive modifier for **friendship: which had never even touched on the subject of marriage.** Even if you judge this modifier to be too complex, keep in mind that judicious use of nonrestrictive elements can enrich your writing.

**13
b**

Exercise 2

1. Combine the two sentences below to suggest that no student in the school is friendly toward Barry. In doing so, turn the second sentence into a modifier for **students.**
   The students shunned Barry.
   Barry had tried to impress the students.

2. Combine the two sentences so that the reader will understand that there is more than one department manager.
   Louise gave the department manager a surprise birthday party.
   Louise had insulted the department manager.

3. Combine the two sentences to indicate that all members of the dance company were rehired.
   The choreographer rehired the dancers for the new show.
   The dancers were over 5'4".

4. Combine the two sentences to indicate that a particular group of engineers worked on the stealth bomber.
   The engineers designed the stealth bomber.

They worked in absolute secrecy for ten years.

5. Combine the two sentences to indicate that all the zoning laws are now being ignored.
   The zoning laws have been enforced for decades.
   These laws are now being ignored.

13c Parenthetical expressions

A *parenthetical expression* interrupts a sentence to provide transition, minor digression, additional information, or explanation. Like the nonrestrictive modifier, it is not essential, and may be deleted without destroying the sentence.

1. This essay, **therefore,** makes no sense at all. [transition]
2. The only thing wrong with your plan, **if I may say so,** is that it can't possibly work. [digression]
3. There are apparent bonanzas (**piles of firewood, for instance**) that provide the termite with only a temporary food supply. [additional information]

13d Effects of parenthetical expressions

Transitional expressions serve the crucial task of relating ideas; they are discussed further in **5e.** Parenthetical expressions can also communicate the presence of the writer and often can give the impression that the writer is tending carefully to the reader's understanding. The transitional device in sentence #1 (**13c**) suggests that the writer is consciously trying to make ideas coherent for the reader. The digression in sentence #2 brings the writer personally into the discourse. And the additional information in sentence #3 demonstrates that the writer indeed wants the reader to understand clearly.

Used with care, parenthetical expressions can be an efficient device to achieve coherence and flavor; used to excess, they will slow the discourse and divert the reader.

Exercise 3

In each sentence below add a parenthetical expression.

1. Love destroyed Anthony's appetite for televised football games.
2. That convenience store sells nothing but junk food.
3. The sergeant showed no mercy toward the recruits.
4. Professor Martinez gave good grades to only a few students.
5. When herbivores overpopulate an environment, they can do more damage than wildfire.

Exercise 4

Combine the sentences in the following passage by using one or more restrictive and nonrestrictive modifiers.

Ads for suntan products appear on TV.
The ads picture well-tanned youths.
The youths are playing volleyball at the
  beach.
The youths leap.
The youths dive.
The youths thrash at the volleyball.
The youths are in a frenzy of
  enjoyment.
The youths never sweat.
The youths' skins never gleam with
  greasy lotion.

14 · Coordinating

14a Coordination

To coordinate, a writer connects two or more language elements that are grammatically equivalent. The connecting may be done with **coordinating conjunctions,** with **commas,** and sometimes with **semicolons.** The coordinated elements may be individual words, phrases, or clauses.

Coordinated individual words must be the same part of speech.

1. "I have nothing to offer but **blood, toil, tears, and sweat.**" [nouns]
   Winston Churchill

2. The girl gazed into the **black, dank, silent** cave. [adjectives]
3. The snake **slithered, hissed, coiled, and twisted** in desperation. [verbs]

Likewise, coordinated phrases and clauses should be of the same type.

4. Our purposes in this advertising are **not only to be honest but also to be persuasive.** [infinitive phrases]
5. **After the burglar had found the gun collection and while he was still looking for the silverware,** Aileen climbed out of her bedroom window. [subordinate clauses]
6. **The workers struck, so the stockholders received no dividends.** [independent clauses]

When elements of the same type are coordinated, they are said to have *parallel construction.* When elements of different types are coordinated, they have *nonparallel construction,* an error discussed in Chapter **47.**

14b Effects of coordination

Unlike subordination, coordination relates elements by giving them equal weight. The effect can be like that of a listing. For example, Churchill's statement quoted above lists the things that the British people in 1940 could expect from the immediate future. Adjective clusters such as **black, dank, silent** can build vivid impressions if the words are chosen carefully (see Chapter **10**). A string of verbs such as **slithered, hissed, coiled, and twisted** can also build impressions while portraying complex actions. Coordinators are especially useful in expressing certain relationships between independent clauses: cause (**for**), exception (**but, yet**), and result (**so,** as in #6, **14a**).

Coordination can easily be abused (see Chapter **17**). Yet when used effectively it has a desirable cumulative effect on the reader, and it makes ideas of equal importance relate coherently. The simplest tactic is to join elements with a coordinating conjunction as in #1, **14a.** When three or more elements are each joined with a conjunction, the effect is to slow down the reading and emphasize each element: **blood and sweat and toil and tears.** When only commas are used to coordinate, the effect is to speed up the reading and to compress the impressions: "**Hopeful, fearful, bewildered** students jostled in front of the new school."

Exercise 1

Underline the coordinators in the following sentences and tell what types of elements they join.

1. The debate was not only boring but also ludicrous.

2. A runaway in the big city faces a life of fear and desperation.

3. The car careened wildly out of control and crashed into the embankment.

4. The new fall fashions were both practical and colorful.

5. The thieves stopped suddenly, for they had left their burglar's tools at the scene of the crime.

Exercise 2

Combine the following groups of sentences by using proper coordination.

1. Lee Harvey Oswald was an exmarine.
   Lee Harvey Oswald was reputed to be a communist sympathizer.

2. Ted Turner owns the rights to hundreds of movies.
   Ted Turner owns the Atlanta Braves.
   Ted Turner owns Cable News Network.

3. Thomas Jefferson wrote the "Declaration of Independence."
   Thomas Jefferson led the United States as its third President.

4. Success in college requires hard work.
   Success in college requires dedication.

5. Newspaper reporters must know how to gather information.

Newspaper reporters must know how to evaluate information.

Exercise 3

Expand the following simple sentences by adding one or
more coordinated elements.

1. Your first year of college can be a wonderful experience.
2. Some students can afford summer-long cross-country
   treks for vacations.
3. The meteor lit up the sky with an unnatural light.
4. *E.T.* was a major box-office attraction in the summer of
   1982.
5. Full appreciation of opera requires a deep sensitivity.

Exercise 4

Combine the sentences in the following passage by using
proper coordination.

Young people face many decisions.
The decisions are difficult.
The decisions are crucial to a young
    person's future.
A young person can pursue an education.
A young person can pursue a career.
A young person can pursue a trade.
Time must be taken with early decisions.
Care must be taken with early decisions.
Mistakes at this stage of life often take
    years to correct.

III

Writing with Precision and Control

15 · Choosing the Best Words

15a Choose words with appropriate denotation and connotation.

Mark Twain is reported to have said, "The difference between the almost right word and the right word is the difference between the lightning bug and lightning." The point of this statement is that while one word may adequately serve the meaning of a sentence, another word may superlatively serve the meaning.

The political importance of "almost right" words and "right" words is illustrated below in two versions of the most famous clauses from the Declaration of Independence. The first is from Thomas Jefferson's first draft; the second is from the final draft sent by the Continental Congress to King George III.

Early draft

We hold these truths to be sacred and undeniable; that all men are created equal. . . .

Final draft

We hold these truths to be self-evident, that all men are created equal. . . .

Comparing the two versions leads us to consider differences in denotation and connotation. A word's *denotation* is what the word refers to in human experience. Denotation is the meaning that scholars identify when they prepare definitions for dictionaries. A denotation of **undeniable** is **that which cannot be declared untrue;** a denotation of **self-evident** is **obvious without need of proof or explanation.** Clearly, the members of the Continental Congress felt that **self-evident** more effectively communicates what they wanted to say because its denotation does more than simply contradict anyone who thinks differently. Saying an assertion is **self-evident** denotes that it carries its own proof within itself and thus forces those who would disagree to search for contrary proof; saying an assertion is **undeniable,** however, can provoke opponents simply to deny the assertion without thinking much about it.

Furthermore, **self-evident** has connotations that must have pleased the Congressional committee that revised Jefferson's first draft. A word's *connotations* comprise the associations and emotional overtones that the word suggests to people. **Self-evident** connotes reasonableness and objectivity. **Evident** things have external evidence that an objective person can perceive. **Undeniable** connotes negativity because of its two negative parts, **un** and **deny.** It suggests closed-mindedness, a reluctance to be open to new information and new perspectives. The Congressional committee thought so well of the term **self-evident** that they deleted the powerfully connotative **sacred** and let **self-evident** stand alone as the only adjective for **truths.**

15b Consult a dictionary and a thesaurus.

One of your most important duties as a writer is to search your vocabulary for words appropriate to your message and audience. When you are not sure of a word, consult a dictionary. When you cannot think of a word, consult a thesaurus.

A dictionary lists a word's denotations so that you may judge if one of them suits the meaning you intend. A thesaurus groups words of similar denotations so that you may judge which of the words is most appropriate for your writing. In choosing a word from a list in a thesaurus, therefore, you should use a dictionary to check the meaning of the words you do not know. For example, in writing about a lazy condition you once enjoyed, you might consult a thesaurus to find a word to describe most accurately this state. The entry in the index under "laziness" would direct you to a list that includes the words "languor" and "lethargy." A dictionary would reveal that while the two words are close synonyms, "languor" can refer to dreaminess while "lethargy" can suggest unhealthy sluggishness. With this knowledge you would then be prepared to judge whether either word is the one you need.

The entry on the opposite page is from the college edition of *Webster's New World Dictionary*.* It illustrates the features of a typical dictionary entry and includes a section that distinguishes among synonyms.

Each word in the dictionary is listed alphabetically, and its *syllables* are set off by dots or dashes. When preparing a final draft, you may break a word at the end of a line by dividing it only at one of its syllables. *Pronunciation* is indicated by accent marks, (´) and phonetic symbols (ərjē). The speech sounds these symbols represent are described at the bottom of each page of the dictionary. *Parts of speech* are abbreviated as they are in Chapter **8.** *Various forms* include noun plurals, verb tenses, and pronoun cases (see Chapter **8**). The *origins* of a word are traced from its most recent ancestor to its earliest. *Definitions* are usually listed in one of two ways: the most common meaning first and the least common last, or the oldest meaning first and the most recently evolved last. Most dictionaries list their words according to the former pattern as does *Webster's New World Dictionary*.

---

*From *Webster's New World Dictionary* © 1984. Used by permission of the publisher, Simon & Schuster, Inc., New York.

Spelling and   *Part of*   *Various*   *Word*
Syllabication   *Pronunciation*   *Speech*   *Forms*   *Origins*

leth·ar·gy (leth'ər jē) *n., pl.* -gies [ME. *litarge <*
OFr. *<* LL. *lethargia <* Gr. *lēthargia < lēthargos,*
forgetful *< lēthē* (see LETHE) + *argos,* idle *< a-,*
not ÷ *ergon,* WORK] 1. a condition of abnormal
drowsiness or torpor 2. a great lack of energy;
sluggishness, dullness, apathy, etc.
SYN.—lethargy implies a dull, sluggish state
brought on by illness, great fatigue, overeating,
etc.; languor now generally suggests an inertia or
limpness that results from indolence, enervating
weather, a dreamy, tender mood, etc.; lassitude suggests a listlessness or spiritlessness resulting from
overwork, dejection, etc.; stupor suggests a state in
which the faculties and senses are deadened, as by
emotional shock, alcohol, or narcotics; torpor implies a temporary loss of all or part of the power of
sensation or motion.

**15
b**

First   *Second*
Definition   *Synonyms*   *Definition*

Exercise 1

Underline the word with the most appropriate denotation in
the sentences below, and compose a sentence that effectively
uses the word you do not pick.

1. In a speech to the stockholders, the president (inferred,
   implied) that the company's financial woes were due to
   narrow-mindedness on the part of management.
2. The burglar alarm rang (continuously, continually) until
   the police arrived on the scene.

3. The doctor instructed us to administer the medication (orally, verbally) every three hours.
4. The (determined, ruthless) negotiator finally worked out an agreement satisfactory to both labor and management.
5. Among all the victims of the earthquake, Marina maintained her (lassitude, equanimity) and so inspired her neighbors.

Exercise 2

Underline the word with the most appropriate connotation in the sentences below, and compose a sentence that effectively uses the word you do not pick.

1. The logic behind the ambassador's carefully worded proposal was (blatant, obvious).
2. The defendant's (statement, allegation) that her victim was to blame for the fatal incident was hard to believe in the face of the evidence.
3. The proud father (chuckled, giggled) softly to himself when he saw his daughter in her first ballet recital.
4. An aggressive sales representative (tapped, pounded) on my door until I finally shouted, "Whatever you're selling, I'm not buying."
5. At the moment the starter's gun sounded, the swimmers (plunged, jumped) into their racing lanes.

15c Choose synonyms with care.

When two words are synonymous, their denotations are similar. Rarely, however, are two words exactly the same in their denotation and connotation. For example, **belief** and **opinion** are synonymous in many respects, but they are not interchangeable in all contexts.

1. Martin changed his political **opinions** after each election.
2. Nell's political **beliefs** could not be shaken by the results of any election.
3. Evita formed her political (**opinions, beliefs**) after voting in several elections.

Because **opinion** denotes judgments open to question, that word is appropriate for sentence #1. Less appropriate would be the word **beliefs,** which denotes ideas held with certainty and consistency. On the other hand, these slightly different meanings make **beliefs** more appropriate than **opinions** in sentence #2. In sentence #3, either word could be appropriate depending on the writer's intent.

When you are faced with a choice of synonyms, a good collegiate dictionary is your best guide. Below is a list of words that have some similarity in denotation, but that are not completely synonymous.

**15
c**

ability (the power to do)
capacity (the ability to take in)

adversary (a hostile force)
opponent (someone taking the opposite side)

anticipate (to look forward to with some emotion)
expect (to believe an event will happen)

belief (an idea to which a person is committed)
opinion (a view held at a particular time)

decline (to politely refuse to accept)
reject (to refuse something as worthless or substandard)

element (a basic part)
factor (a cause)

essential (basic to the essence of something)
necessary (needed with some urgency)

famous (favorably well known)
notorious (unfavorably well known)

fate (a force driving inevitable outcomes)
destiny (an inevitable outcome, usually positive)

fewer (a smaller number)
less (a smaller quantity)

general (not specific)
usual (normal and common)

ignorant (not aware)
stupid (unintelligent)

insignificant (not meaningful)
trivial (of very small importance)

plan (a program for achieving a goal)
scheme (a carefully designed plan sometimes connoting un-
    derhandedness)

**15
c**

thin (lean, small in diameter)
slender (pleasingly slim and trim)

Exercise 3

For the underlined word in the sentences below, substitute a
synonym that more accurately reflects the sentence's flavor
and meaning. Then compose a sentence that effectively uses
the underlined word.

1. The quarterback was known for his tendency to play

   poorly in the big games.

2. The parting lovers gave one another a final passionate

   hug.

3. Before entering the classroom, the students loitered in

   the hall for one more glance at their notes.

4. In the most fast-paced section of the symphony, all the violinists yanked their strings to produce a rush of light, short notes.

5. That late summer afternoon, the maple leaves barely shook in a warm breeze.

15d Use nonsexist language.

Over a quarter century ago a new attitude toward sex-specific words developed among writers and publishers in this country. People had recognized that the way a society characterizes its members shapes their lives by influencing how they see themselves. People saw that "sexism," arbitrarily assigning roles and characteristics solely on the basis of sex, is hurtful to both males and females. Reacting to these perceptions, writers and publishers took responsibility for insuring that published language does not foster a sexist outlook.

Unfortunately, English speakers have traditionally sanctioned sexist usage in some of the most common terms in the language. To aid writers in circumventing these usages, numerous educational institutions, publishing houses, newspapers, journals, and broadcasting companies have devised guidelines. The terms outlined below represent solutions to the problem of sexist usage commonly proposed in these guidelines.

The Problem of Pronouns

Traditional usage has accepted the masculine pronoun (he, him, his) as a "generic" term to represent all people. Such usage, however, subtly discourages the reader from conceiving of women as possible referents for the pronouns. The options below eliminate this problem.

1. Eliminate the pronoun:

Original

A teacher should plan her lessons while keeping her students' abilities in mind.

Revised

A teacher should plan lessons while keeping students' abilities in mind.

2. Use direct address:

Original

After a student has studied hard, he naturally feels discouraged by a low grade.

Revised

After you have studied hard, you naturally feel discouraged by a low grade.

3. Use articles instead of pronouns:

Original

An effective administrator always makes clear his interpretation of policy.

Revised

An effective administrator always makes clear an interpretation of policy.

4. Use plurals:

Original

In learning to read, a child is often his own best teacher.

Revised

In learning to read, children are often their own best teachers.

5. Alternate male and female terms:

Original

At our daycare center we are constantly diagnosing each child's needs. Is he grumpy because he did not eat his lunch? Is he crying because other children have rejected him?

Revised

. . . Is she grumpy because she did not eat her lunch? Is he crying because other children have rejected him?

6. Use modifiers instead of pronouns:

Original

The technician who keeps abreast of the latest developments in his field will maintain job security.

Revised

The technician who keeps abreast of the latest technological developments will maintain job security.

7. Use "he or she" and "his or her" sparingly:

Original

Each member of this student body should take full responsibility for his sexual behavior.

Revised

Each member of this student body should take full responsibility for his or her sexual behavior.

The Problem of Nouns

Numerous male gender English nouns are used generically, but there are nonsexist substitutes. Some options are listed below.

Businessman Entrepreneur, executive, industrialist, manager, merchant, people in business (for *businessmen*).

Cameraman Camera operator.

Chairman   Chair, chairperson, department head, group leader, moderator, presiding officer.

The common man   The average person, ordinary people.

Congressman   Member of Congress, Representative.

Deliveryman   Courier, deliverer, delivery driver, messenger.

Fireman   Fire fighter.

Foreman   Supervisor.

Housewife   Homemaker.

Maid   Houseworker.

Mailman   Mail carrier.

Manhours   Labor, work hours, time.

Mankind   Human beings, humankind, humanity, people.

Watchman   Guard, watch.

Policeman   Police officer, detective.

Repairman   Carpenter, electrician, pipe fitter, plumber, repairer.

Salesman   Salesperson, sales representative.

Spokesman   Advocate, representative, spokesperson.

Sportsman   Golfer, hunter, sports enthusiast.

Sportsmanship   Fair play.

Statesman   Political leader, public servant.

Stewardess   Flight attendant.

Weatherman   Weather reporter, weather forecaster, meteorologist.

Workman   Worker.

Exercise 4

Revise the following sentences using the strategies for non-sexist language outlined in this section.

1. If a businessman wants to participate in a government-supported health care plan, he should have that opportunity.

2. Critics of the criminal justice system argue that the criminal rarely pays a just price for the crimes he has committed.

3. When restrictions are put on art, the artist loses his constitutional right to freedom of expression.

4. I've always resented the student who never comes to class but still makes a "B" or "C" because he's adept at taking tests.

5. The typical student pays his parking fee the first week of class and spends the rest of the semester looking for a place to leave his car.

6. I used to think that if someone is attending college, he must enjoy reading; now I realize that many of my peers never want to open a book.

7. Although a commencement speaker usually says that his talk will be brief, few in the audience believe him.

8. Man now holds the key to survival for all the earth's inhabitants.

9. When a foreman ignores safety standards, he jeopardizes everyone's health.

10. Why should someone who blindly votes with his party as a member of the electoral college be considered more capable of deciding the presidency than a more objective voter casting his ballot for an individual rather than a political party?

15e Choose language as concrete and specific as your topic allows.

Concrete language refers to things and experiences that engage our senses (**apple, hug, sweet**). *Abstract language* refers to ideas, emotions, qualities, and fields of activity (**profit, love, pretty, medicine**). *General* refers to broad classifications (**em-**

ployment, nation), and *specific* refers to particular cases (**computer programmer, France**). Specific wording tends to be concrete, and general wording tends to be abstract. Our language provides a range of meanings from abstract to concrete and from general to specific, as illustrated in the two lists below.

animal—cat—Persian—Abby

move—descend—fall—tumble

A cat is a specific type of animal, a Persian is a specific type of cat, and "Abby" is a particular Persian. Likewise, to descend is to move in a particular way, to fall is to descend in a particular way, and to tumble is to fall in a particular way.

How abstract, concrete, general, or specific your writing should be depends on your topic and your audience. A comparison of two theories on the nature of truth written for readers experienced in philosophical discourse is likely to have a high percentage of abstract and general words. A comparison of two opposing football teams written for readers interested in sports is likely to have a high percentage of concrete and specific words.

Whatever the circumstances, however, a general rule for the philosopher and the sports writer as well as for the college student is to be as concrete and specific as the subject matter permits. Compare the first sentence below with its revised version.

Original

After my mother had waxed the kitchen floor, our dog kept falling down on it.

Revised

For days after my mother had waxed the kitchen floor, our poodle could only slide and trip across the linoleum to his food bowl.

Note that the revision offers the reader the more specific **poodle** for **dog** and describes with the more precise verbs

slide and **trip** instead of **falling down** how the dog fared on the newly waxed floor. It also specifies more details of time and place with the words **for days, linoleum,** and **food bowl.** The basic message is similar in the sentences, but the revision is richer, more memorable, and so more rewarding for the reader.

Exercise 5

Rewrite the following sentences, using more concrete, specific language to convey greater detail and fuller meaning.

1. The field marshal's conception for the northern front called for more men and more equipment.

2. While the employee's attention was diverted, someone removed money from the premises.

3. A loud noise sounded when the player's bat made contact with the ball.

4. After the dance was over the people went home.

5. The administration building was a dangerous eyesore.

15f Use figurative language to intensify the reader's response and to clarify meaning.

The most common figurative devices, *simile* and *metaphor*, express comparisons between two phenomena by linking two images not usually associated or by linking an abstraction with a concrete image.

The *simile* specifies a comparison with such words as **like, as,** or **than.** Note below how the writer uses two similes to convey the stealth of a soldier passing time during a night ambush.

Slower than a caterpillar chews on a maple leaf his fingers tore a small paper packet of Kool-Aid, and quieter than a dandelion loses its fluff his hand shook the light purple powder into his Army canteen.
John Sack

By comparing the actions of opening and mixing Kool-Aid to a caterpillar chewing and a dandelion shedding, Sack gives us a keen impression of this act. Note how much less vivid an impression is given by the sentence below.

Very slowly he tore a small paper packet of Kool-Aid and very quietly he shook the light purple powder into his Army canteen.

A *metaphor* expresses a comparison directly as if the things compared were in fact part of a single phenomenon.

What does education often do? It makes a straight-cut ditch of a free, meandering brook.
Henry David Thoreau

In this statement, Thoreau has treated education *as if* it were an engineering project to convert a stream to a ditch. Also, the statement implicitly compares **stream** and **ditch** to students who are first free and natural but who are later turned into something rigid and artificial. Of course, we do not take metaphor as fact; we know that students are not really ditches, but we accept the metaphor because it is so suggestive. Note how relatively unstimulating is a literal statement of Thoreau's metaphor.

Education can destroy spontaneity and can turn students into conformists.

Another common type of figurative comparison is *personification*, in which something nonanimal or nonhuman is given the characteristics of a person.

The future lurks around the corner, even now making plans to mug me for my youth.

The student who wrote this sentence was trying to make vivid her apprehension and uncertainty about the future, so she personified it as a sinister character plotting a theft.

Hyperbole is exaggeration for effect.

Obviously the mosquitoes had organized an effort to suck every drop of blood from me.

As with metaphor, we know that hyperbole is not literally true. We appreciate the sentence above, therefore, for its figurative truth that the mosquitoes seemed *as if* they had organized to bleed the writer dry.

Successful figurative language gives us a heightened sense of what things are like. Unsuccessful figurative language confuses us. Weak metaphors and similes make vague, inappropriate, or trite comparisons.

Vague

He drove to the hospital like a crazy man.

Inappropriate

He drove to the hospital like a bull in a china shop.

The first sentence is vague because **crazy man** is not specific enough to suggest a clear image. The second sentence is inappropriate because there are too few similarities between a person driving toward a destination and an aimless **bull in a china shop;** this sentence is also trite because of the overused expression about the bull (see Cliché, **15l**).

A *mixed metaphor* combines two incompatible metaphors.

Mixed metaphor

That course in physics was **a dark forest** I couldn't penetrate until Jill began tutoring me; then it became **all sunny weather.**

This passage begins with the figurative idea of a physics course being an impenetrable forest but ends with the unrelated idea of the course being sunny weather. To unmix the metaphor and extend the figurative notion of a course being a type of landscape, **all sunny weather** might be changed to **an open meadow.**

Exercise 6

1. Write a sentence in which you use a simile to describe the atmosphere in a large room where a rollicking party is taking place.
2. Write a sentence in which you use a simile to capture the feeling one might get from finding a hundred-dollar bill in a public place.
3. Use a metaphor to convey the image of a person who has found long-needed hope.
4. Use a metaphor to express your opinion of a popular song or type of music.
5. Use personification in a sentence in which you characterize the '80s (or any other era).
6. Write a sentence using hyperbole to describe a lopsided defeat or victory in an athletic contest or game of some sort.

15g Use a verbal style in preference to a nominal style.

As we suggested in **8j,** expository writers sometimes rely heavily on nouns to convey their messages. For example, note below how many more nouns are used in passage #1 than in passage #2.

1. My preference is for life in a large city because there I have the freedom to do the things that cannot be done in a small town. When I lived in a small town I felt my life had to be like my neighbors'. There was a need for conformity to their beliefs regarding proper behavior. If my actions or thinking was different from their expectations, I was an object of suspicion. My expression of ideas that were in disagreement with those of other people often had the results of their rejection of me and my isolation from the community.

I discovered that abiding by the standards of the town meant imposing limitations on my ways of looking at the world.*

2. I prefer to live in a large city because there I am free to do the things I cannot do in a small town. When I lived in a small town, I felt I had to live as my neighbors did. I needed to conform to what they believed was the proper way to behave. If I acted or thought in a way they did not expect, they suspected me. If I expressed ideas that others disagreed with, they often rejected me and isolated me from life in the community. I discovered that as I abided by the standards of the town, I limited my way of looking at the world.*

Both passages offer the same message; they differ only in style. Because passage #1 depends so heavily on nouns, we say it has a *nominal style:* "My **preference** is for **life.** . . ." Because passage #2 depends on verbs, we say it has a *verbal style:* "I **prefer** to **live.** . . ." Research has demonstrated that noun-dependent writing is more difficult for readers to understand than verb-dependent writing. Unfortunately, writers are sometimes encouraged to compose in a nominal style. Studies of the written language used in government, the professions, and business reveal that some audiences have grown to expect this style. These audiences tend to assume mistakenly that the writer of a passage such as #1 above is a wiser person than the writer of a passage such as #2. In fact, verbal style encourages quicker reading and more extensive recall than does nominal style.

To adopt one of these styles, a writer chooses between verbs and nouns derived from verbs. For example, note the related verbs and nouns in the fifth sentences of passages #1 and #2.

Verbs (5th sentence passage #2)	*Nouns (5th sentence passage #1)*
expressed	expression
disagreed	disagreement
rejected	rejection
isolated	isolation

*Adapted from Rosemary L. Hake and Joseph M. Williams, "Style and Its Consequences: Do as I Do, Not as I Say," *College English* 43 (1981): 447–48.

A nominal style is also characterized by expletive constructions (**9c**), linking verbs (**8b**), and prepositions (**8g**).

expletive constructions: "**There was** a need . . ."
linking verbs: "My preference **is** . . ."
prepositional phrases: " . . . **for** conformity **to** their beliefs **regarding** proper behavior . . ."

To eliminate excessive nominal elements from your writing, first examine your sentences for expletives, linking verbs, and prepositions. Then judge if you can become more forceful and clear by revising those constructions requiring nouns.

Keep in mind, however, that an abstract nominal style may be required by the subject matter. When you have no satisfactory alternative to writing in this way, you can still be forceful and clear by supporting your abstract, noun-dependent statements with examples given in a concrete, verbal style. Note how the two styles complement each other in the following two passages from Colette Dowling's book *The Cinderella Complex.*

1. There is, I have learned, a connection between our feminine urge toward domesticity and those lulling reveries about childhood which seem to lie just beneath the surface of consciousness. It has to do with dependence: the need to lean on someone—the need, going back to infancy, to be nurtured and cared for and kept from harm's way.

2. At night I prepared big meals and spread them proudly on the groaning board of a real dining room. During the days, I laundered, raked, and mulched. At night, playing helpmate, I would type Lowell's manuscripts for him. Oddly, though I'd been writing professionally for ten years, it felt as if typing for someone was what I ought to be doing. It felt *right* (by which, I now know, I meant comfortable and secure).

To state her thesis, Dowling must establish a certain relationship between concepts, so in the first passage she names her concepts with abstract nouns and relates them with linking verbs and prepositions. Subsequently, she goes on to amplify her meaning for the reader with the concrete, verb-dependent example in the second passage.

Exercise 7

Rewrite the following paragraph, which is written in a predominantly nominal style, by converting it to a verbal style.

The regulation and policing of college athletics have become tasks of great difficulty. Officials of the NCAA alone cannot give all the schools the scrutinization necessary for an assurance that no one school gains an advantage through illegal or unethical means. Obviously, there is a need for regulation on the part of the schools themselves. But as long as there is a prevalent attitude of "win at any cost" among many schools, it is unlikely that this self-regulation will exist to any significant extent.

15 h

15h Avoid colloquialisms in formal writing.

To label a term *colloquial* or *informal* is to make a judgment based on experience with language appropriate for different levels of formal and informal discourse. Discourse is colloquial when it is more suitable in conversation than in formal written prose. When dictionaries mark a word *colloq.* or *informal,* they indicate only a judgment that the word is more common in oral than in written language, not an opinion that the word is inferior.

For example, the *American Heritage Dictionary, Second College Edition,* has this entry: "**figure out.** *Informal.* To solve, decipher, or comprehend." Consider the two sentences below.

1. Before Barry had **figured out** the problem, he was **kind of grouchy,** but later he **felt great.**

2. Before Barry had **solved** the problem, he was **rather ill-tempered,** but later he **was in high spirits.**

Each of these statements is suitable for a different context. Sentence #1 would be appropriate in a conversation between two friends discussing a mutual acquaintance; in this context, sentence #2 might sound too formal. On the other hand, sentence #2 would be appropriate in an essay characterizing Barry for an audience of unknown readers; in that context, the readers might find sentence #1 distractingly intimate. Generally, the less familiar you are with your audience or the more formal the occasion, the less colloquial you should be.

15i Avoid slang except in the most informal writing.

Like colloquialisms, *slang* terms are most appropriate in informal discourse. Slang words usually arise within communities whose members desire terms that are vivid and peculiar to their group. By using slang, a person can demonstrate solidarity with group members. Examples of groups that generate slang are ethnic or regional communities, the entertainment world (especially the world of popular music), and young people.

Usually slang terms arise and fade from use quickly. Hippies of the late '60s would **grok** an interesting sight or idea, using the term from the *B.C.* cartoon to mean they would contemplate something; but **grok** is now out of use. Being **hep** meant the same in the '40s as being **hip** in the '60s and '70s. **Twenty-three skidoo** meant a fast departure to young people in the roaring '20s; it was used in a context similar to that of today's **let's split.**

Some slang words, such as **jazz,** have become appropriate in the more formal written discourse. As a rule, though, slang does not serve readers well, least of all readers outside the community that evolved the terms. Imagine trying to understand the sentence below if you did not know that in colloquial basketball discourse, **brick** means a badly missed shot and **to do a face job** means to score on an opposing player in an especially humiliating way.

We had a great game yesterday. The other team put up nothing but bricks, and we did a face job on them every time down the court.

You should keep slang out of your formal writing unless you determine a certain term is appropriate for your audience.

15j Use jargon only for an appropriate audience and always avoid pretentious language.

Like slang, *jargon* is language suitable to an individual community, but unlike slang, it can be appropriate in formal written discourse for the community's members. Most jargon originates in vocational groups. Doctors, lawyers, educators, social scientists, and government agencies all use unique technical terms. For example, consider this sentence from a report of research on the type of prose college students can best understand.

This study investigated the effects of problem-solution rhetorical predicates, intersentential cohesive conjunctions, and reference (lexical cohesion) on reading rate and comprehension.*

Technical terms such as "intersentential cohesive conjunction" are devised by specialists so that they can refer to phenomena as precisely as possible. This term refers to conjunctions, such as **nevertheless,** that occur between sentences and make them cohere in one of four ways specified by the

---

*Duane H. Roen and Gene L. Piché, "The Effects of Selected Text-Forming Structures on College Freshmen's Comprehension of Expository Prose," *Research in the Teaching of English* 18 (1984): 8–25.

research. While such prose may be impenetrable to people not members of the community for which it was written, it can make for efficient, accurate communication among the members.

Jargon obstructs comprehension, however, when it is used needlessly or pretentiously. *Pretentious language* results when a writer is trying to impress readers by flaunting vocabulary. The first passage below is an example of overuse of jargon; the second passage is an example of pretension. Note the *nominal style* (**15g**) of both.

We define motivation . . . as a condition of an organism in which bodily energy is selectively directed in behavioral acts in relation to the environment so as to attain a goal-object that is significant and meaningful to the individual.*

Your subjectively derived belief is not *prima facie* validated as an objectively established construct of reality.

The ideas in these passages can be put more simply.

Creatures are motivated when they try to get something they want.

Your opinion is not necessarily a fact.

A handy principle to guide you in avoiding pretension and unnecessary jargon is that from among synonyms appropriate to the context, you should usually pick the word with the fewest syllables: **part** instead of **component, change** instead of **modify, tell** instead of **relate, ask** instead of **inquire, before** instead of **prior to, use** instead of **utilize** or **employ.**

*J. Galen Taylor and William M. Alexander, *Curriculum Planning for Modern Schools* (New York: Holt, 1966), 207.

15k Avoid using euphemisms to obscure meaning.

A *euphemism* is a word or phrase that indirectly expresses something which is unpleasant in a particular context. We speak euphemistically when we say someone **passed away** rather than **died.** Rather than say a statement is a **lie** we can say it is **untrue,** or we can be extremely euphemistic and say it is **inoperative.** Euphemisms frequently treat sex, violence, death, the body and its functions, and socially and politically sensitive conditions. Below are listed some recently popular expressions with their translations:

civil disorder	riot
control garment	girdle
dentures	false teeth
encore telecast	rerun
misspeak	lie
negative deficit	profit
nervous wetness	sweat
occasional irregularity	constipation
previously owned	used
released	fired
revenue enhancement	taxes
shortfall	error in planning
substandard housing	slum

Expository writing should be direct but not offensive. While you do not want to hurt particular readers' feelings, neither do you want to mask the truth.

15l Avoid clichés.

A *cliché* is an expression that once may have created vivid impressions but has by now become worn out and boring:

break of day	raining cats and dogs
easier said than done	spread like wildfire

fraught with danger   throw your weight around
picture of health   worse for wear
thrill of my life   not playing with a full deck

Such expressions may enliven conversation, but they can
subvert a reader's attention.

Furthermore, like slang terms and euphemisms, clichés
can limit the amount of information that sentences provide.
Compare the two sentences below.

Original

Waiting during late registration in lines **slow as Christmas** made me
sadder but wiser.

Revised

Waiting during late registration in lines creeping one body length an
hour persuaded me never to miss advanced registration again.

15
I

The student who wrote these sentences recognized how
clichés can pop into our minds and give us an easy way to
emphasize a concept such as "slowness" with a phrase such
as **slow as Christmas.** By omitting the cliché and by treating
the subject specifically in the phrase **creeping one body
length an hour,** the student draws readers into empathy
with his frustration. Likewise, by eliminating **made me sadder but wiser,** the student could be much more informative
with a more specific predicate and object: **persuaded me
never to miss advanced registration again.** As writers, we
should follow this example and spend the psychological energy to offer our readers as vivid an understanding as possible.

Exercise 8

1. Rewrite the sentences below, eliminating colloquialisms
   or replacing them with words or terms more suitable to
   formal written prose.

a. Actually, Wally was sort of happy when he was canned from the football team, but he didn't let on to anyone about his feelings.

b. When Faye heard tell of her sister's impending arrival, she lit out for the train station.

c. Marvin was right smart, but he couldn't care less about school.

d. The city manager figured on the zoning commission's cooperation, but she was mistaken.

2. Rewrite the sentences below, replacing inappropriate slang with terms more suitable for a general audience.

a. I thought I had registered for a crib course, but I soon realized that I would have to hit the books or I would flag it.

b. The whole neighborhood was enjoying the big bash until the fuzz made the scene and told everyone to put a lid on it.

c. It is a good friend who will give shelter to someone who needs a place to flop but doesn't have any bread.

3. Rewrite the sentences below, eliminating jargon and pretentious language.

a. Tenatta's superior intimated that the intended course of action was not viable in a profit-wise sense.

b. The post-work life-goals of many people are not in accordance with their future capital intake.

c. This company's promotion policy is predicated on the conviction that employees should receive compensation commensurate with the caliber of their accomplishments.

d. This computer must have more RAM before it can run today's large programs.

4. Revise the following sentences to eliminate clichés.

a. Not being mentioned during the awards ceremony was a real slap in the face for the project's founder.

b. The fog was as thick as pea soup when we stumbled across our missing companion, who was sleeping like a log.

c. I do not want to pass the buck, but I must recommend that someone else rise to the occasion and become committee chairperson.

d. It got under Marcia's skin that she has kept her nose to the grindstone all her life while her children have never done a day's work.

5. Use appropriate euphemisms to soften the effects of unpleasant ideas in the following sentences.

   a. Morris was fired from his job because he was so stupid.

   b. I understand that your father shot your brother-in-law dead.

6. Revise inappropriate euphemisms in the following sentences.

   a. The governor has been accused of providing disinformation to the press.

b. The company did not suffer from the work stoppage

as much as its employees suffered from indigence.

16 · Writing Concisely

To write concisely means to use only words that contribute significantly to your meaning. Much advice on good writing amounts to a recommendation to be concise.

16a Avoid noun-dependent style.

Consider the wordy sentence below.

There is a requirement in the rules for the establishment of procedures which would be of equal help to visiting and home teams.

In this sentence, we can see the characteristics of a noun-dependent style: expletive **there,** linking verbs **is** and **would be,** five prepositional phrases, and four nouns derived from verbs (**requirement, establishment, procedure,** and **help**). Revising these constructions gives us a more concise sentence.

The rules require us to establish procedures equally helpful to visiting and home teams.

Note especially how the objects of the prepositional phrases have been revised. **Rules** has become the subject; **requirement** has become the verb **require; establishment** has become the infinitive **to establish; procedures** has become the object of the infinitive; and **help** has become the adjective **helpful.**

A habit of depending on nouns can thwart concision more subtly and persistently than any other stylistic trait. Sections **8j** and **15e** treat this problem in detail.

16b Avoid needless repetition.

Once you have established a concept for your reader, you usually do not need to repeat it. Note below how the repetitions in the first sentence have been eliminated in the second.

Original

I made the batter first, then **I made** the filling, and last **I made** the topping.

Revised

I made the batter first, then the filling, and last the topping.

The writer has listed three processes, but repeating **I made** slows the sentence and gives unwarranted emphasis to these two words. Needless repetitions often occur in series and are easily revised by eliminating the repeated elements.

Sometimes a word repeated carelessly can retard a sentence.

Original

Marie was worried about her grandfather's **attitude** because a pessimistic **attitude** like his could be dangerous.

Revised

Marie was worried about her grandfather's **attitude** because **pessimism** like his could be dangerous.

Using two or more synonyms is another form of needless repetition.

Original

The parents ceaselessly **pampered** and **indulged** their child.

Pampered and **indulged** have similar denotations, so together they do not build meaning but instead simply repeat it. In the first revision below, the redundant **indulged** has been deleted. In the second, a verb that gives new information has been substituted for **pampered.**

Revised

The parents ceaselessly **pampered** their child.
The parents ceaselessly **shielded** and **indulged** their child.

Repetition of words or synonyms, called *redundancy*, is usually unnecessary, but occasionally writers use redundancy to achieve emphasis and balance (see **17a**).

**16
c**

16c Avoid empty phrases.

Some words and phrases stretch out a simple meaning beyond what it deserves.

Original

Due to the fact that it is raining, we cannot till our garden.

Revised

Because it is raining, we cannot till our garden.

Here are some other *empty phrases:* **at this point in time** (now), **for the purpose of** (for), **in order to** (to), **by means of** (by), **in the direction of** (toward). Such phrases only clutter your sentences.

Often the subjects and verbs of adjective clauses (**which are, who is, that were,** etc.) can be deleted.

Original

Doctors **who are** squeamish about blood are like mountain climbers **who are** afraid of heights.

Revised

Doctors squeamish about blood are like mountain climbers afraid of heights.

In deciding whether or not to write a modifying clause (**who are squeamish about blood**) or a modifying phrase (**squeamish about blood**), you should judge how important the modifier's main ideas are. A clause will emphasize these ideas more than a phrase (see **17b**).

16
c

Exercise 1

Rewrite the following sentences, making them more concise.

1. The idea that Manuel has concerning the problem of security is one that possesses overall merit and worth.

2. There are many different systems in existence which can be employed for the prevention of burglary.

3. There was a bad outlook and attitude displayed by the delegation which led to the impossiblility of a compromise being reached.

4. It is the fault of the government's policies that the rate of unemployment has risen.

5. The inexperienced and green challenger, who was battered and bleeding, stumbled and staggered back to the corner which was his when the bell rang.

6. After she checked her own records and after she checked the records of the bank, the depositor concluded that it was the records of the bank which were incorrect, and she decided her own records were correct.

7. The government of the revolutionaries, which was make-shift, quickly weakened and quickly collapsed when its leader was discovered to be corrupt and no good.

8. It is at this moment in time that we are moving in the direction of being under the power of corporate control in all areas and facets of our lives.

9. There was a tense and strained air and atmosphere on board the ship, and the men seemed to have a mutinous attitude.

16 c

10. There are specific measures that the council could take in order to assist the members of the league in the establishment of credibility in regard to the public.

Exercise 2

Revise the following paragraph, striving for greater conciseness and clarity.

In my opinion, I personally feel that the solution to the problem of illegal drug use among athletes could be achieved in part through the de-emphasis of the "win at any cost" attitude that is so prevalent and widespread in athletics in this day and time. Particularly in individual sports especially, more stress and emphasis should be placed on striving to fulfill and reach individual potential in a way that is whole-

some. If athletes and fans in general would realize that it is
the friendly competitive spirit that is more important in sport
than the "Winning is not everything; it's the only thing" philosophy in sport, then they would be moving positively in
the right direction of eradicating the lamentable and regrettable corruption in sport, of which illegal drug use is the
cause.

**17
a**

17 · Writing with Emphasis

As you plan, write, and revise, you will discern certain ideas
and images that are more important than others. These items
deserve the greatest emphasis. To achieve emphasis, you will
find these tactics useful: repeat the item, put it in an emphatic place or construction in a sentence, or isolate it in com-
paratively brief sentences or after special punctuation.

17a Repeat for emphasis judiciously.

Section **16b** explains that repetition of words and phrases can
destroy conciseness. In special contexts, however, repeated
words and parallel, repeated phrases can be emphatic rather
than dulling.

. . . the party in power should never outrage the minority. That means that it must listen to the minority and be moved by the criticisms of the minority.

Walter Lippmann

Youth, which is forgiven everything, forgives itself nothing; age, which forgives itself anything, is forgiven nothing.

George Bernard Shaw

Lippmann's passage illustrates how a writer can repeat a word (**minority**) as a means of insisting that the reader note its importance. Shaw's passage illustrates how repetition in parallel word order can emphasize comparisons and contrasts. In your prose, you may find that the best place for repeated elements is at climactic points toward which you have led your reader. Remember that repeating words is a risky tactic and should be used sparingly, or it will quickly lose its emphatic effect.

17
b

17b Use emphatic sentence structure.

Emphasis within the English sentence depends on position as well as grammatical function. The most emphatic place is usually at the end. A sentence's final words are likely to be relatively easy to remember because they are the last read. The next most emphatic place is at the beginning. Readers are especially alert when they start a segment of text. The least emphatic place is in the middle. After writing the first sentence below, a college student revised it to achieve the greater emphasis in the second sentence.

Original

I dashed up to Fred waving my arms and making faces before he could make a big fool of himself.

Revised

Before Fred could make a big fool of himself, **I dashed up to him waving my arms and making faces.**

The first sentence leaves the reader with the abstract notion of Fred possibly being a fool, and it nests the vivid image of the writer waving and making faces in the unemphatic middle. The revised sentence is more exciting because the most vivid part is at the most emphatic position.

The revision above de-emphasized the subordinate clause **before Fred could make a big fool of himself.** Modifying clauses and phrases can, however, merit emphatic placement in the sentence.

Original

Eyes ringed and bloodshot, tie askew, shirt sagging over his belt, Jack campaigned throughout our city.

Revised

Throughout our city Jack campaigned, **eyes ringed and bloodshot, tie askew, shirt sagging over his belt.**

The original sentence, with its subject and verb at the end, emphasizes Jack's campaigning, but the revised sentence, with the vivid modifiers at the end, emphasizes his appearance.

Note that the phrases describing Jack are arranged according to space, from his eyes, to his tie, to his shirt. Another way to sequence items in a series is according to significance, with the most significant item in the most emphatic position. Note how the listing of items in the first sentence has been rearranged in the second sentence.

Original

The speech made **most people exuberant, some people indifferent,** and **a few people uncomfortable.**

Revised

The speech made **a few people uncomfortable, some people indifferent,** and **most people exuberant.**

In the revised version, the major effect of the speech (that it made most people exuberant) culminates the sentence. In the original, the fact that the speech left a few people uncomfortable is given the emphatic position.

Emphasis within the sentence is also influenced by which ideas are expressed as independent clauses and which ideas are subordinated in modifying clauses and phrases. Independent clauses are the most emphatic, subordinate clauses are next most emphatic, and modifying phrases are the least emphatic. The sentences below are ordered so that the blizzard receives decreasing emphasis.

A blizzard was rattling the walls, but we continued to celebrate New Year's Eve.

Although a blizzard was rattling the walls, we continued to celebrate New Year's Eve.

With a blizzard rattling the walls, we continued to celebrate New Year's Eve.

**17
c**

17c Isolate and vary for emphasis.

An especially emphatic technique is to isolate an idea or image in a short sentence or after a colon or dash. The passage below illustrates both techniques.

The traditional way of encouraging children to want to learn the things we want to teach is by giving rewards for success: **prizes, privileges, gold stars. Two grave risks attend this practice.**

Margaret Donaldson

Donaldson's listing of the three **rewards** after the colon gives them special emphasis, and the relative brevity of her second sentence gives special emphasis to her point about the **risks.**

Sometimes a writer can emphasize several impressions by making a series of brief points.

They were very poor. Clothes and boots were a problem. They

"made their own amusements." Books were mostly the *Bible* and *The Pilgrim's Progress*. Every Saturday night they bathed in a hip bath in front of the kitchen fire. No servants. Church three times on Sundays.

Doris Lessing

Lessing's passage illustrates the power of the short, emphatic sentence and deliberate fragment. Note, however, that Lessing has varied sentence length and grammatical patterns. The fourth sentence is relatively long and separates the earlier short statements from the two even shorter fragments. A style in which most sentences are of the same length and grammatical pattern will lack emphasis and can make even interesting subjects tedious.

17 c

Original

I made the mistake of my life last week. I had asked my fiancée to get a date for an old high school friend. I learned that the date was a very loud and obnoxious person. I thought that we would all have a miserable time, so I decided to take matters into my own hands.

All the main clauses in the passage above are of similar length and have the same subject-verb-object pattern. This repeated structure makes for dull reading. Note in the revision below how varied sentence structures make the passage more emphatic and thus make us more anxious to know how the writer took **matters into [his] own hands.**

Revised

I made the mistake of my life last week. I had asked my fiancée to get a date for an old high school friend, but then I learned that the date was loud and obnoxious. Thinking we would all have a miserable time, I decided to take matters into my own hands.

Exercise 1

Use repetition or tight parallel structure to create more emphatic sentences below.

1. Janet attended the opera to become cultured; to the seminar she went to become learned.

2. To overcome this problem we need two things, a definition and to understand it.

3. The terrorist was cruel, and he also behaved in a cowardly way.

4. When we want to spread the holiday spirit, the highways beckon us to spread it even though once we are en route, it will be choked to death with traffic.

17 c

5. We cannot improve education without improving physical facilities; teachers' salaries must also increase.

Rearrange or rewrite the following sentences in order to put greater emphasis on the underlined element or idea.

1. "Give the bad news to me straight; <u>don't sugarcoat it</u>," the patient said to the doctor.

2. <u>As it rumbled down the track,</u> the train had smoke pouring from its engine.

3. The pitcher <u>stormed off the field</u>, frustrated with her error-prone teammates.

4. Joint custody <u>may adversely affect the children</u> when the parents are bitterly contesting a divorce.

5. Throughout the night, <u>my roommate cursed under his breath</u> as he patched together a term paper.

Exercise 2

Revise the following sentences by incorporating the underlined words into short, emphatic sentences or phrases.

1. We filled our car with everything we thought we could possibly need for the trip, <u>except for gas.</u>

2. The police finally located <u>his wife</u>, the one person who could reason with the unbalanced hijacker.

3. The graduate thought she would spend her summer visiting relatives and friends, going to the beach, and just relaxing, but her expectations changed two days after the ceremony, because <u>she got a job.</u>

4. The puppy from the animal shelter was painfully thin and weak, and <u>she was obviously a sad case.</u>

5. Tanya was prepared to risk everything she treasured,

   which included her career, her marriage, and her sanity.

Exercise 3

Revise the following paragraph, using the emphatic structures discussed in the chapter to make the paragraph more vivid.

A man who had been badly beaten up staggered from an alley into the lights of a passing squad car. Actually, he would have had an even chance in the fight except for one thing, which was the brass knuckles his opponent carried. The results of his adversary's unfair advantage, a broken nose, a chipped tooth, and a split lip, were evident. In the back of the squad car, he promised himself, as a result of this sobering experience, never again to frequent places where that kind of trouble was likely to begin.

18

18 · Writing in the Active and Passive Voice

Active and passive structures are explained in **9c.** This chapter examines how voice influences style. Compare the two sentences below.

1. Classic novels produced on television can fascinate illiterate people. [active voice]
2. Illiterate people can be fascinated by classic novels produced on television. [passive voice]

While these two sentences express basically the same information, their different subjects suit them to different contexts. Sentence #1 invites the reader to understand something about televised **novels,** and sentence #2 invites the reader to understand something about illiterate **people.** Sentence #1, therefore, would more likely complement a paragraph about novels adapted for television than would sentence #2; sentence #2 would more likely complement a paragraph about people who cannot read.

Often, however, writers resort to the passive voice not to strengthen their readers' understanding but to avoid the active voice. The result is an indirect style that needlessly handicaps the reader. Inexperienced writers rarely invoke a conscious rationale for this avoidance, but we may discern two correlated motives for it. One is the impulse to give readers a feeling that the subject matter is heavy with significance. The more impressed our readers are with the weight of our subject, the more impressed they will be with us. The passive can give a superficial impression of authority by suggesting that events occur as a result of forces known only to the writer. The other related motive is to de-emphasize the *agents,* or those who actually perform acts suggested in the sentence. Sometimes we just do not want to put those responsible for actions in full view. Note how passive constructions burden the simple idea in sentence #3 and how the active voice clarifies it in sentence #4.

3. It is understood that no goals can be achieved until a meeting is held by the full committee.
4. Members of the subcommittee understand that we cannot achieve our goals until the full committee meets.

Without any agents for the verbs "understood" and

"achieved," sentence #3 vaguely implies some sort of universal understanding related to generalized "goals." We are not sure what is going on, but we are briefly tempted to feel it may be pretty deep. And by having the agent for the verb "held" as the object of an adverb phrase, the sentence obscures the full committee's responsibility for meeting. With the use of active voice in sentence #4, agents appear in subject slots preceding verbs, so we get a stronger, more direct statement and a clearer idea of who is doing what. In sentence #4 we lose the stately (if hollow) tone of #3, but we gain forthrightness.

Generally when you face a choice between the active and passive voice, choose the active. To use the passive voice wisely, determine that your context requires the subject of a sentence to receive action. Consider, for example, that the first sentence in this chapter is in the passive voice and the agent (who it was that **explained**) is missing. We can expand this sentence to read,

Active and passive sentence structures are explained in **9c** by the authors.

In the **active,** it could read as below.

In **9c,** the authors explained active and passive sentence structures.

or

Section **9c** explains active and passive sentence structures.

The reason we two authors wrote that first sentence as we did is that we wanted you the reader to focus on the topic of sentence structures, not authors or sections. Note that in the second sentence, we returned to the active voice, and that except for example sentences, the first sentence is the only passive one in this chapter.

Exercise 1

1. Which of the following sentences would be more appro-

priate in an essay focusing on the author's personal feelings and experiences?

  a. While I was sunning on the beach, I sipped cool, refreshing drinks served from a shoreside bar.

  b. Bartenders served me cool, refreshing drinks from a
shoreside bar while I was sunning on the beach.

2. Which of the following sentences would be most effective
in an essay whose purpose is to give pointers on making
a tossed salad?

  a. First wash and drain the produce, and then cut each
ingredient into bite-sized bits.

  b. First the produce should be washed and drained, and
then each ingredient should be cut into bite-sized bits.

3. Which of the following sentences more forcefully emphasizes the action that is described?

  a. When the two boats collided, a shout for help was
heard across the lake.

  b. When the two boats collided, a shout for help rang
out across the lake.

4. Which of the following sentences would seem to be more
appropriate in an introduction to an essay about the practice of voodoo?

  a. Voodoo is still practiced by a number of Jamaicans.

  b. A number of Jamaicans still practice voodoo.

5. Which of the following sentences would be more appropriate in a report about women in athletics?

  a. Little League baseball is now successfully played by
many girls across the United States.

  b. Many girls across the United States now successfully
play Little League baseball.

Exercise 2

The following passage is mainly in the passive voice. Rewrite
it in the active voice, and compare differences in focus, emphasis, and effect.

As the room was entered, I was struck by a joyous sensation. Grandfather was seated in the middle of the room, and the grandchildren were seated around him, laughing and talking. All of Grandfather's birthday presents had already been opened by him, and the wrappings and bows had been scattered about the floor by the kids, creating a colorful and pleasing effect. Great happiness was felt by myself upon having arrived in time to witness this wonderful scene.

IV

Punctuating and Following Mechanical Conventions

19 · Punctuation Overview

Punctuation, though often regarded as a set of arbitrary rules whose mysteries are known only to English teachers, is in fact a system of signals that help writers communicate clearly and efficiently with readers. The system only works, however, when writers and readers agree about what each punctuation mark signifies and how it functions in the context of a particular sentence or paragraph. The chapters that follow examine each mark individually. For an overview of punctuation conventions, study the chart on pages 210–213. The following exercise will give you practice in applying the chart.

Exercise 1

19

For each mark of punctuation highlighted in the passage below, list its use as specified in the chart on pages 210–213. For example, the first mark highlighted is a period used to "terminate and separate."

A Day on Wheels
Cheryl A. Davis

A train ride can be an occasion for silent meditation in the midst of mechanical commotion. Unfortunately, I rarely get to meditate.

I attract attention. I pretend to ignore them, the eyes that scrutinize me and then quickly glance away. I try to avoid the gratuitous chats with loosely wrapped passengers. Usually, I fail. They may be loosely wrapped, but they're a persistent lot.

I use a wheelchair; I am not "confined" to one. Actually, I get around well. I drive a van equipped with a wheelchair lift to the train station. I use a powered wheelchair with high-amperage batteries to get to work. A manual chair, light enough to carry, enables me to visit the "walkies" who live upstairs and to ride in their Volkswagens.

My life has been rich and varied, but my fellow passengers assume that, as a disabled person, I must be horribly deprived and so lonely that I will appreciate any unsolicited overture.

"Do you work?" a woman on the train asked me recently. I said I did.

"It's nice that you have something to keep you busy, isn't it?"

Since we are thought of as poor invalids in need of chatting up, people are not apt to think too hard about what they are saying to us. It seems odd since they also worry about the "right" way to talk to disabled people.

An Overview of Punctuation

MARK	END PUNCTUATION	INTERNAL PUNCTUATION				
	Marks that terminate and separate	Marks that separate and combine	Marks that separate and introduce	Marks that separate and enclose	Marks that indicate omission	Marks that indicate grammatical function
Period	Fill what's empty. Empty what's full. Scratch where it itches. —Alice Roosevelt Longworth				We harpooners of Nantucket should be enrolled in the most noble order of St. George. —Herman Melville	
Exclamation Point	Take my wife, please! —Rodney Dangerfield					
Question Mark	What is this, an audience or an oil painting? —Milton Berle					
Comma		Wisemen make proverbs, but fools repeat them. —Samuel Palmer	When the cat and mouse agree, the grocer is ruined. —Persian proverb	As for me, except for an occasional heart attack, I feel as young as I ever did. —Peter Benchley		

Semicolon	Computers are useless; they can only give you answers. —Pablo Picasso			
Colon		There are two kinds of books: those that no one reads and those that one ought to read. —H. L. Mencken		
Dash		Most Americans have Thanksgiving dinner at the same time-- halftime. —Anonymous	Literature-- creative litera- ture--uncon- cerned with sex is inconceivable. —Gertrude Stein	
Parentheses			If it weren't for Philo T. Farnsworth (inventor of television), we'd still be eating radio dinners. —Johnny Carson	

INTERNAL PUNCTUATION

MARK	END PUNCTUATION Marks that terminate and separate	Marks that separate and combine	Marks that separate and introduce	Marks that separate and enclose	Marks that indicate omission	Marks that indicate grammatical function
Quotation Mark			"Dont' be humble. You're not that great." said Golda Meir to the proud politician.			
Brackets			That cause [slavery] was, I believe one of the worst for which a people ever fought. —Ulysses S. Grant			
Ellipsis Marks					I caught my reflection... polishing my trophies, and... it's easy to see why women are nuts about me. —Tom Ryan	

Apostrophe					I've just learned about his illness. Let's hope it's nothing trivial. —Anonymous	The best way to keep one's word is not to give it. —Napoleon Bonaparte
Slash	Writer/director Woody Allen said "if my film makes one more person miser-able, I'll feel I've done my job."					
Hyphen	The best audience is intelligent well-educated, and a little drunk —Alben Barkley					

Adapted from William Irmscher, *Teaching Expository Writing*. Holt, Rinehart & Winston, 1979, p. 122.

Several marks of punctuation have been omitted in the passage below, taken from a student essay. Enter the correct punctuation according to the chart on pages 210–213.

The monuments in Washington all seemed false in the cool morning mist. They were big and white and extravagant yet the tourists cheapened them somehow as they gawked took photos, and scurried to the next place on their list of things to see. Their attention seemed to focus on what things were rather than on why they were. The scene was a poor sample of Americana Even Honest Abe seemed to frown from his throne. Of all the walls of stone only one seemed real.

This walls long black marble slices into the ground. On it are engraved fifty eight thousand American names from an undeclared war that no one wants to remember in the jungles of a country half a globe away. There are no ornate scrolls or stenciled directions, no fancy faded pieces of parchment, no self-serving sentiments, just names.

Theres also a statue some distance away. Three bronze soldiers stare into the wall, waiting for word of their fellow soldiers or perhaps mourning their loss. The soldiers dont talk they simply stare. They were all just boys, most of them only six years older than I was then nineteen.

Under the statue soldier's gaze, an elderly man lagged behind a tour at the wall. He caressed it and knelt to leave a single rose at its base. He sobbed. He had difficulty standing up. A nearby park attendant helped him and asked, One of yours, sir   The man shook his head and replied, Not just one of them. All of them.

20 · The Period .

20a Use a period to end a declarative sentence (a sentence that makes a statement), an indirect question, or a mild imperative (a directive or command).

For some film makers, special effects are more important than a high-quality script. [declarative sentence]

The quiz-master asked whether any of the contestants knew who was buried in Grant's tomb. [indirect question]

Please cut the grass and trim the hedges. [mild directive]

20b Use periods with abbreviated words ending in a lowercase letter, with initials of personal names, and with most abbreviations in which lowercase letters represent whole words.

Abbreviated words ending in a lowercase letter

1. Personal or professional titles

   Mr. Chavez, Ms. Hahn, Dr. Stein

2. Months and days of the week

   Jan., Sat.

3. Other abbreviations ending in lowercase letters

   English Dept., Time Inc.

Initials of personal names

T. S. Eliot, K. C. Cole

Abbreviations in which lowercase letters represent whole words

a.m., p.m.
e.g. (*exempli gratia*—for example)
i.e. (*id est*—that is)
et al. (*et alii*—and others)

Exceptions are such abbreviations as mph (miles per hour) and rpm (revolutions per minute).

Abbreviations of uppercase letters

Postal abbreviations (CA, FL, etc.) require no periods. For other abbreviations consisting entirely of capital letters (US, AD, BCE), most style guides now recommend omitting periods, although some guides approve periods as optional.

Abbreviations at the end of a sentence

Do not put a second period at the end of a sentence that concludes with an abbreviation.

We are leaving at 5:00 a.m.

20c Do not use a period to separate a part of a sentence from the whole.

Notice how the first period in each of the examples below brings the sentence to a premature close.

Misused

After a long delay. The tennis match resumed.

Misused

A fund-raising dinner will be held in the new civic center. Which seats almost five thousand people.

In the first sentence a period sets off a prepositional phrase, and in the second a period sets off a relative clause.

Each of these sentence parts or *fragments* can be rejoined with the rest of the sentence simply by substituting a comma for the period.

Revised

After a long delay, the tennis match resumed.

Revised

A fund-raising dinner will be held in the new civic center, which seats almost five thousand people.

For a more detailed treatment of how to recognize and eliminate fragments, see Chapter **46.**

21 · The Exclamation Point !

21
a

21a Use an exclamation point to end an emphatic statement.

Forceful statements

"Get out! I don't ever want to see you again!"

Interjections expressing strong feeling

Oh no! I'm going to be late.

Emphatic responses to statements or questions

"Can you come back for an interview next week?" the personnel manager asked.
"Yes!" I enthusiastically replied.

Used judiciously, the exclamation point can be an effective stylistic device, as in this sentence by Dr. Martin Luther King, Jr.

Many men cry "Peace! Peace!" but they refuse to do the things that make for peace.

21b Use exclamation points sparingly.

When used habitually for emphasis, exclamation points can easily become artificial, as in the following example.

Overused

According to recent newspaper reports, a chemical company is planning to build a new factory in this area. I am concerned about how such a business might affect the community. It will produce toxic wastes! It will deplete water supplies! And it will drive smaller companies out of business!

Here, the exclamation points call more attention to the writer's emotionalism than to the arguments against the new chemical plant. Periods, on the other hand, are neutral in tone and would allow the reader to judge the evidence on its own merits.

22 · The Question Mark ?

22a Place a question mark after a direct question.

How many people will be at the party tonight?
Why do you ask so many questions?

22b Use a question mark at the end of a sentence if your purpose is to create a questioning tone.

The library is closing today? I thought it would stay open through the weekend.

22c Do not use a question mark after an indirect question.

Misused

I wonder who will win the Academy Award for best actress this year?

Revised

I wonder who will win the Academy Award for best actress this year.

Exercise 2

In the sentences below, insert or change periods, question marks, and exclamation points wherever necessary. Be able to justify each choice.

1. All complaints, objections, and recommendations should be referred to Dr Leona Williams.
2. The company's representative, Ms Pearson, will be in Mr. Watson's office at 9:00 a m to conduct a seminar on management problems (e g , absenteeism).
3. Tom asked his teachers if he could miss the last day of class before the Christmas holidays
4. I wonder whether Melissa will ever return my call?
5. To my surprise, I received an "A" on my history essay! I have never done that well before! I've decided to change my major to history!
6. Mr Stroud will meet us at the airport at 7:00 p m

22
c

7. How many times have you engaged in conversations with people so boring that you wanted to cry? Even worse, you have to be polite to them and can't tell them to shut up?

8. There were no rules for our game at all, just a free-for-all! Once my brother gave my cousin a bloody nose! Nothing hurts nine-year-olds, however; as he wiped the blood from his face, my cousin just laughed as if my brother only had been tickling him!

9. When the peppers and the onions turn light brown. They are finished cooking. Remove them from the frying pan.

10. You need some more money. I deposited an allowance in your checking account only last week.

<table>
<tr><td>23</td></tr>
<tr><td>a</td></tr>
</table>

23 · The Comma ,

23a Put a comma before a coordinating conjunction (*and, but, or, for, nor, so, yet*) that links two independent clauses in order to indicate the end of the first clause and prepare for the introduction of the second clause.

Many of the new recruits had looked forward to basic training, **but** some could not adapt to the rigorous physical fitness program.

Note: The comma is optional if the two clauses are short.

I looked for you but I couldn't find you.

23b Use commas to separate the elements of a series consisting of three or more words, phrases, or clauses.

Buses, cars, and trucks skidded on the icy road. [a series of nouns]

The dune-buggy **roared across an open expanse of sand, churned up a hill, and disappeared from view.** [a series of verb phrases]

Some films are successful at the box office but fail with the critics, others are acclaimed by the critics but rejected by the general public, and a rare few appeal to both audiences. [a series of independent clauses]

Note: Although current usage allows for the omission of the comma before a coordinating conjunction preceding the last item in a series, a comma in this position does help to prevent misreading—especially in a long, complex series like the one in the final example above.

23 c

23c Use a comma to separate coordinate adjectives (i.e., adjectives that independently modify the same noun).

Draped across the bed was a **tattered, faded** blanket.

There are two simple ways to test for this kind of coordination. If you can reverse the order of the adjectives or insert the word *and* between them without diminishing the clarity or coherence of the sentence, they are coordinate and should be separated by a comma.

Notice that in the example above, neither of these changes would adversely affect the sentence.

Draped across the bed was a **faded, tattered** blanket. [order of adjectives reversed]

Draped across the bed was a **tattered and faded** blanket. [**and** separating adjectives]

Exercise 3

Add commas where necessary in the sentences below. Put a check after any sentences that are correctly punctuated.

1. My brother often returned from school with his clothes torn and his face bruised but he never would talk about what had happened to him.
2. Whenever the crime rate increases, the people who usually get the blame are lawyers judges and the police.
3. I work with a group of happy cooperative people.
4. The pressure of Christmas shopping often makes people irritable and causes them to purchase gifts they cannot afford.
5. The accident occurred on a dark lonely road.
6. So-called intelligence tests are not always an accurate measurement of a child's intelligence and they reveal nothing at all about a person's creative abilities.
7. Many times I tried and failed to stand up on the water skis but by summer's end I could ski across the lake without falling.
8. Shooting a bow and arrow seems quite simple but is more difficult than most people realize.
9. We had to wash our own clothes cook for ourselves and clean up after ourselves for the first time in our lives so my roommates and I had difficulty adjusting to apartment life.
10. I telephoned my father to tell him about the wreck and listened to him nag for at least ten minutes.

11. We hated beer commercials so we always changed the channel when they appeared on television.
12. My sister enjoys classical music, but she also likes jazz and rock.
13. Wimbledon the US Open and the French Open are three of the four Grand Slam tournaments in professional tennis.
14. There is a rich famous fashion designer eating at Chez Ambert's down the street.
15. Dr. Griffen's exam was filled with multiple-choice questions Dr. Field's had several essay questions and Dr. Rose's included both types of questions.

23d Use a comma to set off introductory clauses, long modifying phrases, and certain introductory words.

Introductory modifiers

Walking along the beach, I saw hundreds of sunburned tourists.

After a long hike to the lake, we were ready for a swim.

When the climbers reached their destination, they raised a signal flag.

Plans for the new building having been completed, construction began.

Introductory yes or no

Yes, acid rain is a threat to the environment. **No,** the governments of the US and Canada have not yet reached agreement on how to solve this problem.

A name mentioned in direct address

George, please let me know when you will be home.

Note: The comma is optional after brief introductory modifiers.

Soon[,] the economy may improve.

Without thinking[,] I stepped off the curb.

23e Use commas to enclose parenthetical, nonrestrictive, or contrasting elements (i.e., words, phrases, or clauses that could be deleted without changing the essential meaning of the sentence; see Chapter 13).

Parenthetical words and expressions

This course, **I think,** is going to be more difficult than I anticipated.

In the past, I have always mailed my income tax forms just before they were due. This year, **however,** I am going to finish them early.

Nonrestrictive modifiers

The top of the World Trade Center, **which is over a hundred stories high,** provides a panoramic view of New York City.

The new sports complex, **unlike the old one,** has ample parking.

Nonrestrictive appositives

Ms. Brown, **a local business leader,** was recently elected to the university's Board of Trustees.

Possible ill effects of artificial sweeteners are being studied at Johns Hopkins Hospital, **a well-known research center,** as well as at several other medical centers throughout the nation.

Contrasting elements

Proponents of increased military spending argue that peace, **not war,** is their objective.

Corporal punishment often inspires resentment, **not repentance.**

Exercise 4

Add commas where necessary in the sentences below. Put a check after any sentences that are correctly punctuated.

1. Unless the government acts soon to reduce the budget deficit interest rates will continue to rise.
2. My afternoon classes are all in Taylor Hall which is the hottest building on campus.
3. Some of my friends suffer from the sweat-suit syndrome a malady that can be cured only by purchasing a whole wardrobe of sweat-suits and color-coordinated accessories.
4. As soon as I saw the shaving cream on my pillow and the knots in my sheet I knew that I had been the victim of a practical joke.
5. Some members of Congress have charged that the policies of the Environmental Protection Agency benefit land developers not the people who use public land for recreation.
6. Last year, the School Board presented an award to my parents who led several successful fund-raising drives.
7. Voters should select candidates who have personal integrity.
8. In dead lifting, the fear of injury or heavy weights unless controlled will bring all progress to an abrupt halt.
9. The first technique to learn in hackey sack and probably the most often used technique is kicking the sack gently with the inside of the foot.
10. Christa McAuliffe a New Hampshire school teacher died in the space shuttle Challenger explosion in 1986.
11. No I do not wish to go bungee-jumping this weekend Josh.
12. Although Leona owns numerous audio tapes she prefers compact disks and buys them whenever she can.

13. Caught in the act of dumping raw sewage into the harbor the factory's management was hit with severe fines and became the target of massive protests by environmental groups.
14. After reading <u>Dracula</u>, my roommate slept with his light on for the rest of the week.
15. The new Baltimore baseball facility Oriole Park at Camden Yards has inspired much admiration among baseball fans around the country.

23f Use commas to separate names from titles, cities from states or countries, the day of the week from the day of the month, the day of the month from the year, and the salutation of an informal letter from the text.

23 f

The letter was addressed to Janet Murdock, **Ph.D.**

Boulder, Colorado, is my home.

On **Wednesday, June 1, 1992,** I began a raft trip down the Snake River.

Dear Aunt Minnie,

Note: When a city and state or date is mentioned within a sentence, a comma comes after the state and after the year. Note also that putting the date before the month eliminates the need for a comma: **1 June 1992.**

Exercise 5

Add commas where necessary in the sentences below. Put a check after any sentences that are correctly punctuated.

1. The letter was addressed to Leon Gray MD.
2. Tomorrow we are leaving for San Antonio Texas.
3. One of the most controversial US missions of World War II was the fire bombing of Dresden Germany.
4. July 4 1976 marked the two-hundredth anniversary of the USA.
5. The daughter of Prince Andrew and the Duchess of York was born on August 8 1988 at 8:18 in the evening.
6. Yorktown Virginia was the site of the last battle of the American Revolutionary War.
7. July 4 1826 saw the deaths of both Thomas Jefferson and John Adams.
8. Direct all inquiries to Joellen Sink attorney-at-law.
9. Barcelona Spain was the host city for the 1992 Summer Olympics.
10. Applications received after 13 March 1991 will not be considered.
11. The veterinarian's office is the one at the end of the hall that says "Mark Roberson DVM."
12. The Farnsworths live at 69 McPherson Drive in Pendleton City Pennsylvania.
13. On August 7 1990 Michelle's parents celebrated their twenty-first wedding anniversary.
14. The national office of the Federal Bureau of Investigation is in Washington DC.
15. We feared that our new professor might be a bit arrogant since his door read "Dr. Sigmund Karlheinz von Brandenburg, BA, MS, MB, PhD."

23g Avoid unnecessary commas.

When used for the purposes discussed in the preceding sections, commas help to clarify relationships between sentence elements and guide the reader to an understanding of what the writer seeks to communicate. But if they are inserted where readers who are familiar with the written code expect no punctuation at all or anticipate a different type of punctuation, commas are distracting and confusing.

If you tend to use commas without knowing why or if you insert them wherever you sense a pause, you may need to review the chapters in Part II in conjunction with the conventions discussed in this chapter. The following suggestions about when not to use commas may also prove useful.

1. *Do not put a comma between a subject and its verb or between a verb and its object or complement.*

Unnecessary commas

The luxury liner Titanic, struck an iceberg and sank on its maiden voyage.

I have just read, The Grapes of Wrath.

One of the dreams of every serious actor is, to play King Lear.

In all three of these sentences, the comma should be deleted because it unnecessarily interrupts the progress of the sentence and separates its closely related elements.

2. *Do not put a comma before a coordinating conjunction that links compound subjects, verbs, objects, or complements.*

Unnecessary commas

A degree in mechanical engineering, and an unlimited amount of time are the only qualifications anyone needs to assemble the pieces of a typical do-it-yourself kit. [**and** linking compound subjects]

As we walked along the ridge, a hawk soared high above our heads, and alighted on a distant peak. [**and** linking compound verbs]

When I lived near the airport, I was continually disturbed by sonic booms, and shattering glass [**and** linking compound objects of a preposition]

One summer I was a shoe clerk, and a cook. [**and** linking compound complements]

3. *In general, do not use a comma following a coordinating conjunction.*

Unnecessary comma

This morning, I plan to run five miles, do a few exercises, and, play tennis.

Note: A comma may come after a coordinating conjunction if the comma sets off a parenthetical or nonrestrictive element.

I plan to run five miles and, if I'm not too tired, play tennis.

4. *Do not put commas around restrictive elements: modifiers or appositives that could not be deleted without changing the essential meaning of the sentence (see Chapter **13**).*

Unnecessary comma

Some colleges will not accept students, who rank in the bottom third of their graduating class.

The comma should be omitted because the relative clause limits the category of unacceptable students to those in the bottom third of the class. If this clause were deleted, the sentence would say that some colleges will not accept students.

5. *Do not put a comma before the first element of a series.*

Unnecessary comma

The new car was equipped with, power steering, cruise control, and a stereo system.

6. *Do not put a comma between noncoordinate adjectives (adjectives that you could not logically link with **and**) or between an adjective and the noun it modifies.*

Unnecessary comma

At the entrance to the carnival stood a man holding an enormous, helium-filled balloon.

When the game show host grinned, she revealed a mouthful of white, teeth.

   7. *Whenever you put a comma between two independent clauses, be sure that a coordinating conjunction follows it. The use of a comma alone or a comma plus a conjunctive adverb (***however, therefore, consequently,*** etc.) in this position will result in a comma splice (see Chapter ***45***).*

Comma splice

I dislike mowing lawns, I detest pulling weeds.

Revised

I dislike mowing lawns, **but** I detest pulling weeds.

   8. *When citing only the month and year of a date, do not separate them with a comma.*

Unnecessary comma

The summer theater series begins in June, 1993.

Exercise 6

In the following sentences, delete any unnecessary commas. Put a check after any sentences that are correctly punctuated.

1. At present almost anyone, can buy a handgun, a rifle, or even a machine gun.
2. Some of the most outspoken, critics of television believe that it dulls the intellect, and encourages violence.
3. We watched the national news and, then turned off the TV set.
4. The player, who scored the winning goal, was mobbed by her teammates.

5. A battered, foul-smelling lantern hung from the tree limb.

6. Excellence in education can be achieved only through the coordinated efforts of, teachers, students, parents, and administrators.

7. Ever since my first week at college, the closest I have come to eating a home-cooked meal, is nibbling on Reese's Peanut Butter Cups for breakfast, and grazing on Better Cheddars for dinner.

8. Anyone who could have met my friend, would have known what an altruistic, and compassionate person he was.

9. Fifteen of the seventeen students, who took the state nursing examination, had acceptable scores.

10. In August, 1988, civil rights activists celebrated the twenty-fifth anniversary of Dr. Martin Luther King's "I Have a Dream" speech.

11. A trio of explorers set out, in search of a lost tomb in Egypt.

12. Denzel is interested in, photography, coin collecting, and jogging.

13. My sister was a math and science student, but, she often had trouble in French class.

14. Experts say that any parent, who leaves a sharp object where a child can reach it, is irresponsible.

15. Basketball star Magic Johnson held a press conference where, he informed the public that he had tested positive for the HIV virus.

23
g

Exercise 7

In the sentences below delete unnecessary commas and add needed commas. Be able to explain the reason for each addition and deletion. Put a check after any sentences that are correctly punctuated.

1. The brightly, arrayed chieftain who stood in front of a small stone altar had a stern cold face that belied his cheerful apparel.

2. Joining the Army, seemed to be a good idea to the dissatisfied, restless young man until he met his first drill instructor.

3. Scratching, clawing, and biting, the children had to be separated, and taken from the playground.

4. After seeing the grim, reality of war firsthand, the journalist was forced to wonder what on earth could be worth the misery, and despair, that always accompany conflict.

5. Yes the president of the company, Ms. Danmeyer authorized my transfer but she was not aware of the hidden costs in such a project.

6. The challenger had two advantages: youth, and courage.

7. The answer to our problem is, better organization, more attention to detail, and better communication.

8. Leaping the swollen raging creek, at a single bound the frantically, baying hound raced off into the forest.

9. The possibility of detection, did not seem to alter the thief's demeanor, or behavior in the least.

10. One of the most interesting people I have ever met is my former philosophy professor who left the university on May 15 1977 to search for truth.

11. The lawn, was badly overgrown with dandelions crab grass and chickweed.

12. Les Miserables Phantom of the Opera and Miss Saigon, are three of the most popular musicals to appear on Broadway in recent years.

13. During the late 1980s peaceful demonstrations for democratic reform were brutally suppressed by government forces in Beijing China.

14. The cellist, and the violist, tuned their instruments, and prepared to go onstage for their concert.

15. Civil rights leaders everywhere were relieved when David Duke, a former leader of the Ku Klux Klan and distributor of racist books, failed in his attempt to become governor of Louisiana.

24 · The Semicolon ;

24a Put a semicolon between two independent clauses if your purpose is to combine them in a single sentence without using a coordinating conjunction (*and, but, for, or, nor, so, yet*).

**24
a**

If the two clauses are parallel in form and closely related in meaning, a semicolon alone is sufficient to link them:

Rumor breeds mistrust; mistrust breeds fear.

If the relationship between the two clauses you wish to join is not obvious, add a conjunctive adverb (**however, therefore, otherwise,** etc.) immediately after the semicolon or within the second clause (see **8d**).

I recently bought a new camera; **however,** I am not satisfied with the pictures I have taken with it.

I recently bought a new camera; I am not satisfied, **however,** with the pictures I have taken with it.

or

I recently bought a new camera; I am not satisfied with the pictures I have taken with it, **however.**

Note: If you choose a coordinating conjunction rather than a conjunctive adverb as a connective, place a comma rather than a semicolon in front of the linking word (see **23a**).

I recently bought a new camera, **but** I am not satisfied with the pictures I have taken with it.

24b Use semicolons to separate series items that themselves contain commas.

Looking through a television monitor, the department store detective observed **a young man wearing an enormous, overstuffed backpack; a middle-aged woman carrying a large, bulging purse;** and **an elderly gentleman dressed in a long, loose-fitting topcoat.**

If you are uncertain about the appropriateness of a semicolon in a given context, notice its position in the sentence. Except in those rare instances when semicolons are needed for clarity (as in the last example above), this punctuation mark should always come at the juncture of two independent clauses.

24c Do not substitute a semicolon for a colon or comma.

Semicolon misused as colon

The course syllabus listed three basic requirements**; essays, tests, and oral reports.**

Semicolon misused as comma

Because ice had begun to form on the wings; the pilot decided not to take off.

Because semicolons usually promise the end of one independent clause and the beginning of another, their use as colons or commas is confusing. In the first example above, the reader expects another clause after the semicolon and might initially read **essays, tests, and oral reports** as the subject of this anticipated clause. In the second example, the semicolon simply makes no sense because it does not come at the end of an independent clause. **Because ice had begun to form on the wings** is a subordinate clause modifying **decided.**

Even when you can find a grammatical justification for a semicolon, check to be sure that it is your best stylistic option. Used sparingly and purposefully, the semicolon can be an effective means of creating parallelism and balance and of clarifying sentence relationships that might otherwise be confusing to the reader. But if it is employed repeatedly to link two clauses that are only slightly related, it loses much of its freshness and force.

Exercise 8

**24
c**

In each of the following sentences add, delete, or change semicolons where necessary. If there are no semicolon errors in the sentence, put a check after it.

1. Critics of the two-party political system often complain; that it arbitrarily limits the number of candidates for any public office.

2. If you are looking for something different; scuba diving is for you.

3. Our society needs vast quantities of energy; however, our petroleum resources are dwindling.

4. Rugby has qualities much admired by American sports fans; speed, violence, and strategy.

5. Making speeches does not have to be frightening; sometimes it can even be pleasurable.

6. Conference organizers invited a petroleum engineer from Houston, Texas, an environmental activist from Tacoma, Washington, a farmer from Des Moines, Iowa, and a minister from Elmira, New York, to speak at the forum.

7. The law school dean has appointed a task force to explore possible causes of low bar examination scores; especially inadequate student preparation and nonacademic influences.

8. Newspaper editors generally try to place at least one photograph on each page to generate visual contrast to the columns of news; readers tend to dislike grey pages.

9. Road construction forced us to change our travel route, otherwise, we would have chosen the scenic country roads over the bland interstate highway.

10. As I paddled silently through the salt marsh, I observed
    nature undisturbed; egrets, herons, and gulls sunning on
    mud flats, wild ponies grazing along the island banks,
    and fish jumping up in the air and splashing back into
    the sky-blue water.

25 · The Colon :

25
a

**25a Use a colon immediately after an independent
clause to introduce a list of appositives, a single
appositive, a quotation, or a second independent
clause that illustrates or explains something in the
first clause.**

The student newspaper received the following new equipment: **a
word processor, a short wave radio, and a teletype.** [list of appositives specifying the **new equipment**]

On my last fishing trip, I forgot one very important item: **my fishing
reel.** [single appositive identifying the **very important item**]

From the editors of *Discover* magazine comes a startling announcement: **"Nessie, the Loch Ness Monster, may be nothing more than a decomposing log."** [quotation]

The members of the Budget Committee soon learned the bad news: **tax revenues were lower than expected.** [independent clause explaining what the **bad news** was]

25b Use a colon to introduce the text of a formal letter, divide hours from minutes, separate chapter from verse in biblical references, and distinguish the title of a book from its subtitle.

Dear Dr. Johnson:
9:00 a.m.
Genesis 3:1
Billy Budd: An Inside Narrative

25c Do not assume that a colon is needed in midsentence to signal a series or an example.

Unnecessary colon

For breakfast we had: bacon, eggs, toast, and coffee.

The problem here is that the colon separates the complement (**bacon, eggs, toast, and coffee**) from the verb (**had**), thus forcing the reader to pause unnecessarily before the sentence's line of thought is complete.

25d Do not confuse the colon with the semicolon or period.

Colon confused with semicolon

Barry rushed from the house in anger: several hours later, he returned and apologized.

In this sentence, the colon is misleading because it tells the reader to expect a further explanation or illustration of Barry's anger, but what actually follows is a second independent clause describing Barry's subsequent actions.

25e Test for appropriate use of colons.

One of the best ways to spot such problems is to look closely at the words to the left of the colon and see if they could be punctuated as a coherent sentence. If not, the colon is unnecessary. Applying this test to the first example above, we find that the words **for breakfast we had** make no sense when detached from the complement. Thus, the colon should be deleted:

For breakfast we had bacon, eggs, toast, and coffee.

If the words to the left of the colon meet the first test, as in the example in **25d (Barry rushed from the house in anger** is a complete sentence), notice whether the words following the punctuation mark could also stand alone as a sentence. If there is a second independent clause and it introduces a new idea, change the colon to a period or a semicolon, depending on whether you want to separate or join the two clauses:

Barry rushed from the house in anger. Several hours later, he returned and apologized.

25
e

or

Barry rushed from the house in anger; several hours later, he returned and apologized.

If, on the other hand, you find the second independent clause defines or illustrates the first, the colon is an appropriate mark of introduction.

Barry rushed from the house in anger: he kicked the wall and slammed the door.

Exercise 9

In the following sentences, add, delete, or change colons where necessary. If there are no errors in colon usage, put a check after the sentence.

1. Severe depression can result from feelings of: loneliness, grief, fear, or inadequacy.

2. I have never really enjoyed chemistry: although I do have fun in the laboratory portion of the course.

3. I have developed three areas of my body: my arms, my chest, and my legs.

4. The new Broadway hit was: provocative, enlightening, and entertaining.

5. A swimming instructor can use two techniques to relax a beginner learning to float face up; ask the swimmer to

pretend to lie in bed, and keep one hand beneath the swimmer's back.

6. The crowd stood speechless as it watched the white smoke curl against the clear, blue sky, the space shuttle had disintegrated.

7. A symphony of sneezes, coughs, and sniffs sound throughout the classroom: cold season has hit the campus.

8. Cold sufferers should battle the sniffles with a popular folk remedy, drink hot tea with lemon and honey, eat chicken noodle soup, and get plenty of rest.

9. One of the most famous newspaper photographs ever published is a shot of president-elect Harry S. Truman holding a copy of the November 3, 1948, Chicago Daily Tribune that bears a banner headline; "Dewey Defeats Truman."

10. From the observation tower we could see: the village at the base of the mountain, the skiers gliding down the slopes, and the vast national forest.

26 · The Dash --

26a Use a dash (typed as two hyphens with no space before, between, or after them) as an informal but emphatic mark of introduction.

In a recent biography of Marilyn Monroe, Norman Mailer describes the actress as an angel--a "sweet angel of sex."

I must leave now--without further delay.

26b Use a dash to introduce an independent clause that summarizes the words preceding it.

**26
c**

Shopping malls, condominiums, and convenience stores--these are some of the most prominent features of the modern American town.

26c Use a dash or a pair of dashes to signal an abrupt interruption in thought or an unexpected change of tone.

I am convinced that most--or should I say all--of the claims made by advertisers are exaggerated.

Before every family vacation, my father announced that we could take as many clothes as we wanted--provided that they would all fit in one small suitcase.

26d Use dashes to set off parenthetical elements that warrant special emphasis.

Some members of the Board of Trade--including all the newly elected delegates--are opposed to import quotas.

26e For clarity, use dashes to set off nonrestrictive elements that contain commas.

My aunt--a woman of great charm, intelligence, and patience--has always been one of my favorite relatives.

26f Use the dash for certain stylistic purposes.

When considering a dash, keep in mind that in any given context, it is usually only one of several stylistic options. Both the dash and the colon, for example, are marks of introduction, but each has a different tone and effect. The colon conveys a sense of formality and control, explicitly forecasting what is to follow; the dash, on the other hand, is a freer, less formal mark that usually establishes a more subtle relationship between the introductory statement and the words following it.

Anyone interested in buying a home computer should first learn the meaning of three terms: bits, bytes, and chips.

As the young mathematician contemplated the problem, she closed her eyes and reclined in her chair--gestures that a casual observer might mistake for signs of boredom.

Distinguish also between dashes and other punctuation marks that have the same function of enclosing information. In particular, remember that commas are the standard means of setting off nonrestrictive sentence elements and that habitual use of the dash for this purpose diminishes its value as a mark of special emphasis.

26g Despite its versatility, the dash is not quite the all-purpose punctuation mark it seems to be. It is not, for example, the equivalent of a period or semicolon; thus, it should not be used to separate or link independent clauses.

Dash confused with period or semicolon

The District Attorney argued that the defendant should be held responsible for his actions--the Defense Counsel claimed that her client was temporarily insane.

In this sentence, the dash leads us to expect more information about the District Attorney's views or the defendant's actions, but instead the writer shifts to the Defense Counsel's argument. Thus, the dash should be replaced with a period if the writer intends to separate the two clauses or with a semicolon if the author's purpose is to coordinate them.

27 · Parentheses ( )

27a Put parentheses around figures or words that you want to include as supplemental information.

Death of a Salesman (1949) has been acclaimed as a tragedy of the common man.

In the opening section of the essay "Politics and the English Language" (pp. 1–2), George Orwell argues that political corruption and language abuse are inseparably related.

World War I (the war that was supposed to end all wars) ushered in a century of violence.

Many years ago (I forget just how many) my parents sold their spacious home in the suburbs and moved into a cramped apartment in the middle of the city.

27b Enclose in parentheses numbers or letters that enumerate the items in a series.

To be successful at computer games, a player must have the following skills: (1) good eye-hand coordination, (2) quick reflexes, and (3) the ability to concentrate.

27c If you want to set off a parenthentical expression as a sentence in its own right, put the first parenthesis before the capital letter and the second one right after the period.

More and more species of animal life are becoming extinct. (Soon, human beings may be added to the list.)

27d Whenever you use parentheses to enclose a part of a sentence, place any additional punctuation marks outside the parentheses.

One of the most famous outlaws of the Old West was Bill Harrington (alias Billy the Kid), who started out as the leader of a New York street gang.

27e Do not overuse parentheses.

Parentheses are distracting if overworked or used to set off constructions that do not warrant special emphasis. Both problems are evident in the following passage.

Overuse of parentheses

It was 2:00 (on Wednesday afternoon) when I entered my first college biology class. The teacher (Dr. Harper) was already getting out microscopes as I took my seat. Within a few minutes, everyone (that is, almost everyone) was intently examining slides. I saw nothing but dust particles.

In the first sentence above, the parentheses are unnecessary because there is no apparent reason for calling attention to the day of the week, nor is there any indication why the writer encloses the teacher's name in parentheses rather than using commas—the usual means of setting off nonrestrictive appositives. The last set of parentheses, on the other hand, is functional because the words between them forcefully interrupt the sentence and introduce a personal reflection that helps the reader anticipate the outcome of the incident. Even if all three sets of parentheses were stylistically defensible, the number is excessive, especially in a paragraph this short.

Exercise 10

Add dashes or parentheses as needed in the following sentences. Be prepared to explain your reason for choosing each mark.

1. "There is a growing guilt about the masses of discarded junk rusting automobiles and refrigerators and washing machines and dehumidifiers that it is uneconomical to recycle."

   Anthony Burgess

2. "Whenever I pitched decently a rarity I had to tell her so, and then she would smile and say, 'That's nice, dear.'"

Pat Jordan

3. The final objection to Senator Frampton's appointment and by far the most damaging one is her known ties to underworld figures.

4. Famished by the long ride back to school, I rushed up the stairs, threw open my door, and frantically jerked open the refrigerator door. The bottomless pit my roommate had struck again, devouring all my food.

5. Long hours, little pay, and less respect these are the rewards an educator can expect in the long run.

6. When a weightlifter uses proper form and good judgment two conditions not always present at the same time, the chance for injury is minimal.

7. My first dirt bike was the best piece of machinery on the block black metal finish, dirt tires, coaster brakes, the works.

8. The 1992 US Olympic basketball team the "Dream Team" was the first to include professional players.

27
e

9. The Hal Ashby film <u>Being There</u> 1980 raises questions about the broadcast media's role in creating inaccurate images of national leaders.

10. In <u>Being There</u>, a character named Chance played by Peter Sellers in his final role is completely misunderstood by a cast of powerful and intelligent people.

28 · Quotation Marks " "

28a Put quotation marks around all words that you quote verbatim from an oral or written source so that the reader can distinguish your words from those of the writer or speaker you are citing.

Quotation from an oral source

I was one of the millions of people who watched the inauguration of John F. Kennedy and heard him say, "Ask not what your country can do for you but what you can do for your country."

Quotation from a written source

In the words of noted journalist Caryll Tucker, "Perhaps the most poignant victim of the twentieth century is your sense of continuity."

Quotation within a quotation

If you quote a passage that already contains quotation marks, replace them with single quotation marks and enclose the entire passage in standard double quotation marks.

Jacques Cousteau has observed that, **"**One of the most 'human' qualities of the whale is its intense devotion to other whales.**"**

Indented quotation

When citing a passage longer than four typed lines, set it off
as a block quotation by indenting ten spaces from the left
margin and double spacing. A block quotation requires no
quotation marks unless they appear in the source.

> To a professional violinist such as Victor Aitay, concertmaster
>
> of the Chicago Symphony Orchestra, nothing compares to the
>
> tone that floats from the belly of a Stradivari violin. "Its sound
>
> is rich and smooth, with no harshness or shrillness. Music
>
> erupts from it with just a touch of the bow on its strings, and
>
> its soothing sound carries to every inch of the concert hall,"
>
> says Aitay.

Joseph Alper

28
b

**28b Use quotation marks to distinguish spoken
words from words that are not part of the quoted
dialogue and to set off the words of one speaker
from those of another.**

At night the printed page stood before my eyes in sleep. Mrs. Moss,
my landlady, asked me one Sunday morning:
"Son, what is this you keep on reading?"
"Oh, nothing. Just novels."
"What you get out of 'em?"
"I'm just killing time," I said.
"I hope you know your own mind," she said in a tone which implied
that she doubted if I had a mind.   Richard Wright

28c Use quotation marks to indicate that a word is being used in a special sense.

Some **"convenience"** stores inconveniently run out of the items I always seem to need.

28d Put quotation marks around the titles of essays, short stories, brief poems, short plays, articles in newspapers and periodicals, parts of books, songs and other short musical compositions, and episodes of television and radio shows.

My course in literature and popular culture will begin with a study of George Orwell's essay **"Politics and the English Language,"** W. H. Auden's satric poem **"The Unknown Citizen,"** a one-act play called **"Act Without Words,"** and the **"Economy"** chapter of Thoreau's *Walden*. Later in the year, we will discuss popular music classics such as The Beatles' **"Let It Be"** and analyze some of the **"Point Counterpoint"** debates from the early episodes of *60 Minutes*.

28e Observe the following conventions when punctuating sentences that contain quotation marks.

1. *Always put periods inside quotation marks. Put commas inside quotation marks, too, except when a comma is used to separate the quotation from introductory words.*

"The President's plane is going to be late," the press secretary announced to a crowd of disgruntled reporters.

When I asked my new art instructor if I had to buy a drawing board, she replied, **"Only if you want to pass this course."**

2. *Put semicolons and colons outside quotation marks unless they are part of the quoted text.*

At 11:45 the manager announced, **"As soon as you finish your present assignment, take your lunch break";** by 11:46 the office was empty.

Nathaniel Hawthorne explores several major themes in his story **"Young Goodman Brown":** the nature of good and evil, the relationship between dreams and reality, and the conflict between faith and skepticism.

3. *Place a question mark or an exclamation point inside the final quotation mark if the question or exclamation is conveyed by the quoted words alone. If the quoted material is part of a question or exclamation, the appropriate mark should go outside the final quotation mark.*

In answer to a question about how soon the potholes in the city's streets would be repaired, the mayor responded, **"How long will it take to approve new taxes for road improvements?"**

Why, the reader might ask, does Hamlet picture death as an **"undiscovered country"?**

Irritated by the passengers' constant interruptions, the tour guide shouted, **"Stop talking, or get off the bus!"**

Why is there a movement to adopt a new national anthem? **No ordinary human being can sing "The Star-Spangled Banner"!**

28
f

28f When quoting from secondary sources, proofread carefully to ensure that you have not inadvertently omitted one or both quotation marks.

The omission of a single mark is confusing because it forces the reader to guess where the quotation begins or ends. The omission of both pairs of quotation marks results in an even more serious problem called *plagiarism*—the appropriation of someone else's words or ideas as one's own. (See Chapters **56–57** for a full discussion of how to use and document sources.)

28g Avoid unnecessary quotation marks. In particular, do not use quotation marks with conventional, overworked expressions, with nicknames, or with the titles of your own compositions.

Unnecessary quotation marks

When I was younger, my sister and I fought "tooth and nail."

My brother "Bubba" makes friends easily.

"A Critical Analysis of Three Poems by Emily Dickinson" [from the title page of a student essay]

**28
g**

Exercise 11

In the sentences below, delete unnecessary quotation marks and add needed quotation marks. Put a check after any sentences that are correctly punctuated.

1. "After dinner, my grandmother said, we will take a long walk."
2. Eleanor Rigby, a wistful yet powerful song by "The Beatles," appears in one anthology as an example of modern "poetry."
3. If you don't study for the final exam, you'll be "up the creek without a paddle."
4. The epitaph of John Keats, author of such famous examples of "Romantic" poetry as Ode on a Grecian Urn and La Belle Dame Sans Merci, reads Here lies the body of one whose name was writ in water.

5. One critic has observed that "Edgar Allan Poe's short story The Fall of the House of Usher takes the reader on a journey into the dark recesses of the human mind."

6. Orson Welles's 1938 radio play War of the Worlds sent listeners into as panic when they believed that "Martians" actually had landed at Grovers Mill, New Jersey.

7. A true friend does not think that you are "weird" if your interests vary from those of your peers.

8. I got a lot of "rest" in the hospital—when I wasn't answering telephone calls from well-wishers, receiving visits from the hospital staff, or listening to the television blaring in the room next door.

9. When asked during the 1988 presidential campaign if his administration would raise taxes, George Bush responded, Read my lips; he then mouthed the words, No new taxes.

10. Life on Bath Creek was very "peaceful" with military aircraft roaring almost daily at a low altitude over the length of the creek.

**29
a**

29 · Brackets [ ]

29a Use brackets to enclose information that you have inserted within a quoted source.

The "central characters **[in Ernest Hemingway's A Farewell to Arms]** are caught in a biological trap from which there is no escape."

Whenever possible, integrate quotations with your own sentences in such a way that brackets are unnecessary.

In Ernest Hemingway's <u>A Farewell to Arms</u>, "the central characters are caught in a biological trap from which there is no escape."

29b Substitute brackets for parentheses when parenthetical material occurs within a parenthetical reference.

In <u>A Critical Guide to Leaves of Grass</u>, James E. Miller describes Whitman's "Song of Myself" as "the dramatic representation of a mystical experience" (for a conflicting view, see Carl Strauch's "The Structure of Walt Whitman's 'Song of Myself,'" <u>English Journal</u> 27 [**1938**]: 597–607).

30 · The Elipsis Mark . . .

30a Use an ellipsis mark (three spaced periods) to indicate the omission of part of a quoted passage.

Notice, for example, the way in which the author of the second passage below uses the ellipsis mark to condense the original while preserving its essential meaning.

Passage #1

The health-care system of this country is a staggering enterprise, in any sense of the adjective. Whatever the failures of distribution and lack of coordination, it is the giant scale and scope of the total collective effort that first catches the breath, and its cost. The dollar figures are almost beyond grasping. They vary from year to year, always upward, ranging from something like $10 billion in 1950 to an estimated $140 billion in 1978, with much more to come in the years just ahead, whenever a national health-insurance program is installed. The official guess is that we are now investing around 8 percent of the GNP in health; it could soon rise to 10 or 12 percent.

Lewis Thomas

Passage #2

According to the noted medical researcher and essayist Lewis Thomas, the U.S. "health-care system . . . is a staggering enterprise. . . . Whatever the failures of distribution and lack of coordination, it is the giant scale and scope of the total collective effort that first catches the breath, and its cost. . . . The official guess is that we are now investing around 8 percent of the GNP in health; it could soon rise to 10 or 12 percent."

Three ellipsis dots are sufficient to mark the first deletion above because it occurs within a sentence. But because the second omission comes at the end of a sentence and the third includes an entire sentence, the writer has correctly used a fourth period for terminal punctuation.

Because an ellipsis mark does not tell the reader what or how much has been omitted from a quotation, be careful not to delete words that are essential to meaning or to artificially link widely separated passages.

Notice how the omission of three key words in the second sentence below distorts the first writer's intent.

**30
a**

Source

"Ambition tempered by wisdom is the key to political greatness."

Misleading omission

"Ambition . . . is the key to political greatness."

The first sentence says that those who aspire to political greatness must be wise as well as ambitious. The second states that ambition is the only requirement.

Exercise 12

Read each of the sentences or passages below and follow the

directions accompanying it:

1. "In certain important ways, <u>Moby Dick</u> carried on methods and themes with which <u>Melville</u> was experimenting in his earlier stories."
   Charles Fiedelson

   a. Add in brackets the information that <u>Moby Dick</u> was published in 1851.
   b. Revise sentence #1 again so that you add the date of publication without brackets.

2. "One of William Haast's first jobs, as an airline flight engineer in the 1940s, gave him a chance to pursue both his fascination with snakes at 12, he had kept them as pets and his theories on the value of venom research."
   Ben Funk

   a. Add the punctuation marks needed to indicate that the name **William** has been added by the writer citing the passage.
   b. Punctuate the parenthetical statement **at 12, he had kept them as pets** to indicate that it is part of the original quotation.

3. "Modern English, especially written English, is full of bad habits which spread by imitation and which can be avoided if one is willing to take the necessary trouble."
   George Orwell

   Use the ellipsis mark to condense the passage and at the same time eliminate words that call attention to a type of Modern English.

4. "Salvador Dali (whom, in general, I do not greatly admire) once made the remark that Picasso's greatness consisted in the fact that he had destroyed one by one all the historical styles of painting."

Joseph Wood Krutch

Use the ellipsis mark to condense the passage and also create a more objective tone.

5. "A quarter of century after the introduction of television into American society, a period that has seen the medium become so deeply ingrained in American life that in at least one state the television set has attained the rank of a legal necessity, safe from repossession in case of debt along with clothes, cooking utensils, and the like, television viewing has become an inevitable and ordinary part of daily life."

Marie Winn

Use ellipses to condense the quotation by eliminating a parenthetical passage that could be deleted without changing the meaning of the sentence.

31 · The Apostrophe '

31a Use an apostrophe to mark the omission of part of a date or word.

January of **'89** was unusually warm.

I **don't** want to keep my dental appointment tomorrow.

It's raining.

31b Add *'s* to the singular form of nouns and most indefinite pronouns (*everyone, someone, anyone,* etc.) to form the possessive case.

Overexposure to the **sun's** rays can cause serious skin problems.

The professor lectured on **Keats's** poetry.

The speaker appealed to **everyone's** sense of humor.

31c Use an apostrophe alone to indicate the possessive form of plural nouns that end in *s*.

During the **lifeguards'** convention, the hotel pool was always crowded.

31d Use an *'s* to form the possessive of plural nouns that do not end in *s*.

Several important **women's** rights issues were debated by the legislature.

Children's television viewing habits have been the subject of several recent studies.

31e To denote the possessive case of a compound word (*brother-in-law, someone else,* etc.) or to indicate joint possession, place an *'s* after the last word.

We spent the summer at my **brother-in-law's** beach cottage.

George and Martha's parties are always a great success.

Note: An **'s** after George and Martha would indicate that each gives successful parties.

31f Use an *'s* to indicate the plural form of a letter.

Some parents reward their children for making a certain number of **A's** and **B's**.

31g Do not use an apostrophe with possessive case forms of the pronouns *his, hers, its, ours, yours,* and *theirs.*

The decision is **theirs.**—*not*—The decision is **their's.**

The cat hurt **its** paw.—*not*—The cat hurt **it's** paw.

The insertion of an apostrophe between the **t** and the **s** of the pronoun **its** is particularly confusing because **it's** is the contracted from of **it is** (see also **8c** and **38b**).

31h Do not insert an apostrophe before the *s* ending of a singular verb or a plural noun.

There is a new television network that **show's** famous **film's** of the past.

Revised

There is a new television network that **shows** famous **films** of the past.

In the first sentence above, the first apostrophe misleads the reader into perceiving the verb **shows** as a possessive noun, and the second apostrophe misleads the reader into seeing plural **films** as a singular **film** that possesses something.

31i Do not put an apostrophe before the *s* ending of a plural abbreviation or number.

The university granted 250 **MAs** this year.

My **3s** sometimes resemble **5s.**

32 · The Slash /

32a Use a slash (also called a "virgule") between the conjunctions *and* and *or* to indicate option.

The instruction sheet that came with my new tent informed me that I could use steel pegs **and/or** aluminum braces for support. [The buyer has the choice of using both types of support or only one.]

Note: Although the **and/or** construction is justifiable in an essay that gives instructions or describes a technical process, it is rarely necessary in other types of prose.

32b Use a slash to separate unindented lines of poetry or poetic drama.

Shakespeare's "Sonnet 73" concludes with the lines, "This thou perceivest, which makes thy love more strong, / To love that well which thou must leave ere long."

32c Use a slash (or a hyphen) to link two words that function as one.

Some universities profess support for the ideal of the **teacher/scholar** but reward publication more than teaching. [The **teacher/scholar** is someone who is both a teacher and a scholar.]

33. · The Hyphen -

33a Put a hyphen between two words that function as a single adjective when the modifier comes before the word it modifies.

The **once-popular** resort area had become a ghost town.

The **ill-fated** mission resulted in many casualties.

Note: The hyphen is unnecessary if the first word in the compound ends in **ly** or if the noun precedes the modifier:

The **previously injured** players returned to action before the end of the season.

The resort area that was **once popular** had become a ghost town.

33b Put a hyphen (or a slash) between two nouns to combine them into a single noun.

The **player-coach** took herself out of the game.

If the compound is formed by the combination of a noun and one or more different parts of speech, consult a dictionary for recommended usage. In one recently published dictionary, words such as **break-in, editor-in-chief,** and **ice-skating** are hyphenated, but similar types of compounds are printed as two separate words (e.g., **boundary line, ice water,** etc.) or as a single unhyphenated word (e.g., **bricklayer**).

33c Use a hyphen to form a compound of two numbers that are written as words.

Twenty-five people have already preregistered for organic chemistry.

The **nineteen-sixties** will be remembered as a decade of discontent.

33d Use a hyphen after a prefix when the root word is a proper noun or adjective or when the omission of the hyphen would result in an awkward repetition of letters or confusion of meaning.

Anti-American sentiment had been building in Iran long before the overthrow of the Shah. [The hyphen links the prefix with a proper noun, **American.**]

I want to **re-lease** (i.e., renew the lease on) this apartment next year. [Without a hyphen, **release** would convey the opposite meaning: **give up.**]

33e If you do not have enough space to complete a word of two or more syllables at the end of a line, divide the word after a syllable and insert a hyphen to indicate that the word will be completed on the next line.

If you are in doubt about where to divide a word, consult a dictionary. It will indicate syllable divisions with raised periods, as in the examples below.

ar · chi · tect
bi · ol · o · gist
frac · ture
pre · ven · tion

33f Avoid overusing the hyphen as a mark of syllabication.

Though you might occasionally need to divide a word at the end of a line, a less distracting procedure is to extend the word beyond the right margin or begin it on the next line. Words of one syllable should not be subdivided, nor should words of two or more syllables be split in such a way that a single letter is isolated at the beginning or end of a line. For example, a single-syllable word such as **town** would never be hyphenated, nor would a multisyllabic word such as **amoral** be divided after the first **a**.

33g Do not confuse the hyphen (-) with the dash (--).

Hyphen misused as dash

From my window, I could see a park-a green, fertile oasis in an urban wasteland.

Exercise 13

In the sentences below, delete or add apostrophes, hyphens,
dashes, and slashes wherever necessary. Be able to explain
the reason for each decision.

1. In the brilliant day-light, the man's eyes squinched invol-
   untarily, causing him to look older than his fifty five
   year's.

2. Although many stores sell alcoholic-beverages, few tolerate on premise consumption.

3. Ironically, the police officers salaries were not paid due to
   the robbery of the citys payroll.

4. We are here solely to determine whos to blame for the
   three victim's suffering.

5. Everyones mind was made up about the councils report
   on taxes even before it's release.

6. The on off switch for this unit is located behind the
   counter.

7. The long awaited film finally made it's debut.

8. I cannot recollect what we paid to have our couch re
   covered.

9. Before we could recover our losses, the insurance adjustor asked us to recollect possessions that had been strewn around the neighborhood during the tornado.

10. Many of the so-called wonder-drugs found at the local pharmacy-the cough-suppressants, expectorants, antihistamines, and decongestants-are not so wonderful at relieving the dripping-nose that accompanies the common-cold.

34 · Italics

34a Italicize (underline) the names or titles of books, magazines, long plays, etc.

Books

The Sound and the Fury, Invisible Man, Cosmos

Plays

Hamlet, A Streetcar Named Desire

Long Poems

Paradise Lost, The Waste Land

Magazines and Scholarly Journals

Cosmopolitan, Esquire, Time, Modern Fiction Studies

Newspapers

The Washington Post (or the Washington Post)

Movies, Radio Shows, Television Programs

Gone with the Wind, Mystery Theater, Murphy Brown

Paintings and Sculpture

Van Gogh's Starry Night, Rodin's The Thinker

Major Musical Compositions

Verdi's Requiem Mass, Bach's Brandenburg Concerti

Ships, Planes, Spacecraft

USS Forrestal, Spirit of St. Louis, Columbia

34b Italicize (underline) foreign words that have not yet been fully absorbed into English.

The **carpe diem** theme is one of the central concerns of many seventeenth-century English poets.

I was surprised to find that the chips were covered with combatants, that it was not a **duellum,** but a **bellum,** a war between two races of ants.

Henry David Thoreau

34c Italicize (underline) words, letters, or numbers when you refer to them as such.

The word **evolution** continues to stir people's emotions.

When I write fast, my **t**'s look like **l**'s.

Some people consider the number **6** an omen of evil.

34d Italicize (underline) words that warrant special emphasis.

"I will **never** resign," the coach shouted.

Note: Use italics (underlining) for this purpose only on those rare occasions when the denotation or connotation of a word is not sufficient to convey the desired meaning or tone.

34e In the titles of your own compositions, do not italicize (underline) any words except those you would italicize in a sentence.

Title

Jay Gatsby and the American Dream [italics unnecessary]

Title

A Study of the American Dream in F. Scott Fitzgerald's **The Great Gatsby** [italics needed only for the title of Fitzgerald's novel]

**34
f**

34f Make a distinction between the kinds of names or titles that are customarily italicized and those that are set off by quotation marks.

Robert Hayden's poem "Figure" and Ralph Ellison's novel **Invisible Man** both examine the human suffering caused by racism.

35 · Capitalization

35a Capitalize the first word in a sentence, as well as the first word in the salutation and closing of a letter.

Some people go to a medical doctor when they get sick. Others rely on home remedies or nonprescription drugs. Still others turn to community healers for advice and treatment.

Dear Mrs. Evans,   Dear friends,
Sincerely yours,   Yours truly,

**35
b**

35b Capitalize proper names and their derivations.

Names of People

Monique Richardson, Nick Adams, Eleanor Roosevelt

Personal and Professional Titles

General Patton, Senator McCarthy, Professor Jones,
Dr. Strangelove

Names of Nationalities, Races, and Languages

Scandinavians, Sioux, African-American, Hispanic, English

Names of Religions and Religious Sects
or Denominations

Catholicism, Judaism, Protestantism, Muslims, Mormons, Buddhists, Unitarians

Names for Deity in Different Religions or Cultures

the Holy Ghost, Christ, Allah, Brahma

Names and Abbreviations of Organizations
and Institutions

the Democratic Party, the Republican Party, the Better Business Bureau, **AFL-CIO**, **NATO**, **NOW**, **UNICEF**, **FBI**, the United States Senate, the House of Representatives, the Supreme Court

Names of Roads, Bridges, Buildings, Monuments,
Ships, Planes, Spacecraft, and Other Human-made
Structures

**35
b**

the Blueridge Parkway, the Golden Gate Bridge, the Museum of Natural History, the Tomb of the Unknown Soldier, the battleship Bismarck, the Spirit of St. Louis, the space shuttle Columbia

Place Names and Their Derivatives

Denver, Dade County, New Jersey, the South, Yellowstone National Park, New Yorkers, Europeans, Chinese

Names of Oceans, Rivers, Mountains, and Other
Geological Features

Atlantic Ocean, Snake River, Mt. Whitney, Crater Lake, Niagara Falls

Names of Planets, Galaxies, Constellations, and Related Astronomical Terms

Mars, the Milky Way, Ursa Major, Crab Nebula

Names for Days of the Week, Months, Holidays, Historical Eras, and Geological Periods

Our Christmas holiday begins about the middle of December, usually on a Friday, and lasts through New Year's Day.

Marine invertebrates first appeared during the Paleozoic era.

The eighteenth century was known as the Age of Reason.

35c Capitalize the first word and all other words except prepositions, conjunctions, and determiners in the titles of publications, films and other media productions, speeches, paintings, sculpture, and musical compositions.

**35
c**

The Catcher in the Rye [novel by J. D. Salinger]

The New York Times [newspaper]

Psychology Today [magazine]

"Notes on Punctuation" [a chapter in Lewis Thomas's The Medusa and the Snail]

Casablanca [film]

Wide World of Sports [television series]

Mona Lisa [painting by Leonardo da Vinci]

Bird in Space [sculpture by Constantin Brancusi]

Beethoven's Moonlight Sonata [musical composition]

35d Do not capitalize common nouns, except those which name heads of state (e.g., The President will soon travel to England to confer with the Prime Minister).

One state **senator** has already announced her decision to run for a second term.

Is there a **doctor** on this plane?

At the **high school** I attended, **history** was the most demanding course.

I traveled **south**.

Standing at the rim of the **canyon**, I could see a **river** thousands of feet below.

In all of these sentences, the boldface words are not capitalized because they refer to a general category or class rather than to a specific person, place, or thing. Note, though, that these same words can be used to form proper names, which are capitalized.

One state official, **Senator Kelley**, has already announced her decision to run for a second term.

Is there a **Doctor Johnson** on this plane?

At **Lakeshore High School, Modern American History** was the most demanding course.

I traveled throughout the **South**.

Standing at the rim of the **Grand Canyon**, I could see the **Colorado River** thousands of feet below.

36 · Numbers

36a Use figures rather than words for the numbers in dates, addresses, references to pages or volumes, decimals, percentages, degrees, fractions, and quantities requiring more than two words to spell out.

Dates and Other Specific Time References

December **8, 1960**   **450** BC   **3:00** p.m.

Addresses

PO Box **21**
401 State St., Apt. **6**

Page and Volume Numbers

p. **10**   Vol. **5**

Decimals, Percentages, Degrees, and Fractions

2.75   **60** percent (or %)   **30°** Fahrenheit   **1 3/4**

Quantities That Require More Than Two Words to Spell Out

$255.00   **250,000,000** (or **250** million) people   **125** coupons

36b When using numbers other than those referred to in the preceding section, spell them out if they can be written as one or two words.

thirty-four customers   **six** musicians   **one hundred** dancing bears

   Ordinal numbers (**first, second, third,** etc.) are customarily written out as well.

36c If you begin a sentence with a number, always spell it out.

Thirty degrees below zero is the lowest temperature ever recorded at this time of year.

36d When referring to numbers in a series, treat them all in the same way regardless of the form they would take if used alone.

The manager of the produce department ordered **135** heads of lettuce, **85** cartons of tomatoes, and **10** bushels of apples.

   Whenever you are writing in an academic field and you have a question about which form to use for a given number, consult a manual of style in your discipline for recommended usage.

37 · Abbreviations

37a Abbreviate personal and professional titles
when they precede proper names.

Mr. Lanston, **Mrs.** Clara Pierce, **Ms.** Murdock, **Dr.** Schwartz, **Rev.**
Thomas Barker, **Dr.** Cathy Johnson

Note: The titles **Mr., Mrs., Ms.,** and **Dr.** may be used either
with first name and last name or with last name alone. Titles
such as **reverend, general,** and the like are abbreviated only
when they are followed by the person's first and last name:
General Grant, **Gen.** Ulysses S. Grant; **Reverend** Black, **Rev.**
Gail Black.

37 b

37b Abbreviate words such as *street, avenue,
drive,* and the names of states in addresses.

105 West End **Ave.**
Anaheim, **CA**

Note: Current US postal system abbreviations for each state
are as follows:

Alabama	AL	District of Columbia	DC
Alaska	AK	Florida	FL
Arizona	AZ	Georgia	GA
Arkansas	AR	Guam	GU
American Samoa	AS	Hawaii	HI
California	CA	Idaho	ID
Colorado	CO	Illinois	IL
Connecticut	CT	Indiana	IN
Delaware	DE	Iowa	IA

Kansas	KS	Ohio	OH
Kentucky	KY	Oklahoma	OK
Louisiana	LA	Oregon	OR
Maine	ME	Pennsylvania	PA
Maryland	MD	Puerto Rico	PR
Massachusetts	MA	Rhode Island	RI
Minnesota	MN	South Carolina	SC
Mississippi	MS	South Dakota	SD
Missouri	MO	Tennessee	TN
Montana	MT	Texas	TX
Nebraska	NE	Utah	UT
Nevada	NV	Vermont	VT
New Hampshire	NH	Virginia	VA
New Jersey	NJ	Virgin Islands	VI
New Mexico	NM	Washington	WA
New York	NY	West Virginia	WV
North Carolina	NC	Wisconsin	WI
North Dakota	ND	Wyoming	WY
Northern Mariana Islands	CM		

37
c

37c You may abbreviate names of academic degrees, time references, certain foreign terms, and names of well-known organizations or agencies.

Academic Degrees

BA, MA, MD

Time References

BC, AD, a.m., p.m.

Frequently Used Latin Terms

e.g. (*exempli gratia*) for example

etc. (*et cetera*) and so on
i.e. (*id est*) that is
et al. (*et alii*) and others

Names of Well-Known Organizations or Agencies

UN, US, OPEC, NATO

As the examples in this section indicate, some abbreviations require periods whereas others do not. For guidance in punctuating abbreviations, see **20b.**

Abbreviations other than the kinds listed here are seldom necessary in most forms of expository writing. However, because abbreviation practices vary considerably from one profession and academic discipline to another, you should supplement these guidelines with a study of the conventions recommended by the standard manual of style for your field.

**37
c**

Exercise 14

In the following sentences, correct any errors in the use of italics, capitalization, abbreviations, and numbers.

1. On december seventh, nineteen forty-one, the japanese attacked pearl harbor, destroying a large part of the american fleet.

2. Mark Twain's novel The Adventures of Huckleberry Finn influenced numerous twentieth-century Writers, notably Ernest Hemingway.

3. Yesterday, I had my 18th birthday, but the only present I got was a pop quiz in my History class.

4. A number of people devoted to the TV show star trek fanatically follow "the voyages of the starship enterprise."

5. The word liberal can create very different images and associations in the minds of different people.

6. 40 people began the race, but only a few completed it.

7. On Monday the directors will audition six singers, 10 actors, and 25 dancers for the playhouse production.

8. The President has invited the Governor of his home state to a meeting at the Oval Office.

9. The Scarlet Letter, Moby Dick, and Walden were among the major works of American Literature produced during the mid-Nineteenth Century American renaissance period.

10. Reverend Wallace asked us to send our donations before April twenty-six to Doctor Ellen Vonnegut, five hundred seventeen forty-fifth street, Tyler, Texas.

Exercise 15

Insert and delete punctuation where needed.

To recognize that the writing act is a process shifts the focus of teaching composition, from the product to the producer, it also forces composition teachers to ask more questions; What is the nature of that process, What are the mental juices that have to be squeezed sieved and clarified to make that process work.

To answer thinking goes into the writing process seems to be stating the obvious, however researchers and writing teachers have begun to take that obvious fact, more seriously. The fact, that writers think when they write proposes an interesting question. If students become better thinkers, do they also become better writers. Conversely, if students become better writers, do they also become better thinkers. some researchers think the answer to both questions is yes.

Writing researchers draw scientific support for connections between writing, thinking, and learning from other disciplines; cognitive and developmental psychology, educational theory, and linguistics. The literature on the relationships is speculative or at best descriptive. No studies cite empirical evidence that says "The connection exists!" Art Young and Toby Fulwiler note in their book Writing across the disciplines: research into practice [1986] "(W)e don't know of any studies . . . that prove conclusively that writing improves learning-we are "sure" that it does, but wer'e not sure its been proven." To explore the connections, between writing, thinking and learning requires to a certain extent that we trust the intuition, inferences and even hunches of others, who have studied the composing process.

37
c

V

Avoiding Common
Sentence Errors

38 · Errors in the Case Forms of Pronouns and Nouns

In **8c** and **8d** we discussed the ways in which case inflections (changes in word form) help communicate the role of nouns and pronouns in a sentence. In this chapter, we will explore some common problems of case usage and how to avoid them.

38a Make a distinction between subjective and objective case forms of pronouns.

The only kinds of words that have special forms for the subjective and objective case are personal pronouns and the relative or interrogative pronouns **who** and **whoever.**

Case Forms			*Personal Pronouns*					
Subjective	I	you	he	she	it	we	you	they
Objective	me	you	him	her	it	us	you	them

Case Forms	*Relative/Interrogative Pronouns*	
Subjective	who	whoever
Objective	whom	whomever

A subjective case inflection tells the reader that the pronoun functions as a subject or complement; an objective case form indicates that the word is the object of a preposition, a direct or indirect object, or the object of a participle or infinitive.

subject   object of infinitive
We did not mean to offend **them.**

38
a

direct object
The magician fooled **me** with her hat trick.

In short, uncomplicated sentences such as these, most writers instinctively use the correct case form. It is unlikely, for example, that anyone would write "**Us** did not mean to offend **they**" or "The magician fooled **I**." In certain kinds of sentences, however, the function of the pronoun may be less obvious and the choice of case more difficult.

1. *Case of personal pronouns after linking verbs.* Sentences in which a personal pronoun follows a linking verb are rare in English because such constructions often sound artificial. But if you should find it necessary to structure a sentence in this way, remember to use the subjective case to indicate that the pronoun is a subject complement.

This is **she.**

The winners were **they.**

Note that written usage differs in this respect from such conversational expressions as "It's me" and "This is him."

2. *Case of personal pronouns in compounds.* Another construction that may confuse the reader is one in which a personal pronoun is joined with another pronoun or noun to form a compound subject, complement, or object.

subject
My sister and I took a long vacation.

complement
The winners were **you and they.**

object
The argument between **the cashier and me** was brief but intense.

When you use a personal pronoun in this way, do not be distracted by the other words in the compound; instead, try visualizing the personal pronoun alone in the sentence with-

38
a

out the compound elements. For example, if you wanted to check the appropriateness of the pronoun **I** in "My brother and I took a long vacation," you would rephrase the sentence to read "**I** took a long vacation." If you had written **My brother and me,** your rephrased sentence, "**Me** took a long vacation," would make the error obvious. When you cannot appropriately isolate the problem pronoun, as in the third example above, you can test for correctness by substituting the plural pronouns **we** and **us** in the same case as the pronoun in the compound. Applying this test to the sentence "The argument between the cashier and me was brief but intense," you would substitute the objective case form **us** for **the cashier and me.**

The argument between **us** was brief but intense.

If you had originally written **between the cashier and I,** rephrasing the sentence with the subjective plural—"The argument between **we** was brief but intense"—would indicate a need for revision.

Note: If the compound is an appositive, both elements should be in the same case as the word(s) to which they refer.

The supervisors, **Ms. Simpson and I,** will conduct a workshop next week.

I is in the subjective case because it is part of a compound appositive that refers to **supervisors,** the *subject* of the sentence. Like all appositives, this one can be substituted for the words to which it refers.

Ms. Simpson and I will conduct a workshop next week.

Similarly, when a pronoun appositive refers to an object, the pronoun is in the objective case:

The teachers condemned their supervisors, Ms. Simpson and **me,** with faint praise.

3. *Case of personal pronouns after **than** or **as**.* When you use a personal pronoun after **than** or **as** in an elliptical sentence, think about how the sentence would read with the omitted word(s) included. If the pronoun is the subject of the omitted words, use the subjective case; if it is the object, choose the objective case.

The waiter was more upset with my friends than **I** [was]. [pronoun as subject]

The waiter was more upset with my friends than [he was with] **me.** [pronoun as object]

Note that in these statements, the case of each pronoun leads the reader to a different conclusion. The first sentence explains that both the waiter and the speaker were dissatisfied with the latter's friends. The second sentence states that the waiter was upset with both the speaker and his/her friends.

4. *Case of relative/interrogative pronouns **who/whom, whoever/whomever**.* **Who** and **whom,** plus their derivatives **whoever** and **whomever,** are the only relative or interrogative pronouns that have different inflections for the subjective and objective cases. Difficulties with these inflections usually arise in three types of sentences.

Although the usual pattern of English sentences is subject-verb-object, this pattern is sometimes reversed in questions. Thus, an interrogative pronoun at the beginning of a question can be in either the subjective or the objective case, depending on its function.

Who are you?

Whom were you calling?

In the first sentence, **who** is in the subjective case because it is the subject of the sentence. In the second sentence, the writer correctly uses the **m** inflection of the objective case to indicate that pronoun is the object of the verb **were calling.**

The function of an interrogative or relative pronoun may

also be obscured by a parenthetical expression that separates the pronoun from the rest of its clause. To determine the case of a pronoun in this context, disregard the parenthetical expression and concentrate on the grammatical relationship of the other words.

Who **do you think** will win the election?

Some people will vote for whoever **they believe** will reduce taxes.

Omitting the words **do you think** and **they believe,** we can see that **who** is the subject of **will win** and **whoever** is the subject of **will reduce.** Thus both inflections are correct.

Even more troublesome for most writers are sentences in which the function of a relative pronoun within its own clause is different from the function of the clause within the sentence:

Several people saw **who stole the car.**

I want to know the identity of **whoever found the stolen property.**

In the first sentence, the clause in bold type is a direct object, but **who** is in the subjective case because it is the subject of the clause. In the second sentence, the clause in bold type is the object of the preposition **of,** but here, too, the writer has correctly used the subjective case form of the relative pronoun (**whoever**) because it is the subject of the clause.

Another test for **who/whom** inflections can be applied in these three simple steps:

Step 1 Examine only the words following the **who** or **whom** in the sentence. For the sentence "Several people saw who stole the car," the pertinent words would be **stole the car.**

Step 2 Note where a word is needed to make the remaining words a complete sentence: _____ **stole the car.**

Step 3 Fill this slot with **he** or **him, they** or **them.** If **he** fits the slot, **who** is appropriate; if **him** fits the slot, **whom**

38
a

is appropriate. Since **he** fits the slot above, **who** is the correct word for the sentence.

38b Become familiar with possessive case inflections.

Like the subjective and objective cases, the possessive case has only a few inflections:

Nouns	Indefinite Pronouns (someone, anyone, everyone, etc.)	Relative/ Interrogative Pronouns	Personal Pronouns
's or s'	's	whose	my/mine your/yours his, her/hers, its our/ours their/theirs

Many errors in possessive case usage are caused by the writer's failure to recognize which inflections have an apostrophe and which do not. Two of the most frequent errors are evident in the sentences below.

38 b

Omitted apostrophe

The bankers account was overdrawn.

Unnecessary apostrophe

The coyote sounded it's mournful cry.

In the first sentence, the writer has omitted the apostrophe before the **s** in **bankers,** thus giving the impression that the word is a plural subject rather than a possessive. The insertion of an apostrophe in **it's** in the second sentence is equally misleading because the apostrophe signals a contraction (**it**

is) rather than the possessive case inflection **its,** which never has an apostrophe.

In most contexts, the need for a possessive case inflection is fairly obvious (Few people would write **John** car, for example, or **me** books). The case of a noun or pronoun is more difficult to determine, however, when it comes immediately before a verbal ending in **-ing** (**running, dancing, driving,** etc.). In general, use the posessive case if the verbal is a gerund (i.e., if it functions as a noun) and the objective case if the **-ing** word is a participle (i.e., if it functions as an adjective).

Tom**'s driving** worries me.

Yesterday, I saw **him weaving** in and out of traffic on the freeway.

In the first sentence above, **Tom's** is in the possessive case because **driving** is a gerund used as the subject of **worries.** In the second sentence, the personal pronoun **him** is in the objective case because it is a direct object modified by the participle phrase **weaving in and out of traffic on the freeway.**

In some constructions you may use either the objective case or the possessive case depending on how you want the reader to interpret the sentence.

I heard **John's** snoring.

I heard **John** snoring.

In the first sentence, **snoring** is a gerund naming what **I heard.** In the next sentence, **snoring** is a participle modifying **John**—John, who is snoring. See Chapter **31** for further discussion of the apostrophe.

Exercise 1

Underline the correct form of the pronoun within the parentheses, and indicate whether it is the subjective, objective, or possessive case.

1. (Who, Whom) do you think portrays superspy James Bond more convincingly, Timothy Dalton, Roger Moore, or Sean Connery?

2. Just because you score higher on that standardized test than (I, me) doesn't mean you are smarter than (I, me).

3. I knew that Karen was working in the cafeteria, but I didn't know that it was (she, her) who was responsible for the luncheon menu.

4. To (who, whom) should I give this paperwork?

5. The coach lost her temper when Tanya and (I, me) were late for basketball practice.

6. Working in the community volunteer program gave Sherry and (he, him) a sense of self-worth.

7. Unfortunately, the rare, old baseball card lost much of (its, it's) value when it was creased.

8. The race for secretary ended in a run-off between the incumbent and (me, I).

9. When Meg saw the giant deluxe pizza she had ordered,

**38
b**

she realized that (her, she) and her friends could never

eat all of it by themselves.

10. Although I had been working a month longer than my

brother Derrick, our employers gave me a smaller Christ-

mas bonus than (him, he).

Exercise 2

In the following sentences, correct all errors in case form. Put
a check after any correct sentences.

1. I wondered if this puppy belonged to whoever had left
   the nearby bicycle.

2. Cathy and Wandria are two friends of mine who dream
   of singing in Broadway muscials after they graduate.

3. Alyssa drove Jake, Tracy, and I to school last week because my car had broken down and was being repaired.

4. This writing competition is open to whomever wishes to
   enter, as long as the entrant is a resident of the United
   States.

5. My cousin Eduardo, who recently came to the United
   States from Costa Rica, speaks Spanish much better than
   me.

6. Whom has seen the latest Spike Lee film?

38
b

7. Jennifer visited Guy and I often even though we refused to listen to her Iron Maiden and Def Leppard tapes and played Pink Floyd recordings instead.

8. Who said "Ask not for who the bell tolls, it tolls for thee"?

9. The summer camp counselors, Brian and me, showed the kids how to play mudball after the volleyball pit was drowned in a rainstorm.

10. Our's is the only committee to have it's own stationery.

Exercise 3

Find and correct the case errors in the following passage:

Just between you and I, I believe that all the turmoil over whom gets elected president every four years is pointless. Who the voters choose makes little difference. It seems that no matter how hard our leaders try to bring about positive change, their efforts are of no more consequence than the efforts of ordinary citizens such as you and I. Although some presidents might disagree, our country is truly led and controlled by systems and institutions, not by people. The day might come for we Americans when our president, like the royalty of England, is more of a symbol than a power.

39 · Pronoun-Antecedent Disagreement

A pronoun and its *antecedent* (the word or words that the pronoun refers to) should always agree in number. A singular pronoun requires a singular antecedent, and a plural pronoun requires a plural antecedent.

The antique **collector** placed **her** bid.

The antique **collectors** placed **their** bids.

A pronoun and its antecedent *disagree* grammatically if one is singular and the other is plural.

Disagreement

singular   plural

An **idealist** will never abandon **their** principles.

Before our eyes reach the direct object in the sentence above, we have construed a singular **idealist** who **will never abandon** something; however, when we read the plural pronoun **their,** our concept of the singular idealist is contradicted, and our reading is temporarily confused.

The causes of such errors in writing vary, but they are most likely to occur when the antecedent is a *collective noun,* an *indefinite pronoun,* or a *compound.*

39a With collective nouns such as *committee, team, jury,* and the like, use either a singular or a plural pronoun depending on whether you want the reader to think of the members of the group as a unit or as individuals.

The **committee** submitted **its** report to the governor.

The **committee** disagreed about whether **they** should submit **their** report to the governor.

The singular pronoun in the first sentence tells the reader that the committee acted as a single body; the plural pronouns in the second sentence, on the other hand, refer to the members of the committee.

Whenever you use a collective noun, check to be sure that you have not treated it as both singular and plural in the same sentence. For example, a sentence such as "The committee **has** decided to submit **their** report to the governor" would be confusing because the verb **has** signifies that **committee** is singular, but **their**—a plural pronoun—sends the reader a contradictory signal.

39b When using an indefinite pronoun as an antecedent, note whether it is singular or plural and make any pronoun that refers to it agree in number.

39
b

Like collective nouns, some indefinite pronouns (**any, all, most, none, some**) may be singular or plural.

Some of the baggage was damaged when **it** fell out of the trunk. [**Some of the baggage** is conceived as a single amount.]

The graduating seniors gathered in the auditorium. **Some** wore **their** robes, and **some** wore **their** school clothes. [**Some** refers to several individuals.]

Several other indefinite pronouns (**both, several, few**) are always plural:

Few remained in **their** homes during the earthquake.

Most indefinite pronouns, however, are always singular. These include such words as **each, every, either, neither, everyone, someone,** and **anyone.** Confusion can arise when words intervene between an indefinite pronoun and its antecedent.

Disagreement

Each of the members of the women's caucus had **their** own motives.

Agreement

Each of the members of the women's caucus had **her** own motives.

Agreement errors are most likely to occur when a singular indefinite pronoun is the antecedent of a personal pronoun. In a sentence such as "**Somebody** left **their** car in the middle of the street" or "**Everyone** has **their** own theory about how to prepare for tests," for example, the plural pronoun **their** is inconsistent with the singular antecedent (**someone** and **everyone** respectively).

Because singular third person personal pronouns referring to humans (he and she) specify sex, constructions such as these pose a dilemma for skilled and inexperienced writers alike.

The **somebody** who left a car in the street could be a man or a woman, and **everyone** is a word that includes people of both sexes. The writers of both sentences have attempted to avoid the gender problem in the same way that speakers often do in informal conversations—by using the plural **their.**

A better alternative is simply to delete the pronoun or substitute a plural noun or pronoun for the singular antecedent.

39 b

Somebody left a car in the middle of the street.

Students have different theories about how to prepare for tests.

A third option is to join masculine and feminine pronouns with a hyphen, a slash, or the conjunction **or.**

Everyone has **his or her** own theory about how to prepare for tests.

Note, though, that such compounds can convey a stilted tone—an effect that becomes even more pronounced if the combined pronouns are used more than once:

Everyone has **his or her** own preference about how to study for **his or her** tests.

Section **15d** further discusses the problem of sexist language.

39c To decide whether a pronoun with a compound antecedent should be singular or plural, notice what type of conjunction links the elements in the compound.

In general, a pronoun should be plural if its antecedent is a compound consisting of two or more words joined by **and.**

My brother and his wife like cold weather, but **they** are having second thoughts about moving to Alaska.

Exception: If the elements joined by **and** refer to the same person or thing, treat the entire compound as a singular antecedent and use the singular form for any pronouns that refer to it:

The famous **actor and director** recently completed **his** new film.

Here, the pronoun **his** is singular because the **actor and director** are the same person.

If the antecedent is a compound in which the elements are linked by **or, nor, either . . . or, neither . . . nor,** or **not only . . . but also,** the pronoun should agree with the part of the antecedent that is closest to it.

Neither the lifejacket nor the **flashlight** was in **its** proper place.
Neither the lifejackets nor the **flashlights** were in **their** proper place.
Neither the lifejackets nor the **flashlight** was in **its** proper place.

Note: If the elements of a compound antecedent are different in number, as in the last example above, you can express the relationship between pronoun and antecedent more effectively by changing the connective and—if necessary—the pronoun and verb.

The lifejackets **and** the flashlight were out of **their** proper places.

Exercise 1

39
c

Revise each of the following sentences to eliminate pronoun-antecedent disagreement errors.

1. Each instructors has a philosophy of teaching that they

   follow.

2. The encounter group meets every Tuesday in their room

   on the third floor.

3. Neither of the campers was very happy with the weather

   they encountered during the backwoods trip.

4. The committee makes their recommendations for new by-laws after their last meeting of the year.

5. The entire coin collection was stolen from their hiding place.

6. Everyone who has finished their warm up can begin their floor exercise.

7. The great doctor and scientist Paula Muller will take a vacation only after the completion of their research.

8. Some of the logs spilled from its bin on the back of the truck.

9. Few of the students had finished his or her argumentative essays.

10. Either a clarinetist or an alto saxophone player forgot to tune their instrument.

**39
c**

Exercise 2

Revise each of the following sentences to eliminate pronoun-antecedent disagreement errors.

1. The new set of rare jewels resided in their own special safe.

2. World-class swimmers, such as Janet Evans, must frequently sacrifice her personal pleasures for competitive success.

3. In front of the White House, a group of demonstrators argued over its opposing opinions.

4. Everyone remained in their offices during the fire drill because some thoughtless prankster had pulled the alarm twice last week.

**39
c**

5. Our weekend guests, Mr. Hassam and the Wilsons, left some of his or her belongings at our house when they went home.

6. The Los Angeles riot of 1992 was the worst in the United States during the twentieth century; they caused more than fifty deaths and billions of dollars in damage.

7. Neither Martina nor Phyllis was in their seat when the late bell rang.

8. The student government association filed their annual report one month late.

9. Almost everyone misplaces their car keys sometimes.

10. The driver's education program in the city's public schools lost their accreditation.

Exercise 3

Correct the pronoun-antecedent disagreement errors in the following paragraph.

Everyone has their favorite kind of music, but few can tell specifically what makes it appealing. Like the kids on American Bandstand, the average music lover can describe their reactions to the music only in general terms, such as "I like the beat" or "It's easy to dance to." These people fail to realize that each of the songs they admire has their distinctive features. By analyzing the appeal of a song, both the enthusiast and the average listener derive greater enjoyment and appreciation.

**39
c**

40 · Subject-Verb Disagreement

In standard written English, a singular subject takes a singular verb, and a plural subject requires a plural verb. When a writer uses a singular form for one and a plural form for the other, the subject and verb disagree grammatically.

Disagreement

Military **advisers has** been sent to Central America.

Fast, effective medical **service are** one of the major goals of an Area Health Center.

In the first sentence, the plural subject **advisers** leads us to expect a plural verb, but instead we find the singular verb **has.** In the second sentence, the singular subject **service** prepares us for a singular verb, yet the next word is the plural verb **are.**

To avoid such inconsistencies in your own writing, follow closely the conventions discussed in the sections that follow.

40
a

40a Do not confuse the plural *s* ending of a noun with the singular *s* ending of a verb.

An **s** at the end of a noun almost always signals that the word is plural, whereas an **s** at the end of a verb indicates that it is singular. Therefore, if you have written a sentence in which the subject and verb both end in **s,** they probably disagree in number.

Disagreement

In the latest air disaster film, two **planes** flying over a large city **collides.**

Here, the **s** at the end of **collide** is unexpected because the **s** at the end of **plane** prepares us for a plural verb.

Exceptions

1. A few nouns (**news, economics,** etc.) are plural in form but singular in meaning. When one of these singular nouns functions as a subject, its verb should also be singular.

The **news** from Washington **was** all bad.

Economics attracts many students on this campus.

2. When a title is the subject of a sentence, the verb should always be singular—even if the title includes a plural noun or pronoun.

James Fenimore Cooper's ***The Pioneers* takes** place in the West.

***Jaws* has made** some people afraid to go in the water.

Note that in both of these sentences the subject is the title itself, not the words comprising it.

40b When the subject of a sentence is a collective noun, use a singular verb if the noun refers to a group as a unit and a plural verb if the noun refers to the individuals comprising a group.

Collective noun referring to members as a unit

The negotiating **team disagrees** with the ambassador's policy statement.

Collective noun referring to individual members

The negotiating **team disagree** about how to respond to the ambassador's policy statement.

In the first sentence above, the verb is singular because the negotiating team is unified in its disagreement with the ambassador's policy statement. In the second sentence, the verb is plural because the members of the negotiating team respond differently to the ambassador's statement.

Note: If a plural verb following a collective noun sounds unnatural or awkward to you, modify the sentence slightly by adding **the members of** just before the noun:

The members of the negotiating team **disagree** about how to respond to the ambassador's decision.

40c When using an indefinite pronoun as subject, choose a verb form that tells the reader whether the pronoun is singular or plural in meaning.

Some of the liquid in the beaker **has spilled** on the floor. [**Some** is a singular quantity and therefore needs a singular verb.]

40 c

Some of the skateboard artists **were doing** flips as they glided along the sidewalk. [**Some** refers to more than one skateboard artist and therefore needs a plural verb.]

Be sure to make a distinction between these indefinite pronouns and the two other classes of indefinite pronouns: those which are always plural (**several, few, any**) and those which are always singular (**each, every, everyone, everybody, somebody, anybody, either, neither**).

Many speak, but **few listen.**

Everyone has the same problems.

40d Make the verb in a relative clause agree in number with the antecedent of the relative pronoun.

Because a relative pronoun (**who, which, that**) does not have distinctive singular and plural forms, you must locate the antecedent in order to determine the number of the pronoun. You can then make a decision about the verb's number and communicate that information to the reader.

The **person who has** the most experience will receive first consideration. [singular antecedent—singular verb]

The **people who have** the most experience will receive first consideration. [plural antecedent—plural verb]

40e To determine the number of a verb with a compound antecedent, note the type of conjunction(s) used to unite the elements of the compound.

If you form a compound subject with **and,** make the verb plural; if you join the subjects with **or, nor, either . . . or, neither . . . nor,** or **not only . . . but also,** make the verb agree with the part of the compound closest to it.

1. *Compound subjects joined by* **and.**

The highway patrol **and** the national guard **were** available for emergency duty.

Use a singular verb with such constructions only on the rare occasions when you want to indicate that the elements joined by **and** function as one.

The famous **pirate and smuggler was** capable of evading even the swiftest of his pursuers.

Here the singular verb is appropriate because it tells the reader that the pirate and the smuggler are the same person. On the other hand, the use of the singular verb **was** in the previous example would be confusing because the highway patrol and the national guard are separate agencies.

2. *Compound subjects joined by* **or, nor, either . . . or, neither . . . nor,** or **not only . . . but also.**

Neither **reason** nor **intuitions are** infallible.

Either **thunderstorms** or heavy **fog makes** driving difficult.

Though technically correct, both of the above sentences would be improved stylistically if both parts of the compound were the same number.

Neither **reason** nor **intuition is** infallible.

Either a **thunderstorm** or a heavy **fog makes** driving difficult.

**40
f**

40f When you use either a single word or a compound as the subject of the verb *be*, make the verb agree with the subject, not the complement.

A constant **threat** to my garden **is insects.**

In this sentence, some writers might be tempted to use the verb **are** because the noun closest to it, **insects,** is plural. Readers, however, would be confused by **are** because the subject **threat** is singular.

40g If you invert the usual subject-verb order in a sentence or begin with the expletive *there* or *here*, look to the right of the verb for the subject.

   1. *Inverted word order.*

Alongside the highway **were** two abandoned **automobiles.**

In this sentence, the verb **were** is plural because its subject is **automobiles,** not **highway.** The prepositional phrase **alongside the highway** serves as an adverb. A good way to test for subject-verb agreement in an inverted sentence is to consider how the sentence would read if the subject came first.

Two abandoned **automobiles were** alongside the highway.

   2. *Expletive constructions.*

There is an extra chair on the porch.

Here are the most colorful, exciting real estate ads.

Notice that in each of these sentences the first word is not the subject but a means by which the writer defers the subject (**chair** and **ads** respectively) until later in the sentence.

   To test for subject-verb agreement in clauses beginning with **here** or **there,** follow one of these procedures:

   If the sentence begins with **there,** think about how the sentence should read with the word deleted.

An extra chair is on the porch.

   If the sentence begins with **here,** try moving the word to the end of the sentence and repositioning the verb.

The real estate ads **are here.**

40h Do not be distracted by words that come between a subject and its verb.

1. **Representatives** of a large hotel chain **are** planning to meet with the Builders' Association.
2. The **turntable** as well as the speakers **is** defective.
3. **Postponing** decisions **is** one of my worst faults.

Writers who determine the number of a verb by the number of the noun closest to it might use **is** instead of **are** in sentence #1 and substitute **are** for **is** in sentences #2 and #3. In sentence #1, however, the verb should be plural because its subject is **representatives; chain,** the word immediately before the verb, is the object of the preposition **of.**

In sentence #2, the verb **is** agrees with the singular subject **turntable,** not with **speakers,** the object of the preposition **as well as.** One option here would be to substitute a coordinating conjunction for the preposition and make the verb plural:

The turntable and the speakers are defective.

In sentence #3, the subject is a verb phrase consisting of a gerund (**postponing**) and its object (**decisions**). In such constructions, the verb should agree with the **-ing** word, not with its object. Thus **is** is the appropriate verb because **postponing** names a single act.

Exercise 1

Correct the errors in subject-verb agreement in the following sentences without changing verb tense.

1. Neither the chief airport official nor the president of the

   airline were certain that the strike could be averted.

2. If either of the rescue teams get through in time it will be a miracle.

3. <u>Star Wars</u> were a picture that spawned numerous inferior imitations.

4. Statistics are a required course for computer science majors.

5. The source of the lawyer's problems were the apathy and mistrust of her client.

6. Always lurking in the back of the prisoner's mind was thoughts of escape.

7. Reducing the inefficiencies in production lines were the main concern of the newly hired consultants.

8. There is several ivory chess sets in the wall safe.

9. The dancers and their director gives a benefit performance yearly for the community.

10. Some outspoken professors at the university has been attacked in recent newspaper editorials.

40 h

Exercise 2
Correct the errors in subject-verb agreement in the following sentences without changing verb tense.

1. I thought the beach, not the mountains, were the most beautiful part of our state.

2. Near my grandmother's house was ponds with dragonflies and minnows.

3. <u>Jumpers</u> are a play by the famous modern playwright Tom Stoppard.

4. Kelly, along with numerous other tourists, were mugged while walking in Central Park at night.

5. Either St. Louis or Memphis were to be awarded a new team that would join the struggling National Wiffleball League.

6. Talking on the phone every hour of the weekend with Monica and Heather are among Trent's favorite occupations.

7. Neither Mr. Adams nor Ms. Budryck are expecting any holiday visitors this year.

8. Kerry's dogs always plays with the new kitten instead of trying to start a fight with it.

9. Basic mathematics are generally believed to be an important foundation for higher learning.

10. The beautiful forests of the Pacific Northwest has been threatened by disease and uncontrolled logging.

Exercise 3

Correct the errors in subject-verb agreement in the following passage.

Two of the biggest problems a college freshman face are homesickness and loneliness. Freshmen on their own for the first time often experiences feelings of anxiety and insecurity until they adjust to their new independence. However, once the newest members of the campus community makes the necessary adjustments, solitude and new-found freedoms becomes enjoyable rather than frightening.

41 · Errors in Verb Usage

Subject-verb disagreement, a problem discussed in the preceding chapter, is only one of several common errors involving verb forms. Others include omission or misuse of the **d/ed** inflections; use of nonstandard forms of **be;** confusion of verbs such as **sit/set, lie/lay,** and other words that are similar in sound but different in meaning; and unnecessary shifts in tense or voice.

41
a

41a Do not omit the *d* or *ed* ending of a regular verb in the past or perfect tense.

Because a final d sound is often inaudible in speech, writers who are guided by the sound of a word rather than by a knowledge of its grammatical form and function are likely to omit the inflection in the past or perfect tenses of regular verbs.

Confusing omission of inflections

I **finish** my research paper yesterday.

The delegates to the convention have **propose** several changes in the constitution.

Whatever the cause, the omission of the **ed** inflection of **finish** and the **d** ending of **propose** in the sentences above is confusing because both verbs have a present tense form, yet they describe actions that have already occurred.

41b Do not use *d* or *ed* to form tenses of irregular verbs.

Misuse of d/ed inflections with irregular verbs

The department store manager **choosed** the most successful salesperson for the new customer relations job.

Though common in some spoken dialects, such nonstandard verb forms are distracting to readers who are able to distinguish between regular and irregular verbs and expect to find **chose** in this context.

41c Follow the conventions of written English when using forms of *be*.

Although in some oral dialects the verb **be** has as few as two forms (**be** and **been**), in standard written English it has eight different forms (**am, are, is, was, were, be, being, been**). Therefore, a speaker addressing a listener conversant in the same dialect might say "I **been** to town" or "We **be** ready," but a writer addressing a diversified audience accustomed to the conventions of the written code should conform to that code.

We **are** ready.

I **have been** to town.

41d Distinguish between *sit* **and** *set*, *lie* **and** *lay*, **and the forms of other irregular verbs that look and sound alike but have different meanings and different inflections for each tense.**

Consider the following examples:

Confusing

My grandfather likes to **set** in his rocking chair every afternoon.

I **laid** on the sofa and fell asleep.

Each of these sentences is confusing because the verb conveys a meaning different from that which the writer intended to express.

In the first sentence, the writer has confused **set,** which means **put,** with **sit,** which means **take a seat.** In the second sentence, the writer makes a similar error, using **laid (placed)** instead of the expected **lay (reclined).**

The chart below shows the basic forms of these verbs.

Infinitive	*Past Tense*	*Past Participle*
sit (take a seat)	sat	sat
set (place)	set	set
lie (recline)	lay	lain
lay (put)	laid	laid

Note that **set** and **lay** are transitive verbs and take objects, while **sit** and **lie** are intransitive verbs (see **9b**). One way to tell the difference between **lay** and **lie** is to remember that "I laid down on the grass" means "I put feathers on the grass."

41e Avoid unexpected and unnecessary shifts in verb tense.

Unexpected shifts

As I **parked** my car, someone **runs** into it.

The runner **circles** the track each time she **won** a race.

Both of these tense shifts are puzzling because they cannot be predicted or explained by anything in the sentence. Notice how much clearer the time relationships in each sentence become when verb tenses are consistent.

As I **parked** my car, someone **ran** into it.

The runner **circles** the track each time she **wins** a race.

Verb tenses should also be consistent within a paragraph and from one paragraph to the next. Look closely at the two passages below and observe how the writer has handled verb tenses.

As a child, I dreamed of all the wonderful things that would happen to me when I became sixteen. Most of all, I looked forward to owning a car and becoming more independent. But when I turned sixteen, I realize that I can't afford to put gas in a car, much less own one, and that my dream of independence is also an illusion. I still had to do homework, mow the lawn, and abide by my parents' rules. In no sense do I feel like an adult.

As a child, I dreamed of all the wonderful things that would happen to me when I became sixteen. Most of all, I looked forward to owning a car and becoming more independent. But when I turned sixteen, I realized that I couldn't afford to put gas in a car, much less own one, and that my dream of independence was also an illusion. I still had to do homework, mow the lawn, and abide by my parents' rules. In no sense did I feel like an adult.

The first passage moves unpredictably between the past and the present. These frequent shifts in verb tense suggest that the writer is unsure about the perspective from which this account of personal experience should be related. At the outset, the point of view seems to be that of an older person reflecting on an earlier time (notice the past tense verbs **dreamed, became, looked, turned**). In sentence 3, however, the writer seems to assume the role of the young person, recording the conflict between dreams and reality in the present tense (**realize, can't, is**). Two additional tense shifts that occur in sentences 4 and 5 add to the confusion, further undermining the writer's authority and the reader's sense of continuity. In the revised version, the writer resolves these problems simply by changing the present tense verbs to past tense.

Note: Some shifts in verb tense are logical and necessary, as in sentences such as the following:

Shakespeare **died** in 1616, but his plays **live** on.

Once, great herds of buffalo **roamed** the West; now only a few **remain.**

Exercise 1

In the following sentences, revise nonstandard verb forms and make verb tense sequence consistent and logical.

1. I laid in the sun all day and got burned.

2. I use to be shy before I took a course in self-confidence.

3. We been writing for at least an hour.

4. The irate fans had came to the conclusion that their team would never be a winner.

5. The banking industry was shook by the revelations of corruption in high places.

6. The guests were told to sit their gifts on the hall table and then to set down in the den.

7. The archeological team spared nothing in their efforts to rise the sunken galleon from the harbor bottom.

8. As I walked into the hotel, I spies the man I had been looking for.

9. I saw many beautiful trees and lakes as I runned through the park.

10. When the writer was alive, nobody knows her; when she dies, suddenly everybody would proclaim what a genius she is.

Exercise 2

In the following sentences, revise nonstandard verb forms and make verb tense sequence consistent and logical. Put a check after any correct sentences.

1. We been to the arcade to play video games.

2. Several years ago, Jill's father won a prize in the state lottery, and ever since he buys a lottery ticket each Monday.

3. John lay the book beside the sofa and fell sound asleep.

4. AIDS researchers reported that they had failed in their most recent efforts to produce an effective vaccine.

5. Last week my little sister decides she wants to be an astronaut.

6. As ruthless governments in Eastern European countries fell in 1989 and after, thousands of citizens rejoice.

7. The great poet laid down on his bed after scribbling the rough draft of a potential masterpiece in a fit of inspiration.

8. The errors in the student's essay been corrected by the teacher.

9. Elaine, Craig, and Carl be the best foosball players in our school.

10. No sooner had we sat the heavy boxes down in the stockroom than we were called back for another load.

Exercise 3

In the following paragraph, revise nonstandard verb forms
and eliminate inconsistencies in verb tenses.

Only a month after I bought a new car, it was stole while I
am attending a party. I been at the party just a short while
when I decided to leave because I was not feeling well. My
date and I went to where we remember parking the car, but it
was not there. After our initial shock, we decided to check
and make sure we weren't on the wrong street. However, after we had went up and down all the nearby streets, we
knew that the car was lost. Luckily, my car was recover the
next day by the police, out of town and out of gas. Apparently someone had merely wanted to take a one-night joy
ride; unfortunately, my car happens to be the most joyful one
available.

42 · Errors in Adjective and Adverb Forms

Most problems with the forms of adjectives and adverbs can
be traced to the differences between spoken and written English.

42a In writing, do not omit the *ly* ending of adverbs such as *surely, really, easily.*

Though common in spoken English, such omissions are un-expected and distracting to most readers because the form of the modifier is inconsistent with its function.

Adjectives misused as adverbs

I can pass the driving test **easy.**

People in coastal areas are **real** unhappy about the government's plans to dispose of hazardous wastes in the ocean.

In these sentences, **easy** and **real** have the form of adjectives, but they are used as adverbs (**easy** modifies the verb **can pass** and **real** modifies the adjective **unhappy**).

Such inconsistencies can be eliminated simply by chang-ing the adjective to an adverb.

I can pass the driving test **easily.**

or

I can **easily** pass the driving test.

People in coastal areas are **really** unhappy about the government's plans to dispose of hazardous wastes in the ocean.

42 b

42b In writing, do not omit the *d* or *ed* inflection of the past participle of a regular verb.

Confusing omission of inflection

The goods **produce** by the Fly-by-Night Hardware Company were defective.

The picture on the woodworking kit bore no resemblance to the **finish** product.

Although **produce** and **finish** are spelled the way the writer might pronounce **produce*d*** and **finish*ed*,** the form of each word conveys a meaning different from that which the writer intends.

In the first sentence, the reader may initially assume that **produce** is the predicate of **goods** rather than an adjective modifying it. The omission of the **ed** ending of **finish** in the second sentence is also misleading because the word at first appears to be a noun. Only after reading further do we discover that the writer intended this word to be an adjective.

42c Follow written rather than oral conventions when using comparative and superlative forms of adjectives.

In some regional dialects, expressions such as **most happiest** and **more prettier** are commonplace, but such redundancies are distracting in an essay and should therefore be revised.

Redundant

I am **most happiest** when I am alone.

The flowers are **more prettier** in the spring than in the summer.

Revised

I am **happiest** when I am alone.

The flowers are **prettier** in the spring than in the summer.

Keep in mind, too, that the written code makes a distinction between the comparative and the superlative that is seldom observed by speakers. Writers conventionally use the comparative when referring to two people or things and the superlative when referring to more than two.

Claire is the **more** experienced of the two laboratory technicians on duty this summer. She is also the **most** intelligent member of a large and diversified department.

Someone speaking informally about Claire, on the other hand, might say she was the **most experienced of the two lab technicians.**

Oral and written usage are not always incompatible, of course. In fact, your familiarity with the spoken language will often help you decide the specific form to use for the comparative or superlative degree of a particular adjective—to recognize, for example, that the superlative of **famous** is not **famousest** but **most famous.** If you have doubts about the appropriate comparative or superlative form of any adjective, consult a dictionary.

Exercise 1

Eliminate the incorrect uses of adjectives and adverbs in the following sentences.

1. All the model ever had for lunch was toss salad.

2. The disgruntled employee did not feel that the lie detector test he was forced to take was administered fair.

3. Both of the cars were quite practical, but the imported model was most beautiful.

4. Marsha sure was pleased by the results of her aptitude test.

5. Even though the jacket was on sale, the reduce price was still far beyond the means of most shoppers.

42
c

6. The survivor's tale was one of the more bizarre stories ever told.

7. The awesome lightning forked crazy across the sky.

8. Many drivers who routinely violate the speed limit believe they can't be caught easy.

9. The calculus test was so difficult I became real frustrated.

10. Critics felt that some of the new fall television shows were more likelier to succeed than others.

Exercise 2

Correct the faulty uses of adjectives and adverbs in the following passage.

**42
c**

Aerobic dancing involves performing a series of increasing difficult exercise routines to the beat of popular songs. For the initial ten minutes of class, participants move slow, preparing their muscles for the upcoming workout. Then they warm up by doing jumps and twists to the beat of a relative slow song. Finally, they dance specific aerobic routines to the driving beat of hard rock. By the time the session is over, the dancers feel like accomplish performers.

43 · Vague Pronoun Reference

The reference of a pronoun is clear if the pronoun has a specific, immediately recognizable antecedent.

Standing at the door was a stern looking **man who** glared at the **customers** as **they** filed past **him** into the theater.

Some products are marked with a special sale **price,** but **this** can be misleading.

At a slower pace, after the flash, came the **sound** of the explosion, **which** some people have no recollection of hearing, while others described it as an earth-shaking roar, like thunder or a big wind.

Alexander Leighton

The reference of a pronoun is *vague* under the following conditions: if the pronoun refers broadly to the idea of a sentence or paragraph rather than to a specific word or word group; if the pronoun normally has an antecedent but none is expressed or implied; or if the pronoun refers ambiguously to more than one antecedent.

43a Avoid excessively broad reference when using the pronouns *this, that, which,* and *it.*

Some of the effects of such vague references can be seen in the following sentences:

Broad reference

1. One recent report on American education concludes that schools should stay open all year. **This** appeals to some parents.
2. Donnell was annoyed because his friends were late, but **that** did not bother them.

3. The judge ruled that the accident victim's whiplash injury was a hoax, **which** pleased the defendant.

After reading sentence #1, we still cannot be certain what **this** refers to. The only possible antecedent actually expressed in the sentence is **report,** but the report itself does not seem to be what some parents found appealing. The word might refer to the conclusion of the report or to the concept of a longer school year or to the longer year itself. The lack of a specific antecedent for **that** in sentence #2 raises similar questions. **That** could refer to Donnell's annoyance, to his friends' lateness, or to the fact that he was angry with them for being late. And in sentence #3, the reader may at first mistake **injury** or **hoax** for the antecedent of **which** before realizing that the pronoun refers to an unstated antecedent—the judge's ruling.

Vagueness problems of this kind can be eliminated in several different ways.

1. *Include an exact antecedent.*

A recent report on American education concludes with the **recommendation** that schools should stay open all year. **This** appeals to some parents.

2. *Add a noun immediately after the pronoun if the latter is* **this, that,** *or one of the other demonstrative pronouns.*

Donnell was annoyed because his friends were late, but **that reaction** did not bother them.

3. *Restructure the sentence to eliminate the need for an antecedent.*

The defendant was pleased at the judge's ruling that the accident victim's whiplash injury was a hoax.

Note: The fact that a demonstrative or relative pronoun does not have a one-word antecedent does not necessarily mean that its reference is vague. But if you use a pronoun in this way, its meaning must be clear from the content, as in the following passage.

Most of us are too tired or too harassed to take a computer, a slide rule, and an M.I.T. graduate to market and figure out what we're buying. The makers of the goods we buy know **this**.

Marya Mannes

43b Do not use a personal pronoun such as *they* or *you* as if it were an indefinite pronoun.

Vague reference

I have always wondered when the old house at the edge of town was built. **They** say that George Washington once slept there.

No amount of searching will yield an antecedent for **they** in this sentence. If the writer's intent is to make only a general reference to the townspeople, an indefinite pronoun such as **some** would better serve the purpose.

I have always been curious about when the old house at the edge of town was built. **Some** say that George Washington once slept there.

If the writer has in mind a more specific group of people, that information should be shared with the reader.

I have always been curious about when the old house at the edge of town was built. **People whose families have lived within the area since the Revolutionary War era** say that George Washington once slept there.

A similar problem arises when the second person pronoun **you** has only a general reference.

When **you** join the college's marching band, **you** must give up other extracurricular activities.

Here the writer seems to be projecting his or her personal experience into a generalized **you** rather than addressing a second person audience as the pronoun leads us to expect. With the substitution of a first person pronoun, an indefinite pronoun, or a plural noun, the meaning of the sentence becomes clearer.

When **I** joined the college's marching band, **I** gave up other extracurricular activities.

Anyone who joins the college's marching band must give up other extracurricular activities.

Students who join the college's marching band must give up other extracurricular activities.

43c Avoid ambiguous reference.

Ambiguous reference

When Kellen accused Scott of cheating, **he** was very angry.

Mrs. Posey told her sister that **she** was irresponsible.

43
c

In the first sentence, the reference of **he** is ambiguous because its antecedent could be either **Kellen** or **Scott.** The same problem occurs in the next sentence, where **she** may refer to either **Mrs. Posey** or **her sister.**

If you find that you have used a pronoun in this way, rephrase the sentence to eliminate the ambiguity:

Scott was angry when Kellen accused **him** of cheating.

Mrs. Posey criticized **her** sister for being irresponsible.

Exercise 1

Rewrite the following sentences to eliminate vague pronoun references.

1. The driver thought he could beat the train to the railroad crossing, but this was fatal.

2. The village was located on top of a peak; it was like climbing Mount Everest after a hard day's journey.

3. The children ate like perfect ladies and gentlemen, and they even talked politely during the meal, which surprised the camp counselor.

4. When the police arrived, the mob dispersed, and that was a relief to the townspeople.

5. Ms. Farnsworth's estate is worth over a million dollars; they say she started out without a dime to her name.

6. While I was camping in the Appalachians, the first thing I saw every chilly morning was my breath; they say that the temperature often drops below freezing even in the summer.

43 c

7. When the bride walked down the aisle past her mother, she winked.

8. Eric excitedly called Louis to announce that he had won the state lottery.

9. They say that everyone who falsifies an income tax return will eventually be caught.

10. By the end of the season, Jordan had almost 500 rebounds. This was amazing for a guard.

Exercise 2

Rewrite the following passage to eliminate vague pronoun references.

If you are thinking about investing in a cable television hookup or a video recording system, you should consider the disadvantages as well as the advantages of owning such equipment. For instance, you will be able to spend many pleasurable hours in the presence of interesting screen and stage characters, but this will reduce the amount of time available for socializing with actual people. They also say that the sports fare available through cable is varied and excellent. Of course, the more time you spend watching and rewatching sporting events, the less time you will have to participate in them; in fact, the most exercise anyone will get will probably consist of punching the buttons on the remote control ap-

43
c

paratus. The basic rule to remember in this is that if you have a desire to spend more time sitting idly in front of a TV screen, then invest. Otherwise, don't have it installed.

44 · Dangling and Misplaced Modifiers

An adjective, an adverb, or a phrase or clause used as an adjective or adverb should refer to a specific word in the same sentence and be placed close to the word modified so that the relationship is clear to the reader. A modifier is *dangling* if it has nothing to modify, and it is *misplaced* if intervening words obscure the relationship between it and the word it modifies.

44a Avoid dangling modifiers.

44
a

Typically, a dangling modifier comes at the beginning of a sentence and takes the form of a participial phrase, a prepositional phrase, an infinitive phrase, or an elliptical clause (a clause with one or more words omitted).

Dangling modifiers

Having cleaned the apartment, the next job was to wax the floor. [dangling participial phrase]

After adjusting the microscope, a slide was placed under the lens. [dangling prepositional phrase]

To lose weight, rich foods should be avoided. [dangling infinitive phrase]

While discussing theories of insect behavior, a fly lit on Mr. Worthington's desk. [dangling elliptical clause]

All of these sentences are confusing for essentially the same reason: they begin with a reference to someone we expect to be identified at the beginning of the following clause, but in each instance this expectation is frustrated. Obviously, a job cannot clean an apartment, a slide does not adjust a microscope, foods do not lose weight, and a fly is incapable of discussing insect behavior. Yet that is what the structure of these sentences implies.

To avoid such confusion in your own writing, ask yourself this question whenever you use a modifying phrase or clause: To whom or what does this group of words refer? If you cannot find a word in the same sentence that gives you a logical answer, either revise the phrase or clause so that its reference is clear or use an appropriate noun or pronoun as the subject of the independent clause.

After the microscope was adjusted, a slide was placed under the lens.

or

After adjusting the microscope, **the scientist placed a slide under the lens.**

A dangling modifier at the end of a sentence can be corrected in the same way.

Dangling modifier

A ball hit me in the head **while waiting for a tennis court.**

Revised

A ball hit me in the head while **I was** waiting for a tennis court.

44b Avoid misplaced modifiers

A misplaced modifier is often confusing because the reader may associate it with the wrong word.

Misplaced modifier

A cloud of foul-smelling gas ruined our lunch **from a nearby paper mill.**

By placing the prepositional phrase at the end of the sentence rather than immediately after **gas,** the noun it modifies, the writer seems to be saying that the lunch, not the gas, came from the paper mill.

The solution to such a problem is simply to move the modifier to its appropriate position in the sentence:

A cloud of foul-smelling gas **from a nearby paper mill** ruined our lunch.

Another kind of misplaced modifier (sometimes called a *squinting modifier*) is one that refers ambiguously to the word on either side of it.

The spectators who had been shouting **angrily** confronted the officials.

In this sentence, the adverb **angrily** is next to the word it modifies, but we cannot tell which word that is. The writer may mean either that the spectators had been shouting angrily or that they confronted the officials angrily. Such ambiguity can usually be eliminated by a shift in the position of the modifier or by a slight change in the wording.

44 b

The shouting spectators **angrily** confronted the officials.

The spectators who had been **angrily** shouting confronted the officials.

The spectators who had been shouting confronted **angrily** the officials.

Exercise 1

Rewrite the following sentences to eliminate dangling or misplaced modifiers.

1. Having missed the flight, the trip was postponed.

2. The charred papers were exhibited at the official proceedings that were salvaged from a lit fireplace.

3. To become a professional dancer, pain and setbacks must be endured.

4. When studying, noise must be kept to a minimum.

5. After accelerating recklessly through the final turn, the race was easily won by the Italian team.

6. Only the staff members who had prepared diligently completed their tasks.

7. Failing to sell enough tickets to break even, the concert was canceled.

8. As I looked out the window, I saw a man walking his dog in a tuxedo.

9. An injury to the camera operator occurred while photographing a street riot.

10. After receiving a bomb threat, the school building was cleared.

Exercise 2

Rewrite the following sentences to eliminate dangling or misplaced modifiers.

1. Running well ahead of everyone in the marathon, the new shoes began to hurt Randy's feet.

2. To win the prize, the balls must be thrown directly against the target.

3. While driving to work, a cat just missed being hit.

4. Despite being an excellent dramatic actor, Ruth's premedical studies are more important to her now.

5. Having finished the main course, the dessert was eagerly consumed.

6. While still a child, my mother made me rake the yard every week.

7. The artist who had just finished painting gleefully phoned her boyfriend to tell him she was through at last.

8. Leaving the broken down truck on the beach, a single dune buggy transported all six of us back to town.

9. The little boy asked questions of the political leader with a blue balloon and a thumb in his mouth.

10. Dodging the bullets whizzing overhead, the latest news on the ethnic struggle was filed by the network correspondent.

Exercise 3

Rewrite the following passage, eliminating misplaced and dangling modifiers wherever they occur.

**44
b**

After attending the wedding, a search for the bride and groom's car was undertaken. We soon found it parked about three blocks from the church in an alley. Armed with cans of shaving cream, the windows were quickly covered with foam. Next, we tied tin cans to the rear bumper filled with marbles. Finally, as the newlyweds approached, everyone who had participated enthusiastically shouted, "Surprise!"

---

45 · Comma Splice and Fused Sentence

The *comma splice* and the *fused sentence* are sentence errors that result from the mispunctuation of independent clauses.

45a Do not link or "splice" two independent clauses with a comma alone or with a comma plus a conjunctive adverb such as *however, therefore,* or another such connective (see *8h* for a list of conjunctive adverbs).

Comma splices

The coach paced nervously along the sidelines, the kicker sat calmly on the bench.

The coach paced nervously along the sidelines, **however,** the kicker sat calmly on the bench.

Both types of comma splices frustrate readers' expectations. A comma alone following an introductory independent clause, as in the first sentence above, prepares the reader not for a second independent clause but for a nonrestrictive modifier or a series.

The coach paced nervously along the sidelines, **where the kicker sat calmly on the bench.** [nonrestrictive subordinate clause modifying **sidelines**]

The coach paced nervously **along the sidelines, behind the bench, and among the cheerleaders.** [series of prepositional phrases]

Remember that two independent clauses may be joined by a comma plus a coordinating conjunction (see **14a** and **23a**).

The coach paced nervously along the sidelines, **but** the kicker sat calmly on the bench.

A comma followed by a conjunctive adverb, such as **however,** is also misleading because such words are set off by commas only when they occur within a clause.

The coach paced along the sidelines; the kicker, **however,** sat calmly on the bench.

Note that if the conjunctive adverb were moved to a position between the two clauses, it should be preceded not by a comma but by a semicolon—a punctuation mark that does have the function of linking independent clauses.

45b Do not fuse or run together two sentences by omitting the punctuation mark or connective that marks the boundary between them.

**45
b**

Fused sentence

To some people home remedies are more effective than prescription drugs to others they are a waste of time.

In this sentence, the writer fails to indicate where the first clause ends and the second one begins. As a result, we are likely to misconstrue the words following **drugs** as a continuation of the first clause rather than as a new statement that completes the contrast between the people who value home remedies and those who scorn home remedies.

The key to eliminating both comma splices and fused sentences is being able to recognize independent clauses and to choose the most appropriate means of linking them.

1. *If you want to give separate emphasis to each clause, put a period between them:*

Wind and water erosion are destroying more and more beachfront property every year. People continue to build houses close to the ocean.

2. *If you want to establish a closer but still balanced relationship between the two clauses, link them in one of these three ways:*

With a comma plus a coordinating conjunction (and, but, or, for, nor, yet, so)

Wind and water erosion are destroying more and more beachfront property every year, **yet** people continue to build houses close to the ocean.

With a semicolon alone

Wind and water erosion are destroying more and more beachfront property every year; people continue to build houses close to the ocean.

With a semicolon plus a conjunctive adverb

Wind and water erosion are destroying more and more beachfront property every year; **however,** people continue to build houses close to the ocean.

3. *If, after thinking about the problem, you decide that one clause warrants more emphasis than the other, subordinate the less important one.*

**45
b**

For example, if you wished to emphasize the folly of the people who persist in building houses on the beach, you might subordinate the first clause.

Although wind and water erosion are destroying more and more beachfront property every year, people continue to build houses close to the ocean.

Specific decisions about which construction to use will depend on the context in which the sentence occurs (see Chapters **11, 13,** and **14** for additional suggestions).

Exercise 1

Eliminate comma splices and fused sentences by adding or
changing punctuation, or by subordinating one part of the
sentence to the other. Put a check after any sentences that are
correctly punctuated.

1. We spent several weeks preparing for the admissions
   exam, but it was much more difficult than we had imag-
   ined.

2. Oysters are good at any time of the year some people like
   to eat them only in the summer.

3. I could see the trail winding toward the bottom of the
   canyon, about halfway down, something darted across
   the path and disappeared in the underbrush.

4. Physical changes can be documented rather easily, psychological growth, on the other hand, is difficult to measure.

5. Something may appear to be amiss; however, our procedures are correct.

6. Fog engulfed the airport no planes were allowed to land
   or take off.

7. Interest rates have declined slightly during the past month, unemployment, however, has increased.

8. Many stores begin selling Christmas toys right after Halloween, some people are predicting that in the near future we will be putting up Christmas trees on Labor Day.

9. Organized efforts to censor have increased dramatically, two of the chief targets have been <u>The Grapes of Wrath</u> and <u>Catcher in the Rye</u>.

10. One of the most popular oral legends is a story called "The Vanishing Hitchhiker," it concerns a woman who returns from the grave each year on the anniversary of her death, hitches a ride with some motorist, and then disappears.

Exercise 2

45
b

Eliminate comma splices and fused sentences by adding or changing punctuation, or by subordinating one part of the sentence to the other. Put a check after any sentences that are correctly punctuated.

1. Each year, someone leaves a rose and a bottle of cognac at the grave of Edgar Allan Poe on Poe's birthday, however, no one knows who the donor is.

2. On last night's news, the weatherforecaster predicted rain, the sports reporter interviewed tennis star Jennifer Capriati.

3. Regina felt that Mr. Talbot's teaching emphasized little that was of actual use, Kim thought he was an effective teacher who provided a great deal of useful knowledge.

4. Our air conditioner ran smoothly all summer, our neighbor's clattered and wobbled every time it came on.

5. In 1992, Johnny Carson left television after years of hosting the Tonight Show, and when Jay Leno took over, the show lost no ratings points during his first official week as host.

6. My mother's guitar playing is atrocious, luckily, her saxophone playing is very good.

7. The court's decisions satisfied neither of the litigants therefore, both sides are sure to continue to seek remedies.

8. Mrs. Burnett did not pick her daughter up from school yesterday her husband did.

9. Kevin took up juggling in his spare time, Derrick debated between watching television and playing billiards.

10. Nelson Mandela had been jailed for decades as a political prisoner by the South African government, he was seen as a threat to the apartheid system.

Exercise 3

Eliminate comma splices and fused sentences in the passage below.

We wear garments of East Indian origin our pajamas are made of cotton, a material that was first domesticated in India. The beds that most of us sleep on are built on a pattern that originated in ancient Persia, the eiderdown quilts that keep us warm were invented in Scandinavia. After awakening in the morning, we walk into the bathroom there we wash with soap, an invention of the ancient Gauls, we then dry ourselves with Turkish towels. Returning to the bedroom, we remove our clothes from a chair, which was invented in the Near East. We put on close-fitting garments, which derive their form from the skin clothing of Asiatic nomads, we fasten our clothes with buttons, which have been in existence since the close of the Stone Age.

Adapted from Ralph Linton's "One Hundred Per Cent American"

46 · The Sentence Fragment

A *fragment* is an incomplete sentence that has been punctuated as if it were a sentence. It either lacks a subject or a verb, or its subject and verb are part of a dependent clause.

The *causes* of fragments vary. Some occur because the writer is following the oral rather than the written code of punctuation, translating a prolonged or emphatic pause into a period. Fragments can result from the mistaken assumption that verbals have the same function as verbs. Still others stem from uncertainties about the role of subordinating conjunctions or the careless omission of a subject or verb.

Whatever the specific cause, fragments are confusing because a capital letter at the beginning of a group of words signals the reader that a complete sentence follows, and a period at the end of the word group indicates that the sentence with all its additions is over. When there is no complete sentence between the capital letter and the period, the reader must stop and decide what purpose these words serve. Are they part of a neighboring sentence? Are they meant to express an independent thought as a sentence? Are they part of a sentence not in the text, but in the writer's head?

46a Do not punctuate a modifying word, phrase, or clause as a sentence.

Fragments

Suddenly. The door opened. [fragment: adverb modifying the verb **opened**]

The best musician in the orchestra is the lead violinist. **Who practices six hours a day.** [fragment: relative clause modifying **violinist**]

After a two-week strike. The workers returned to their jobs. [fragment: prepositional phrase modifying the verb **returned**]

I couldn't study for my electrical engineering exam. **Because the lights went out.** [fragment: subordinate clause modifying the verb **couldn't study**]

46b Do not punctuate an appositive as a sentence.

Fragment

My cousin is a professional wrestler. **The winner of several championships.**

46c Do not confuse a verbal (a gerund, a participle, or an infinitive) with a verb.

Fragment

As we looked out the window, we saw a rabbit leaping across a ravine. **And a turtle plodding across the highway.** [fragment: a group of words with a subject, **turtle,** but no verb; **plodding** is a present participle]

**46
d**

46d Revise fragments.

After identifying a fragment, decide which of the following methods of revision best serves your purpose:

1. *If a fragment belongs in the preceding or following sentence, make it a part of that sentence by deleting the period or changing it to a comma.*

The best musician in the orchestra is the lead violinist, **who practices six hours a day.**

2. If you want a sentence to be a sentence in its own right, then change, delete, or add words to make it an independent clause.

The best musician in the orchestra is the lead violinist. **He practices six hours a day.**

Note: Skilled writers sometimes use a fragment purposefully for stylistic effect, as in the following excerpt from Gail Sheehy's book *Passages:*

Without warning, in the middle of my thirties, I had a breakdown of nerve. It never occurred to me that while winging along in my happiest and most productive stage, all of a sudden simply staying afloat would require a massive exertion of will. **Or of some power greater than will.**

This fragment is meaningful because the passage is about psychological fragmentation and because the lack of grammatical completeness calls attention to the "power greater than will." Functional fragments are rare, however, and inexperienced writers should strive for complete sentences until they are relatively certain of English syntax.

Exercise 1

In the examples below, underline each fragment and revise the sentence to eliminate the error. If there is no fragment, put a check after the sentence.

1. For many European explorers, America was El Dorado.

   The legendary city of gold.

2. Before making a difficult decision. I like to consider all

   my options.

3. I have tried hard to talk to my sister. And understand her.

4. The storyteller related an amusing tale about a hermit. Who did not enjoy living alone.

5. Lines began forming at 5:00 in the morning. Most people were disappointed, however, because all the remaining tickets for the U2 concert were sold within minutes after the box office opened.

6. The professor lectured on several characters from <u>The Canterbury Tales.</u> Giving particular emphasis to the Wife of Bath.

7. The Trojan War began. Because Paris stole Helen from her husband.

8. According to one noted author, under a government that imprisons any of its citizens unjustly. The only place for a just individual is a prison.

9. Prospective home buyers should have a good under-standing of their special needs before signing a contract. To avoid having to move in a year or two.

10. A family that has no hardships or problems can be found nowhere. Except on television.

Exercise 2

In the examples below, underline each fragment and revise the sentence to eliminate the error. If there is no fragment, put a check after the sentence.

1. Surely one of the greatest athletes in the world today is Jackie Joyner-Kersee. Who for years has dominated her competition in the demanding heptathlon and long-jump events of track and field.

2. After the launch, scientists found numerous defects in the lens of the extraordinarily expensive Hubble Space Telescope. A huge, orbiting platform that was supposed to view deep space from above the interference of the earth's atmosphere.

3. We stared at the Jackson Pollock painting. It was built with layers and layers of color streaks and looked different from every angle.

4. The intrepid explorer began to sink after she stood on a patch of moist ground. Which she realized too late was quicksand.

5. The Amazon rainforest, the largest in the world, is being depleted by timber cutting, farming, and mining. And may be gone within a decade or two, leaving no hope of survival for thousands of rare animal species.

6. The Venus flytrap snapped shut. Around a squirming insect.

7. I do not want to go to the mall today. Because I am reading a great book and I want to finish it.

8. After fixing an exotic meal of Afghan food, my roommate made me wash the dishes because, he said, such was the Afghan custom.

9. My friends and I rented <u>Sewer Wombat Massacre IV: The Annihilation</u>. The worst movie ever made, in our opinion.

10. On Wednesday, I babysat for some kids. Who were playing with Teenage Mutant Ninja Turtle dolls when I arrived.

46
d

Exercise 3

In the following passage, revise each fragment by changing or deleting punctuation or by making the fragment a sentence.

Advertisers use many different strategies to persuade the public to buy new cars. One company proclaims that its cars are works of classic grace and beauty. Sleek and elegant. Another manufacturer emphasizes comfort. Extolling the plush carpeting and leather upholstery. According to the ads, these cars making a pleasure cruise out of the longest and most boring drive. A third firm asserts that its luxury cars are so well engineered they last indefinitely. And operate at peak efficiency without regular maintenance. I have pondered these claims all morning. While waiting to get my own new car out of the shop.

47

47 · Nonparallel Constructions

A *nonparallel construction* is one in which sentence elements of unequal grammatical rank are joined in a compound or series.

47a Be alert to the possibility of nonparallel constructions in compounds and series in which the connective is a coordinating conjunction (*and, but, for, or, nor, so, yet*).

Nonparallel constructions

1. **The house was old,** but **its foundation being solid.**
2. The sun was **bright** and **with intensity.**
3. My chemistry professor is someone **with a photographic memory** and **who also has a dynamic personality.**
4. The porch was littered with **faded newspapers, old clothes,** and **it had broken glass.**

The writers of these sentences seem to be either unable to recognize that an imbalance exists or unaware of its adverse effect on readers. In sentence #1, the comma and the coordinating conjunction **but** immediately following the first independent clause prepare us for a second independent clause. But the expected pattern breaks down at the point where the writer uses the verbal **being** instead of the anticipated past tense verb **was.** Similarly, the **and** after **bright** in sentence #2 seems to forecast another one-word adjective, but instead we find a prepositional phrase (**with intensity**). The relative clause (**who also has a dynamic personality**) at the end of the third sentence also comes as a surprise because the words on the other side of the coordinator—**with a photographic memory**—alert us to look for a second prepositional phrase or another object of the preposition **with.** The third element of the series at the end of sentence #4 frustrates our expectations in much the same way because the clause **it had broken glass** is inconsistent with the adjective-noun pattern established by the first two items, **faded newspapers** and **old clothes.**

47
a

If you compare these sentences with the revised versions below, you can see how parallel structure adds coherence.

independent clause   independent clause
The house was old, but **its foundation was solid.**

        adjective   adjective
The sun was **bright** and **intense.**

                                    adjective-noun
My chemistry professor is someone with a **photographic memory**
        adjective-noun
and a **dynamic personality.**

                              adjective-noun   adjective-noun
The porch was littered with **faded newspapers, old clothes,** and
adjective-noun
broken glass.

47b Whenever you use correlative conjunctions such as *either . . . or, neither . . . nor, both . . . and, not only . . . but also,* place them so that the words following them are parallel.

Nonparallel constructions

I will **either** take a bus **or** a cab.

The speaker **both** addressed the members of the press corps **and** millions of television viewers.

In the first sentence, we expect the words following **or** to have the same grammatical form as the words following **either,** but **take a bus** is a verb phrase and **cab** is a noun. There is a similar imbalance in the second sentence, where the writer attempts to connect a verb phrase (**addressed the members of the press corps**) with a noun plus a prepositional phrase (**millions of television viewers**).

In both sentences, a slight shift in the position of the first conjunction would eliminate the problem.

noun   noun
I will take **either** a bus **or** a cab.

noun + prepositional phrase
The speaker addressed **both** the members of the press corps **and**
noun + prepositional phrase
millions of television viewers.

Exercise 1

In the following sentences, eliminate nonparallel constructions by adding, changing, deleting, or shifting words. If no revision is required, put a check after the sentence.

1. After the initiation ceremony, the pledges were shown a movie about the club's role in the community, its social activities, and presented with a club pin.

2. The agent's mission was to seek out and the destruction of secret documents.

3. The philospher not only commanded respect from his followers but also from his opponents.

47
b

4. The star of the drama performed her part with grace and showed style.

5. The castle was ancient but still having great majesty.

6. Having reviewed all the available evidence, the jury decided the defendant neither had motive nor opportunity to commit the crime of which he was accused.

7. The accountant performed her job quietly and with efficiency.

8. Worried and having doubts, the job applicant paced the waiting room floor.

9. The university research team studied the environmental effects of coastal development but refusing to release the results to the media.

10. The personal director had a reputation for being critical but fair.

Exercise 2

Revise the following paragraph to eliminate nonparallel constructions.

The day was warm and the waves being perfect, so the water was crowded with surfers. There were short surfers and tall surfers, male surfers and female surfers, and surfers who were old and surfers who were young. They all had one common goal, however: seeking that "perfect ride" of surfer lore. Nothing kept these enthusiasts from careening wildly down every wave they could catch, bodies plunging and the surfboards would sail. Foolhardy swimmers both had to watch for people and fiberglass. When the last ray of sunlight disappeared, the surfers disappeared also, exhausted but having a feeling of exhilaration.

VI

Eliminating Spelling Problems

48 · Spelling

48a Understand the nature of English spelling.

English suffers the reputation of having a difficult, even capricious, spelling system. Writers sometimes despair over the different ways particular sounds are spelled. The **f** sound, for example, can be spelled **f, ph,** or **gh.** Why, we might wonder, can we not simply write **fone** instead of **phone** and **ruf** instead of **rough?**

The reason for our rather complex spelling system is that written English reflects more than a sound-symbol relationship. A word's spelling also carries information about smaller units of meaning within it, about families of words to which it is related, about its history in the language, and about its grammatical role in the sentence.

Phone, for example, relates to the family of words derived from the Greek word for "sound," which the Greeks spelled with their letter called "phi." **Rough** comes from the Anglo-Saxon word which ended in a guttural **gh** sound unlike today's **f** sound. We write **forebode** instead of **forbode** because **fore,** an Old English prefix, communicates the idea of **before**hand. Writing **health** instead of **helth** keeps the root word **heal** intact for the reader.

If English words were spelled strictly according to sound, we would lose such extra information. Indeed, a purely phonetic spelling system would make English more difficult to read. In such a system, for example, we might spell **huts** as we do now, but **hubs** might be spelled **hubz.** Our current system assures readers that they need only perceive **s** or **es** at the end of the vast majority of English nouns to understand that the nouns are plural. Plural **s** is thus a grammatical sig-

**48
a**

nal to the eye as well as a signal of sound for the ear. Like-wise **ed** in regular verbs signals past time regardless of the sound; so we write **heaped, arched,** and **peeked** rather than **heapt, archt,** and **peekt.** (Irregular verbs depart from this pattern, but often do so in systematic ways: **sleep-slept, keep-kept,** etc.)

48b Use special techniques for learning spelling.

Research has shown that good spellers tend to apply knowledge acquired by seeing and understanding words in meaningful contexts. In fact, alert experience with written English discourse seems to be the most powerful teacher of spelling. By being alert to words as you read and write, you naturally develop a feel for the systematic nature of English spelling. When you do encounter trouble with spelling, therefore, you will want to exploit learning strategies that most efficiently increase your understanding of how a word's letter pattern is systematic and meaningful. The techniques below can be helpful in learning to spell words difficult for you.

1. *Study the word in a context that suggests its meaning.* If you have time, write the word in several sentences.

My **intelligence** will help me learn.

Cats have less **intelligence** than dogs.

Intelligence is influenced by environment.

2. *Relate the word to other words having the same spelling pattern.* Try to remember the word as a member of a group.

-ence words

intellig**ence**
differ**ence**
perman**ence**
refer**ence**

**48
b**

The criteria you develop for classifying a word group can be any that help you see a consistency.

Words with short i after double consonant

inte**ll**igence
i**rr**itable
mi**ss**ile
i**mm**igrant

3. *Identify meaningful word parts.* Use a dictionary that gives etymologies (word histories). Study the way the word itself imparts meaning.

The verb **persevere** is composed of **per,** a prefix meaning "thoroughly," and **severe,** which as an adjective means "strict, stern, serious." The verb means to remain seriously committed to a goal. Note that **persevere** fits in an **-ere** spelling group: **revere, atmosphere, interfere, adhere.**

The noun **repetition** is composed of the prefix **re** meaning "again," the suffix **-ion** meaning "the act of," and a root from the Latin word **petitius** meaning "gone toward." The word parts add up to the meaning "the act of going to something again," which relates to the modern meaning of the word, "the act of doing something again." Note also that **repetition** is related in spelling and meaning to **petition.**

4. *Pronounce the word accurately.* In conversation we sometimes drop syllables from words, pronouncing "accidently," "probly," and "temperture." If you misspell such words as you pronounce them conversationally, you should study them by learning the pronunciation given in a dictionary. The words below are among those frequently misspelled because of faulty pronunciation.

accidentally	government
athlete	laboratory
chocolate	library
disastrous	lightning

probably	temperature
strictly	umbrella

5. *Use memory aids.*   You can learn some pesky words by making especially memorable associations. These memory aids will be most effective if you think up the associations yourself. Some examples are given below.

The princi**PAL** is my **PAL.**

On station**E**ry we find l**E**tt**E**rs.

Old **AGE** is a tr**AGE**dy.

Weak gram**MAR MAR**s my speech.

He was persis**TEN**t **TEN** times in **TEN** days.

Bury all your **E**'s in a c**E**m**E**t**E**ry.

48c Learn those spelling rules pertinent to the problems you may have.

1. *Prefixes.*   Adding a prefix to a word does not change the spelling of the word.

mis + spell = misspell

pre + fabricate = prefabricate

un + necessary = unnecessary

Prefixes sometimes require hyphens: **K-car, anti-hero, de-emphasize.** See Chapter **33** for hyphen conventions.

2. **ie** *and* **ei.**   The rule is **i** before **e** (fr**ie**nd, rel**ie**ve) except after **c** (rec**ei**ve, c**ei**ling) and when the sound is **a** (sl**ei**gh,

ei**ther**	h**ei**ght	s**ei**ze
for**ei**gn	l**ei**sure	w**ei**rd
forf**ei**t	sh**ei**k	

48
c

3. *Suffixes and final consonants.* Some types of words ending in a consonant double the final consonant when a suffix (a word ending) is added, and some types do not. No words ending in **c** (frolic) or **x** (fix) double the final consonant. When the word is one syllable long and a single vowel precedes any final consonant (except **c** and **x**), *double* the final consonant.

jab—ja**bb**ed
p**u**t—pu**tt**ing
h**o**t—ho**tt**er

When the word is one syllable long and either a pair of vowels or a vowel and a consonant precede the final consonant, *do not double* the final consonant.

p**ea**led—pealed   l**if**t—lifting
h**ur**t—hurting   l**ea**k—leaking
l**oo**k—looking   h**ow**l—howling
Exception: **real**—rea**ll**y

When the word is two or more syllables long, *double* the final consonant *if* one vowel precedes the final consonant *and if* after the suffix is added the last syllable of the root word is stressed.

handi**cap**—handica**pp**ed
be**gin**—begi**nn**er
dis**pel**—dispe**ll**ing

When the word is, two or more syllables long, *do not double* the final consonant *if* more than one vowel or a vowel and another consonant precede the final consonant (app**ear**—appearing; res**ort**—resorting). Do not double the final consonant *if* after the suffix is added the last syllable of the root word is *not* stressed (p**ar**don—pardoned).

re**join**—rejoined
ent**reat**—entreating
m**ar**ket—marketing

4. *Suffixes and final* **e.** Some words ending in a *silent* (unsounded) **e** drop the **e** before a suffix, and some words keep the **e.** If the suffix begins with a vowel, drop the **e.**

rise—ri**s**ing
measure—measu**r**ing (but, of course, measur**ed**)

Sometimes silent **e** is retained before a vowel to help in word recognition and pronunciation.

mil**e**—mil**ea**ge (instead of milage)

Words ending in **ce** and **ge** usually keep silent **e** to retain the soft **c** and **g** pronunciation.

courage—coura**geou**s
peace—pea**cea**ble
knowledge—knowled**gea**ble
change—chan**gea**ble (but changing)
dance—dan**cea**ble (but dancing)

If the suffix begins with a consonant, keep the **e.**

disgrace—disgrac**ef**ul
endorse—endors**em**ent
moderate—moderat**ely**

But sometimes when preceded by a vowel, silent **e** is dropped before a suffix beginning with a consonant.

arg**ue**—arg**um**ent
tr**ue**—tr**ul**y

5. *Final* **y.** Most words ending in **y** preceded by a consonant change the **y** to **i** before all suffixes except the possessive **'s,** suffixes beginning in **i,** and the suffixes **-like** and **-ship.**

dut**y**—dut**i**es—dut**i**ful
likel**y**—likel**i**hood
def**y**—def**i**ant—def**y**ing (**y** kept before **ing**)
somebod**y**—somebod**y's** (**y** kept before **'s**)
librar**y**like (**y** kept before **like**)

Most words ending in **y** preceded by a vowel do *not* change the **y** before any suffix.

conv**oy**—conv**oy**ing
depl**oy**—depl**oy**ing
gr**ay**—gr**ay**ing—gr**ay**ness

Some exceptions are d**ay**—d**ai**ly, l**ay**—l**ai**d, p**ay**—p**ai**d.

6. *Plurals.*   Most nouns are made plural by adding **s** to the singular form.

election**s**	studio**s**
pipe**s**	visit**s**
ring**s**	

Nouns ending in **s, z, x, ch,** or **sh** are made plural by adding **es.**

bu**ses**	bun**ches**
buz**zes**	bu**shes**
bo**xes**	

Most nouns ending in **o** preceded by a consonant add **es** in the plural.

buffa**loes**
he**roes**
toma**toes**

But some nouns ending in **o** preceded by a consonant add only **s.**

e**gos**
pia**nos**
t**wos**

Some nouns ending in **f** or **fe** are made plural by changing the **f** or **fe** to **ves.**

calf—cal**ves**
kni**fe**—kni**ves**

Nouns ending in **y** preceded by a consonant are made plural
by changing the **y** to **i** and adding **es.**

ar**my**—arm**ies**
ba**by**—bab**ies**
s**ky**—sk**ies**

But nouns ending in **y** preceded by a vowel simply add **s.**

b**oy**—boy**s**
k**ey**—key**s**

When a compound term is made up of two nouns, the plural
is formed on the last noun.

book club**s**
city-state**s**
fairground**s**

When a compound term is made up of a noun and another
part of speech, the noun is made plural whatever its position
in the term.

mother**s**-in-law
runner**s**-up

Vowel changes signal some plurals.

m**a**n—m**e**n
g**oo**se—g**ee**se

Some nouns retain their Latin, Greek, French, and Italian
forms in the singular and plural.

datum—data (Latin)
medium—media (Latin)
analysis—analyses (Greek)
beau—beaux (French)
bambino—bambini (Italian)

48d Learn to distinguish homonyms.

Homonyms are words that sound alike but are spelled differently and have different denotations (e.g., **here** and **hear**). Like tense and number markers (**ed** and **s**), homonyms are examples of how the visual appearance of a word can be as important as the sounds it represents. To learn to spell homonyms, you must be sure of the meaning of each similar word and then use an effective study strategy. Below is a list of commonly confused homonyms and near homonyms.

accept (to receive)
except (to leave out)

affect (concerning feelings)
effect (concerning results)

all ready (prepared)
already (previously)

ascent (a rising)
assent (to agree)

brake (to cause to slow down)
break (to shatter)

capital (the city that is the seat of government)
capitol (a legislative building)

censor (to delete or forbid)
censure (to rebuke)

cite (to specify)
sight (vision)
site (a place)

coarse (rough)
course (a direction)

complement (to improve or reinforce)
compliment (to praise)

descent (a going down)
dissent (to disagree)

48
d

desért (to abandon)
désert (an arid area)
dessert (the last course of a meal)

discreet (secretive)
discrete (separate)

elicit (to draw forth)
illicit (illegal)

emigrate (to move away from a country)
immigrate (to move to a country)

ensure (to make certain)
insure (to guarantee)

formally (in a formal way)
formerly (previously)

loose (not tight)
lose (to suffer defeat)

persecute (to harass)
prosecute (to bring legal action)

principal (of prime importance or head of a school)
principle (a basic law)

stationary (still)
stationery (writing paper)

strait (a narrow passage)
straight (not curved)

to (toward)
too (also)
two (sum of one plus one)

waist (a body part)
waste (to use without benefit)

weather (atmospheric conditions)
whether (a conjunction)

48
d

Exercise

Using the guidelines in this chapter plus a dictionary, proofread each of the following paragraphs and correct any misspelled words.

1. For years, I was an only child. Then, all of a sudden their
   was a new baby on the sene geting all the attention.
   Eventualy, I learned to except the fact that he was small
   and helpless and needed constant care. I changed him,
   fed him, washed him, and played with him. Within a
   short time, I became almost like a second mother, and
   when my parents divorsed several years later, I took over
   the father's role to.

2. Reading is one of the tresures of existeance, a rich fruit of
   life. Most people begin at an early age and continue untill
   their dieing days. But some foolish people use it only to
   get through school and then cast it aside as dead wieght.
   This truely is a tradgedy.

3. All my life, I have been unlucky. So it was with considerable reluctance that I accepted my first blind date. My
   worst fears were soon realized. When I first met my date,

**48
d**

I was so nervous that I missed the step onto the sidewalk and almost fell on my face. We both laughed, which helped to lesson the tension for the moment, but my bad luck came back to haunt me at the restrant where we went for diner. I was undecided about what to order and got so caught up in reading my menu that I didn't hear the waitress ask me what I wanted. When I realised that she was standing there waiting for me to answer, I just blurted out, "I'll have gravy." When I realized that everyone seated around us was stareing at me, I was so embarased that I felt like crawling under the table.

VII

Writing for Special Purposes

49 · Writing About Literature

Writing that deals with literary subjects is almost always analytical or argumentative. Its purpose is not merely to summarize the surface details of a work but to explore some aspect of its meaning or artistry that would not be apparent to the casual reader.

49a Employ critical reading skills.

To write effectively about literature, you must read analytically. When you read analytically, you ask and tentatively answer questions that help you see beyond the literal circumstances of the story, play, or poem you are examining. You may ask some general questions about any work of literature, and you will ask others about the particular genres of fiction, drama, or poetry.

General questions

1. *What is the relationship between the title and the work itself?* The title can be a valuable aid to interpretation because it usually identifies the central character, situation, or subject—the general issue with which the work is concerned (e.g., love, fate, pride, etc.). It may also foreshadow the outcome or introduce a key image or symbol that is repeated throughout the work.

2. *What are the tone and theme of the work?* Tone (the author's attitude toward the subject) and theme (an underlying meaning that readers construe from the total work) are integrally related concepts. When analyzing tone of fiction and poetry, first think of the word or words that best express what you consider the *narrator's* or *persona's* attitude toward the subject (e.g., skeptical, condescending, sympathetic,

49
a

questioning, etc.). Then judge whether the values suggested by the work as a whole support or contradict the narrator's attitude. Remember that the speaker of the story or the poem may have different values than the author.

Because drama rarely uses a narrator, you must determine the tone from the nature of the characters and from what happens to them. In fact, the good or ill that befalls characters in any genre has significance only in terms of the character's values and motives.

3. *How was the work influenced by the context within which it was produced?* Consider the historical era during which the writer lived as well as the writer's gender, ethnic identification, social class, and political orientation. These factors typically influence a writer's choice of subject and attitude toward the subject.

Questions for reading fiction

1. *Who tells the story?* Although your immediate instinct may be to say "the author," the question and the answer are more complex than they at first appear. In some novels and short stories, especially those told from the third person point of view, the author and the narrator are indeed difficult to distinguish. But in others, particularly first person narratives, the voice the reader hears is that of a fictional character who may look, think, and act very differently from the author. A writer may even choose to tell a story from the vantage point of someone whose statements and judgments are so obviously unreliable that the reader cannot accept at face value anything the narrator says.

2. *What events comprise the plot or action of the story, and what is the significance of this narrative structure?* In a traditional plot, the action begins at a certain point, builds through a series of conflicts or complications to a climax, then diminishes in intensity, and finally comes to a resolution. It would be a mistake, however, to expect this type of narrative

**49
a**

structure in every story or to find fault with an author for varying from the traditional pattern, for there are many artistically satisfying ways to tell a story. The writer may shift back and forth in time rather than proceeding chronologically, explore the consciousness rather than the actions of a character, or even abandon the conventions of plot altogether by presenting incidents in disconnected fashion. Although plot is seldom the center of interest in a serious work of fiction, it nonetheless deserves thoughtful analysis because it is both a means of characterization and a vehicle for developing theme.

3. *What are the distinctive traits of the characters and what problems do they face?* Judgments about characters should take into account not only what the narrator says about them but also what they say about one another, what they reveal about themselves through words and actions, and what conflicts they are involved in. When analyzing conflict, keep in mind that characters may be pitted against environmental, social, or psychological forces as well as against other human beings.

4. *What is the setting and why is it significant?* To answer the first part of this question, look for specific indications of time and place: dates, references to season or time of day, allusions to historical events or other contextual details, the names of cities, countries, or geographical regions, and so on. The results of this analysis, together with a close examination of other details, will help you decide whether the setting is merely a backdrop for the action or whether it plays a more significant symbolic or thematic role.

Questions for reading drama

Most of the questions we raise about fiction are relevant to the study of drama. For example, in writing an essay about a play, you would find the fiction questions about plot structure, character traits, and setting (and the general question of theme) all very useful. Keep in mind, however, that in a play, no one tells the story as a fiction narrator does. Instead, the dramatist withdraws from the action, allowing the characters to speak for themselves. Because dramas are meant to be produced on stage, your analysis must take into account the way a performance looks and sounds.

1. *What is the appearance of the stage?*   If you have only the script of the play to study, you must imagine how the play would be staged for a performance. Pay special attention, therefore, to stage directions and to the way characters describe each other and the setting. By indicating what the stage sets look like and specifying how and when special effects such as lighting, music, props, and other theatrical devices should be used, stage directions can help you imaginatively recreate the play. If you have the opportunity to see a production of the play, take careful note of how the script has been translated into a performance.

The sights and sounds of a play have significance beyond their surface appearance. For example, harsh lighting on a set showing a few shabby furnishings might suggest the characters' poverty and alienation; a subsequent shift toward softer lighting might suggest a shift in the material status or psychological condition of the characters.

2. *How do characters look, move, and sound?*   Stage directions may also indicate when and where characters should enter or leave the stage, where they should stand in relation to one another, and even how they should speak their lines. To imaginatively recreate a production, you must envision the actors moving, gesturing, speaking, and portraying emotions. Also interpret the motives of the characters and any changes in motives. Understanding the reasons for a character's behavior is crucial to understanding the play as a whole.

3. *How is the play structured?*   Playwrights conventionally segment their dramas into acts and scenes so they can focus audience attention on those events essential to convey plot

49
a

and character. The end of a scene signals a shift in time or space. As acts and scenes follow one another, the audience can discern significant patterns of actions and consequences.

4. *What is the plot of the play?* Plot is the backbone of all that occurs in the play. Once you imaginatively enter the world of the play, you will want to know from moment to moment what will happen next. When the play ends and you find out the last answer to that question, you can deepen your understanding of the drama by reflecting on the plot: What conflicts generate the plot? What are the outcomes of the conflicts? What is significant about the outcomes? To answer this last question you should reconsider prior questions, especially those about characters' motives. The success or failure of a character is significant in terms of the values he or she represents.

Questions for reading poetry

1. *Who is the speaker (persona)?* To identify the speaker of the poem, notice the title and look for any other details that aid in identification. Note particularly the pronoun references (**8d**). First person pronouns not enclosed within direct quotations usually identify the speaker. If there are no first person pronouns, note details that indicate whether or not the voice of the persona is similar to the poet's. If the speaker is not fully described, the poet may be focusing directly on the subject, on an interpretation of it, or on the audience. Sometimes a poem has more than one speaker. Look for quotation marks and other indications that distinguish one speaker's words from another's.

2. *Who is the speaker's audience?* Second person pronouns often indicate the audience, but you must determine whether the persona is addressing the reader directly or a listener within the poem. If there are no second person pronouns, you can assume the persona is addressing you, the reader. What attitude toward the audience does the speaker have?

3. *What situation does the poem portray?* To envision the situation (e.g., a funeral, a sports event, a domestic scene), note signals of time, place, and events. The absence of these signals suggests that readers may construe their own specific situations or should leave specifics of time and place vague.

4. *What is the poem's structure?* Poems have both a thematic structure (pattern based on meaning) and a formal structure (pattern based on the rhythm and sound of words). To determine the thematic structure, notice whether the poem tells a story (narrative), analyzes or explains an idea (expository), presents an argument, or simply paints a picture (descriptive). To determine the formal structure, notice whether the poem has a consistent meter, rhyme scheme, and stanza pattern. Note how the structural features advance the thoughts and feelings of the poem.

5. *How does the poem sound when read aloud?* As you read a poem aloud for the first time, listen to the sound of the words and the natural cadences of the lines. Then reread the poem, this time with an eye and ear to the details of sound and meaning. If, during your reading, you were aware of vowel repetitions (assonance) or consonant repetitions (alliteration and consonance), notice whether any pattern takes shape. You may find that sound correspondences link key ideas, call attention to important words, or arouse pleasant or repellent associations.

6. *What use does the poet make of imagery, figurative language, and symbols?* Imagery appeals to our senses, figurative language renders new meaning by linking two subjects not usually associated, and symbols take on significance within the context of the poem. Although prose writers and dramatists also make use of these devices, they are particularly important to poets because poetry is such a condensed medium. As you read a poem, pause to consider the sensations its words evoke and how these sensations affect your response to the poem's subject. Be alert to signals of

49
a

figurative language, such as the words "like" or "as," words giving human characteristics to nonhuman phenomena, and words that explicitly equate unlike things, such as the flight of a bird and the passage of time. Watch also for particular images that seem unusually prominent, that act as symbols representing a complex of meaning beyond what you can explain by a literal reading. For example, in the context of a poem, the image of birds migrating might symbolize dying.

49b Decide on a topic and a critical approach.

By the time you complete your analytical reading, you should have sufficient knowledge of the work to decide on a topic and a perspective from which to approach it. Here are just a few of the many options available to you:

1. *Decide what the tone or theme of the work is, and write an essay in which you present and analyze the evidence that supports your interpretation.*

Sample topics

Irony in *Desire Under the Elms*

The theme of lost innocence in Gerard Manley Hopkins's "Spring and Fall: To a Young Child"

2. *Explain the purpose and meaning of one of the literary elements you examined in your critical reading of the work.*

Sample topics

The symbolism of the letter *A* in Hawthorne's *The Scarlet Letter*

The role of figurative language in Langston Hughes's "Dream Deferred"

3. *Write an essay that explains the relationship between a part of a work and the whole.*

Sample topics

The drunken porter scene in *Macbeth*

The flawed ending of *Huckleberry Finn*

If your assignment requires you to examine more than one work or to investigate secondary sources (e.g., critical articles and books, biographies, literary histories, etc.), the number of options increases.

4. *Place the work in its biographical, social, historical, or social context.*

Sample topics

Emerson's attitudes toward abolitionism

Social realism in Kate Chopin's *The Awakening*

5. *Approach the work from the perspective of another discipline, such as psychology, philosophy, the physical sciences, or fine arts.*

Sample topics

A Freudian interpretation of *Death of a Salesman*

The role of music in Wallace Stevens's "Peter Quince at the Clavier"

6. *Compare two or more works on the basis of theme, tone, or technique.*

Sample topics

Conflicting views of death in Emily Dickinson's "Because I Could Not Stop for Death" and "I Heard a Fly Buzz"

The concept of honor in Hemingway's *A Farewell to Arms* and Heller's *Catch 22*

49c Formulate and develop a thesis.

Once you have settled on a topic and a critical approach, formulate a thesis statement that will enable you to analyze and interpret some significant but limited aspect of the topic.

Thesis statement

The letter *A* in Hawthorne's *The Scarlet Letter* is a complex symbol that signifies not only adultery but also ableness, angelhood, and Arthur, the name of Hester's lover. [Topic: The symbolism of the letter *A* in Hawthorne's *The Scarlet Letter*]

The ending of *Huckleberry Finn* is flawed because it is disproportionately long, unrealistic, and inconsistent with the events leading up to it. [Topic: The flawed ending of *Huckleberry Finn*]

If your thesis is precise and restricted, as in the examples above, it will both suggest a plan of organization and guide your selection of supporting examples. To support your thesis, you will want to quote from the text and summarize portions of the work. Your composition should not, however, be merely a string of quotes and summaries. Rather, it should communicate your understanding of the work as a whole and your interpretation of the specific details you cite.

49d Sample essay with preliminary notes

The following essay and the notes on which it was based represent one student's response to a critical reading and writing assignment for a college composition class. Using procedures similar to the ones discussed in the preceding sections of this chapter, the writer began by reading several poems in the class text; raising questions about speaker, audience, situation, structure, language, context, and other aspects of literature; and making marginal notations. When he had finished, he reread the poems and his notes in an effort to find the work and topic he wanted to write about.

The poem he eventually decided on was Amy Lowell's "The Taxi," which he had annotated in the manner shown on page 377.

As the student restudied the poem and his responses to it, he made several important discoveries: (1) Most of his comments were concerned with imagery. (2) The images he

The Taxi

Speaker is the person leaving (or about to leave) in a taxi

Title refers to the type of vehicle we usually associate with travel to airports, railroad depots, bus terminals, etc.

Auditory imagery —
Speaker's entire world at this moment described in terms of the dead, muffled, inharmonious sound of a slackened drum

When (I) go away from <u>you</u>
The world beats dead
Like a slackened drum.
(I) call out for you against the jutted stars,
And shout into the ridges of the wind.
Streets coming fast,
One after the other
Wedge <u>you</u> away from me,
And the lamps of the city prick (my) eyes
So that (I) can no longer see your face.
Why should (I) leave you,
To wound (myself) upon the sharp edges of the night?

Sound again important ("call out," "shout") Also visual and tactile images ("jutted stars," "ridges of the wind") emphasize futility of effort to communicate

Images of sight, touch, movement — creates sense of panic, emptiness, pain

Night pictured as something threatening — with "sharp edges" that can wound

Structure — Four sentences. Each seems to treat a different aspect of her emotional state.

tone — Generally one of depression and despair — though the question at the end suggests that the speaker may have some control over the situation — separation may not be inevitable.

theme — Separation from a loved one can create deep emotional disturbance that affects perceptions of everything else.

had identified all seemed related to the speaker's thoughts and feelings. (3) The patterns of imagery in the four sentences comprising the poem each revealed a different emotional dimension.

At this point, the writer was able to formulate a thesis (see the final sentence of the introductory paragraph in the sample essay), devise a plan of organization (a sentence-by-sentence analysis of imagistic language and its emotional

49
d

overtones), and write the first draft of his paper. Later, he revised and edited the paper and submitted the version below for evaluation.

Sample paper

Imagery in "The Taxi"

In "The Taxi," Amy Lowell explores the thoughts and feelings of a person who is attempting to cope with the reality of being separated from a loved one. We can't tell whether the speaker is talking directly to the unnamed "you" of the poem or addressing this individual imaginatively while traveling in a taxi toward some unspecified destination, but there can be no doubt of the speaker's emotional condition. For throughout the poem, Lowell uses vivid images to make us aware of this person's frustration and pain.

In the first three lines of the poem, the speaker's mood is one of extreme depression--a feeling that Lowell captures in the auditory imagery of lines 2 and 3: "The world beats dead/Like a slackened drum." A slackened drum is one on which the cover has been loosened, and in this condition it can produce only hollow, muffled sounds. The implication is that the speaker too feels empty and out of harmony with the external world.

In the second sentence (lines 4–5), the speaker calls out to the person left behind. The frustration remains, though, because there is no one to hear the words. The futility of this attempt at communication is reinforced by other images. The distant stars seem "jutted" and threatening, and the wind has "ridges" that shouts cannot penetrate.

In the third sentence (lines 6–10), the poem speeds up as the speaker becomes aware of the "Streets coming fast,/One after another." Images of motion ("coming fast," "Wedge you away from me") convey a sense of panic, which is soon replaced with even stronger emotions in lines 9 and 10: "And the lamps of the city prick my eyes/So that I can no longer see your face."

The poem slows down in the final sentence (lines 11–12). Here the speaker pauses to ask, "Why should I leave you . . . ?" but the last line brings the poem to a close as pessimistically as it began. For even the night seems a weapon with "sharp edges" capable of inflicting a "wound" on anyone who has experienced the pain of separation.

Exercise

Read the following poem carefully, and answer the questions that accompany it. When you have finished, choose one question that you consider especially interesting and important, formulate a thesis statement that answers it, and develop it into a short analytical essay.

Ozymandias

I met a traveller from an antique land
Who said: Two vast and trunkless legs of stone
Stand in the desert . . . Near them, on the sand,
Half sunk, a shattered visage lies, whose frown,
And wrinkled lip, and sneer of cold command,
Tell that its sculptor well those passions read
Which yet survive, stamped on these lifeless things,
The hand that mocked them, and the heart that fed:
And on the pedestal these words appear:
"My name is Ozymandias, king of kings:
Look on my works, ye Mighty, and despair!"
Nothing beside remains. Round the decay
Of that colossal wreck, boundless and bare
The lone and level sands stretch far away.

Percy Bysshe Shelley

Questions for Analysis

1. Who tells the story of Ozymandias and his statue? Is this account reported directly to the reader or related at second hand by someone else? What does Shelley accomplish by using this point of view?
2. What is the physical setting of lines 2–14, and why is it important?
3. Approximately how much time has elapsed between the traveler's discovery and the days of Ozymandias's kingship? What contrast between past and present does Shelley develop throughout this poem?

**49
d**

4. What was the nature of the relationship between Ozymandias and the sculptor? How did the sculptor make known his attitude toward the king? What is the evidence on which the traveler bases this inference?
5. What does the inscription on the pedestal of the statue reveal about Ozymandias's character and ambitions? Does the rest of the poem support or contradict the message carried by this inscription? Consider especially the condition of the statue at the time the traveler sees it, the particulars of the physical setting, and the effect of the repeated *b, l,* and *s* sounds in the last two lines.
6. What do your answers to the preceding questions suggest is the tone of the poem?
7. What comment does the poem make about the human dream of earthly immortality?

50 · Writing Answers for Essay Examinations

50a Objective tests and essay examinations

Objective tests ask students either to indicate a correct answer from among alternatives (as on multiple-choice and matching items) or to provide a correct answer in a phrase or a brief statement (as on fill-in and short-answer items). Because such tests require only simple marks or a few written words, they may treat a wide range of topics during a relatively short examination time, and they may be scored quickly and objectively. This efficiency makes objective exams a popular type of academic evaluation.

**50
a**

Often, however, college courses endeavor to increase students' ability to communicate at length using new knowledge. Such a goal is not served by tests requiring students simply to indicate a preestablished right answer. Only an *essay item* confronts students with an exam problem requiring them to recall pertinent information and to develop a coherent response. Such writing tasks are similar to those in professional service and commerce, fields which depend on people able to communicate quickly and accurately about problems.

You should respond to essay exam items as you would to other essay assignments, except, of course, you must be faster. Despite time constraints, therefore, you should undertake all stages of the writing process outlined in Chapter **1.** The one stage of the process students most often overlook is revision. Even if you have only a few moments, read over your essay answers not only to correct grammar and usage, but to strengthen points you have made and to add points you have omitted. College professors generally prefer to have significant information added between the lines and incorrect information scratched out than to have neatly written but incomplete answers.

50b Types of essay items

Most essay items involve one of the four types of tasks discussed below.

1. *Recalling knowledge.* This type of item requires the student to write down information in a form similar to previously expressed material. The material might be in a textbook, in class notes, or in a non-print medium such as film. The correct answers written by students would differ little from each other in wording. To do well on such an item you simply recall the information requested and organize it either

50
b

as it was originally given or as its points relate logically to one another.

Sample item

1. What type of people constituted the major social classes in the eighteenth-century American colonies and what values differentiated these classes?

A good answer to this question would be organized as a brief classification essay (see **4c**). The first paragraph might identify each social class and tell the type of people found in it; a second and final paragraph might describe the social values peculiar to each class. Or each paragraph in the essay might treat the people and values of a particular social class. Recall items do not request judgments or inferences; they simply request evidence that the student remembers the information.

2. *Demonstrating understanding.* Another type of item requests thought in addition to recall; students are asked to demonstrate comprehension of course content by interpreting it. Interpretation can involve translating content into your own words or inferring a main idea and its relationship to supporting details. Items that test comprehension may also ask you to discuss implications that are not expressed in the content but that follow directly from it.

Sample items

2. Paraphrase Shakespeare's description of aging in Sonnet 60, and explain what conclusion he draws from these observations.
3. Specify the intent of Section 3 of the Fourteenth Amendment to the US Constitution and the implicit justification for this intent.

Read such items carefully, paying special attention to the words identifying the approach you should take ("paraphrase," "specify") and to words giving the focus of the answer ("description," "conclusion," "intent," "justification").

A good answer to item #2 would translate Shakespeare's images of old age into original wording and would express the poet's conclusion that although passing time inevitably takes away all beauty, these verses written by the poet will preserve a record of his beloved's beauty for future generations.

A good answer to item #3 would explain that Amendment XIV, Section 3 pertains to former officials of the United States who have taken part in rebellion against the government. The answer would go on to draw the inferences that such individuals will have broken an oath they took upon becoming officials, and so Section 3 assumes they justly forfeit their right to hold office in the United States again.

3. *Analyzing.* Questions requiring comprehension or recall refer to course content as it may be interpreted or as it is given. Questions requiring you to apply your understanding by analyzing a topic refer to the content's structure (the relations between its parts). Recall and comprehension exam items specify the particular content you are to treat; you do not have to search your memory for relevant generalizations or evidence because the exam items either identify or provide the actual text of the content you are to treat (e.g., a sonnet or a government document). Analysis items, however, can pose problems requiring that you search your knowledge for information about a topic, select points relevant to the question, and establish a coherent relationship between the points. When an analysis problem does specify the content, it demands that you take a critical view of the way its parts relate to the whole. For example, instead of simply requesting a demonstration of understanding of Shakespeare's Sonnet 60 as in sample item #2, a question could request an analysis as follows: "Discuss how the images portrayed in Sonnet 60 help develop the poem's theme." To respond to this question, you must not only comprehend the images and the theme but also demonstrate how the images work together to

help communicate the theme of the effects of aging on the speaker's attitude toward his beloved.

Types of thinking commonly required by analysis are identifying and describing parts or features, comparing and contrasting subjects, tracing causes and effects, and explaining the principles or patterns according to which content is organized. Because analysis demands such extensive thought and careful exposition, be especially alert in planning your answer. The six-stage planning procedure recommended in **4a** can be particularly helpful.

Sample items

4. Contrast divergent and convergent problem solving.
5. Considering the text and history of Amendment XIV, Section 3 of the US Constitution, explain what the amendment's framers apparently hoped to achieve by its adoption.
6. Study the map given below. Note that features of rainfall, terrain, mineral resources, and natural vegetation are portrayed. Describe how the various geographical features would influence the economy of a community made up of people with iron-age skills.

A good answer to item #4 will exploit the principles of comparison given in **4c** (4). Most important, you should identify bases for comparing the two types of thinking; for example, you might contrast them according to differences in (a) the contexts of divergent and convergent problems, (b) the ways information is used in solving the two types of problems, and (c) the types of solutions that result.

Note that sample items #4 and #5 would require only recall if their answers were specified elsewhere in course materials. As an analysis item, #5 would require you to call up pertinent facts from history and to show how they explain the motives behind this section of the Constitution. You might note that Amendment XIV was proposed in 1866 and ratified in 1868, having originated in a US Congress embittered by four years of civil war. Certain members of Congress not only wanted to exclude former rebels from political office and to punish the old Southern power structure, they also wanted political power in the South for their own Republican Party. Thus they found it useful to disenfranchise the South's former leaders.

Item #6 would, of course, require you to apply your map-reading skills. You would also have to recall information about the type of agriculture and craft suitable to the geography depicted and to the technological level given for people living in the area. You would then incorporate your information in a description of the ways the various geographical features would influence the economy.

4. *Evaluating.* Questions asking students to evaluate content are relatively rare because the answers can be difficult to grade fairly, especially if the questions invite students to offer personal opinion. Sometimes, though, professors want you to demonstrate that you can apply criteria in describing the quality of something. Evaluative questions require you to explain such standards as how good or true or effective or valuable something is. The general criteria you are to apply will be stated in the question, which will specify whether you are to treat such notions as "goodness" or "effectiveness." To respond to this kind of question, you must first make specific criteria clear to yourself and then apply them systematically to the content to be evaluated.

Sample item

7. Explain why according to Lawrence Kohlberg one of the two adolescents described below would be acting on a higher level of morality than the other.

The general criterion requested in item #7 is degree of morality. The specific criteria are psychologist Kohlberg's descriptions of six stages of moral development. Your task would be to call up your understanding of these stages, analyze the behaviors in terms of them, and demonstrate the higher morality of one of the behaviors.

50
b

51 · Writing Business Letters

Business letters are written and read to help make transactions possible. Clear, direct, careful, grammatical letters
typed in a standard format increase the ease of transactions;
wordy, vague letters with nonstandard language written in a
format that does not conform to readers' expectations make
transactions more difficult.

51a Use standard block format.

The most obvious feature of a business letter is its format,
commonly called a *block format*. An example of a block format
letter with its parts labeled is given on page 387.

1. *Heading.* If you are using *letterhead paper* (stationery
with the name and address of a company or institution at the
top), the only entry for your heading should be the date; otherwise, include your mailing address.

2. *Inside address.* This should be identical to the address
on the envelope. Be sure to use an appropriate personal title
(**Mrs., Ms., Dr.**) and, if pertinent, the business title (**Director,
Treasurer**). If the business title is long (**Director of Research
Department**), you may put it under the person's name.

3. *Salutation.* The person's or firm's name in the salutation should agree with the name in the inside address. For
example, if the letter is addressed to **Dr. Carla Brown,** the
salutation should read **Dear Dr. Brown,** *not* **Dear Professor
Brown.** If the letter is addressed to a firm, repeat the firm's
name in the salutation: **Dear Sears, Roebuck and Company.**

4. *Body.* This is the letter's message. You may indent
the first line of each paragraph as you would in an essay, or

**51
a**

Sample business letter

10–15 spaces

Heading

324 River Road
Oak Grove, NJ 07014
January 10, 1994

4–8 spaces

Inside Address

Mr. Robert Williams, Director
Oak Grove Recreation Department
1101 15th Street
Oak Grove, NJ 07014

Salutation   **2 spaces**

Dear Mr. Williams:

1 space

Thank you for the Blue Springs Park schedule of events and
the guidelines for groups using city recreation facilities.

Body   **1 space**

Please reserve the open-air theater for the annual picnic
of the Oak Grove Little Theater on June 2 from 6:00 to
8:00 p.m. Our group will use the theater to present skits
and to make awards to actors and patrons of the 1992-93
season. We will not need any recreation department
equipment.

1 space

We are grateful for the opportunity to enjoy this facility,
and we gladly agree to abide by the guidelines for its use.

Complimentary Close   **1 space**

Sincerely,

Signature Block

Cecilia Rhodes   **4 spaces**

Cecilia Rhodes, Chairperson
Board of Directors
Oak Grove Little Theater

2 spaces

Enclosure List

Encl. Completed reservation form
      Signed contract

51
a

you may type the first line flush with the left margin as is common in business correspondence. In either case, you should single space within paragraphs and skip a line between each paragraph.

5. *Complimentary close.*   Capitalize only the first letter of the complimentary close and put a comma at the end:

Sincerely,   **Sincerely yours,**
Very truly yours,   **Best wishes for the holiday season,**
Best regards,

6. *Signature block.*   Your name, title, and the name of your department and organization should appear four spaces beneath the complimentary close. Omit the names of your organization and department if this information appears in a letterhead on your stationery. If you represent only yourself, put just your name in the signature block.

7. *Enclosure list.*   Two spaces below the signature block, list any materials you are sending with the letter. If these materials do not have titles on them, give them descriptive titles. The abbreviation **Encl.** precedes the list, and the enclosures are listed one per line to the right of **Encl.** In the example below, the first entry is the title printed at the top of an application form, and the second entry is the writer's description of a check.

Encl.   Application for Teacher Certification
Certified check for $30.00

51b Write in a direct, friendly style.

Remember that a business letter's main purpose is to make business easier to conduct. People become willing to do business if they feel a letter treats them as people, not as abstractions; if the letter seems to be written by an individual they might like to meet, not by a computer; and if the attitude of the writer is positive and understanding, not accusing or self-justifying.

You should, therefore, empathize with the recipient of your letter. How might the content affect someone in the position of your correspondent? Might the content worry, anger, or bore the person? The golden rule of correspondence is to write to others as you would have others write to you. Avoid putting your correspondent on the defensive even if you are frustrated. Instead of writing "Despite my last letter, you still seem confused," write "I believe this letter will make my point more clearly." Instead of writing "Your lack of co-operation has been discouraging," write "I look forward to our cooperation."

Business is also inhibited by letters that ramble or obscure the writer's intent. Get to the point immediately. Compare the wasted words in the first introductory paragraph with the direct appeal of the second introductory paragraph below.

Original

All of us in this department are busy, and surely you are no exception. Nevertheless, I hope you will take the time to consider the crucial needs of the United Fund.

Revised

The annual United Fund Drive, which begins next week, funds 24 charitable organizations in our community. Without the support of people such as you, these organizations would have to cease their work.

While succinctness is desirable for composition in general, it is essential for business correspondence. Pay special attention, therefore, to the strategies for concise writing in Chapter **16.**

Try to keep your letter to one page in length. The prohibition against one-sentence paragraphs common in freshman English courses does not apply in business; if you've made

**51
b**

your point in one sentence, go on to the next paragraph. In general, remember that succinctness, politeness, and straightforwardness are more than ethical matters in business; they can make the difference between doing and not doing business. These characteristics are illustrated in the letter on page 387.

52 · Preparing a Résumé

A résumé is a carefully arranged summary of a person's qualifications for employment. Usually it is mailed with a cover letter by an applicant who is responding to a job opening. Employers read over all the applications they receive and then decide which people to invite for interviews. Obviously, the more clearly your résumé communicates your qualifications, the greater your chances for employment.

Organize your résumé according to categories of information. The eight entries given below and illustrated in the sample on page 392 are generally suitable, but your entries should be tailored to your circumstances. One page is the length most welcomed by employers in business and industry.

1. *Give basic information to identify yourself.* Include name, school address (if appropriate), permanent address, and the phone numbers (with area codes) of both addresses.

2. *State your career objectives.* You might write one major objective or write short-range and long-range goals. Word them generally so you can use the same résumé for numerous job applications.

3. *Outline your educational background.* List your educational credentials chronologically, putting your most recent experiences first and your earliest experience last. Include only those details relevant to your career objective.

4. *Cite any honors you may have received at school.*

5. *Outline your work experience.* If you have been out of school for a few years, you may want to put work experience right after your objectives, especially if experience is a strong feature of your application. For each job include the title, the place, the dates, and a brief description of your accomplishments.

6. *List professional and extracurricular activities.* Specify organized activities that suggest your ability to help achieve group goals.

7. *List other interests and abilities that indicate an active involvement in the world at large.*

8. *Indicate at the end of your résumé that you will furnish the names of your references on request; there is no need to give the names themselves.*

With your résumé, send a cover letter that relates your qualifications to the particular job you are applying for. Your letter should be a business letter in style and format (Chapter **51**). It might open with a reference to how you came to learn of the company or the job. It should include a brief summary of your goals and qualifications most clearly relevant to employment with the firm. It should end with a statement of your availability for further contact with the company.

52

Sample résumé

MARTIN ALVAREZ

Permanent Address
1405 Crestline Blvd.
Oak Park, NJ 07012

School Address
992 Ripley Rd.
Fenner, NJ 07112

Professional Objective
  To become a successful manager of advertising and promotion.

Education
  B.B.A. Degree, Fenner State University, Fenner, NJ, May 1992;
    marketing major. Completed an invitational "Topics in
    Management" course, concentrating on marketing management.
    Average in major 3.4/4.0.
  High School Diploma, Oak Park H.S., Oak Park, NJ, June 1988.

Academic Honors
  Recipient during junior and senior years of Adele MacIntosh
    Scholarship administered by Fenner State University
    Scholarship Fund.
  Dean's List, Spring 1991 and Fall 1991.

Work Experience
  1991–present: First State Bank, Fenner, NJ. Teller (part
    time during academic year, full time during summer).
  1990–91: Passmore's Men's Shop, Oak Park, NJ. Salesperson
    and stock clerk (full time during summer).
  1987–90: Oak Park, NJ Recreation Department. Lifeguard (full
    time during summer).

University Activities
  Residence Hall Counselor, 1990–91, 1991–92. Duties involved
    supervising dormitory facilities and counseling
    resident students.
  Member FSU Racquetball Club.

Interests and Skills
  Racquetball, swimming, photography.
  Proficiency in Basic computer language.

References
  Available upon request.

Letter to accompany résumé

1405 Crestline Blvd.
Oak Park, NJ 07012
June 8, 1992

Mr. William B. Simpson
Highland Advertising Agency
4828 Market Road
Newark, NJ 07011

Dear Mr. Simpson:

Professor Fred Baker of the Fenner State University
School of Business has told me of a recent opening in
your firm. I am applying for this position.

Because the job involves soliciting and managing
advertising accounts, I feel especially qualified. In my
marketing studies, I have specialized in the design and
management of just such accounts. Furthermore, working
at the First State Bank in Fenner and at Passmore's Men's
Shop has given me practical experience in finance, record
keeping, and sales.

I am available for an interview at any time on a day's
notice. My telephone number is 609-555-2971.

Sincerely,

Martin Alvarez

Martin Alvarez

Enc. Résumé

52

VIII

Writing the Research Paper

53 · Guides for Library Research

53a Approaches to research

Research is a systematic process of exploration and discovery—a means of attaining new knowledge and gaining fresh insights to previously held beliefs. Thus, it is both an essential human activity and an indispensable scholarly tool.

Some research activities involve laboratory experimentation. Others require field investigations such as interviews, surveys, and observations of natural phenomena. Still others lead researchers into libraries and archives to explore published and unpublished sources of information.

Different types of research can be reported in different ways. Researchers in the physical and biological sciences usually depend on mathematic notation, tables, and charts as well as prose to present their findings. Psychologists, sociologists, and other social scientists also report quantitative results in tables and charts; like scientists, they often use prose to describe the processes of gathering data and the results of analysis of the data.

Scholars in the humanities, on the other hand, are usually more concerned with qualities than with quantities. Historians, literary critics, and philosophers use exposition and argument to propose insights usually derived from a search of written material. These researchers use prose less to describe than to interpret and judge.

Although specific methods may vary from one research activity to another, most nonexperimental research tasks will depend on these basic steps:

1. Choose a subject that interests you, and narrow it until it becomes a topic that you can investigate thoroughly and write about convincingly.

2. Find out what style of documentation is appropriate for this piece of research writing and familiarize yourself with the conventions for documenting sources and preparing a bibliography or list of works cited.

3. Use the resources in your college library to identify books, articles, and other materials pertaining to your topic.

4. Compile a preliminary bibliography of the sources referred to above.

5. Locate, read, and take notes on the sources listed in the preliminary bibliography.

6. Develop a thesis statement and outline based on the evidence you have accumulated.

7. Present results and conclusions in systematic, well-documented written form.

8. Prepare a list of works cited from the preliminary bibliography.

A survey of all types of research-based writing would far exceed the scope of this text. The chapters that follow will, however, introduce you to the fundamentals of library research—a form of scholarly investigation that is basic to all disciplines—and help you to develop the skills needed for one important kind of academic research writing, the documented essay usually referred to as a *research paper* or *term paper*.

Although some research topics require interviews, surveys, or the study of documents in off-campus archives, the center for most academic research is the college library. There you will find *primary sources* (examples of the actual subjects being investigated, such as literary works, letters, and the texts of speeches and interviews); *secondary sources* (biographies, scholarly books and monographs, periodical articles, and other works about the subject); and the various reference tools needed to identify and obtain these sources.

53b The library catalog

One indispensable research tool is the library catalog, which indexes all the books and bound periodicals in the library's collection. Most catalogs consist of a computer catalog, which indexes recent acquisitions, and a card catalog, which indexes earlier holdings. Each catalog is usually divided into three sections: (1) an author file, which contains entries for all books arranged alphabetically by author; (2) a title file, which consists of entries for all books and bound periodicals arranged alphabetically by title; and (3) a subject file, which includes entries for all books arranged alphabetically by subject. The entries in the library catalog provide several kinds of information that will aid you in your research:

1. A Library of Congress or Dewey Decimal System **call number** that indicates the exact location of the work in the library.

Sample Entries from Library Catalog

Card catalog: author entry

378.1981
W676a

      Williamson, Edmund Griffith, 1900–
        The American student's freedom of expression; a research appraisal, by E. G. Williamson and John L. Cowan, with the editorial collaboration of R. George Crawford and Virginia Willems. Minneapolis, University of Minnesota Press [1966]

        xi, 193 p.   illus.   24 cm.

      On cover: George Rockwell. Interracial marriage laws. Jail for C.O.'s. Petitions. Picketing. Martin Luther King. Censorship. Sit-ins.

      1. College students—U.S.—Political activity.   2. Liberty of speech. I. Cowan, John L., joint author.   II. Title.

LA229.W5   1966   378.19810973   66-29069

Library of Congress   [5]

Card catalog: title entry

378.1981   The American student's freedom of
W676a   expression.

Williamson, Edmund Griffith, 1900–
　　The American student's freedom of expression; a research
appraisal, by E. G. Williamson and John L. Cowan, with the
editorial collaboration of R. George Crawford and Virginia
Willems. Minneapolis, University of Minnesota Press [1966]

　　xi, 193 p.　illus.　24 cm.

　　On cover: George Rockwell. Interracial marriage laws. Jail for C.O.'s.
Petitions. Picketing. Martin Luther King. Censorship. Sit-ins.

　　　1. College students—U.S.—Political activity.　　2. Liberty of speech.
I. Cowan, John L., joint author.　　II. Title.

LA229.W5　1966　　　　378.19810973　　66-29069

Library of Congress　　　　　　　　[5]

Card catalog: subject entry

378.1981 Liberty of speech.
W676a

Williamson, Edmund Griffith, 1900–
　　The American student's freedom of expression; a research
appraisal, by E. G. Williamson and John L. Cowan, with the editorial collaboration of R. George Crawford and Virginia
Willems. Minneapolis, University of Minnesota Press [1966]

　　xi, 193 p.　illus.　24 cm.

　　On cover: George Rockwell. Interracial marriage laws. Jail for C.O.'s.
Petitions. Picketing. Martin Luther King. Censorship. Sit-ins.

　　　1. College students—U.S.—Political activity.　　2. Liberty of speech.
I. Cowan, John L., joint author.　　II. Title.

LA229.W5　1966　　　　378.19810973　　66-29069

Library of Congress　　　　　　　　[5]

**53
b**

2. Author, title, and publication data for the book.
3. Brief notes about the book's contents.
4. Cross-references to other headings under which each book is listed.

Computer catalog: opening screen

```
Enter the NUMBER of search you wish to perform
        1-By AUTHOR
        2-By TITLE
        3-By SUBJECT-TOPIC OR PLACE
        4-By SUBJECT-PERSON'S NAME
        5-By RESERVES-COURSE NUMBER/NAME
        6-By OTHER Searches

                OR

Enter a KEY WORD to see possible matches
Choice:  ___

Enter ? for GENERAL INSTRUCTIONS. To ENTER, type
number then press RETURN.
```

Computer catalog: subject—topic or place screen

```
SUBJECT-TOPIC OR PLACE:  FREEDOM OF SPEECH
                FOUND:  93

REF   DATE   TITLES                              AUTHOR
R1    1992   Revolutionary sparks:               Blanchard, Margaret A.
R2    1992   Free speech in an open society/     Smolla, Rodney A.
R3    1990   Liberty denied:                     Demac, Donna A.
R4    1990   The First Amendment, democracy,     Shiffrin, Steven H.
R5    1990   First Amendment:                    Encyclopedia of the Ameri
R6    1990   Corporate first amendment rights    Wolfson, Nicholas.
R7    1990   Freedom of speech/                  Evans, J. Edward.
R8    1990   The future of free speech law       Wright, R. George.
R9    1989   A legal guide to the public emp     Allred, stephen.
R10   1970   Academic freedom/                   Smith, Robert.

(MORE)

    Enter a REF number to select a heading; or /ES to restart.
```

Computer catalog: author/title screen

```
AUTHOR:        Shiffrin, Steven H., 1941-
TITLE:         The First Amendment, democracy,
               and romance/Steven H. Shiffrin.
PUBLISHER:     Cambridge, Mass.: Harvard
               University Press, 1990.
PHYSICAL DESC: viii, 285 p.; 25 cm
SUBJECTS:      Freedom of Speech - United States
               Dissenters - Legal status, laws,
               etc. - United States
               Romanticism - United States
LOCATION       CALL#/VOL/NO/COPY        STATUS
J/STK/BK       KF 4772 .S45 1990        Available
(END) Press RETURN to continue or /ES to start
a new search: ___
```

53c General encyclopedias and biographical dictionaries

Articles in encyclopedias and other general reference works usually treat their subject so briefly and superficially that there is seldom any need to cite them in a formal research paper. However, they do often provide useful background information, as well as bibliographical references that may lead you to more promising sources.

General Encyclopedias

Collier's Encyclopedia. 24 vols. 1982.
The Encyclopedia Americana. International Edition. 32 vols. 1980.
The New Encyclopædia Britannica. 32 vols. 1985.
The Random House Encyclopedia. Revised ed. 1983.

Biographical Dictionaries

American Men and Women of Science. 1971– .
American Writers. 1974–.
Contemporary Authors. 1962–.
Dictionary of American Biography.
Dictionary of National Biography (English). 22 vols. 1882–1953.
International Who's Who. 1935– .
New Grove Dictionary of Music and Musicians. 20 vols. 1980.
Notable American Women 1607–1950. 3 vols. 1971.
Webster's New Biographical Dictionary. 1983.
Who's Who's in America. 1899– .
Who's Who in Finance and Industry. 1972– .

53d Specialized reference works

Many of the subjects covered in general reference works are
treated in greater detail in books such as the ones listed below. For additional titles consult such works as Eugene
Sheehy's *Guide to Reference Books,* Gavin Higgens's *Printed Reference Material,* or G. Chandler's *How to Find Out: Printed and
On-Line Sources.*

The Sciences

McGraw-Hill Encyclopedia of Science and Technology. 15 vols.
    1975. Supplemented by *McGraw-Hill Yearbook of Science
    and Technology,* 1971–.
*Encyclopedia of American Agriculture: A Popular Survey of Agri-
    cultural Conditions, Practices, and Ideals in the United States
    and Canada.* 4 vols. 1907–1909.
The Cambridge Encyclopedia of Astronomy. 1977.

The Encyclopedia of the Biological Sciences. 2nd ed. 1970.
Grzimek's Encyclopedia of Ecology. 1976.
The Encyclopedia of Chemistry. 3rd ed. 1973.
Encyclopedia of Physics. 1981.
The Planet We Live On: Illustrated Encyclopedia of the Earth Sciences. 1976.
Universal Encyclopedia of Mathematics. 1964.

The Social Sciences

International Encyclopedia of the Social Sciences. 18 vols. 1968.
Dictionary of Anthropology. 1970
A Dictionary of Education. 1982.
Encyclopedia of Education. 10 vols. 1971.
Encyclopedia of Physical Education, Fitness, and Sports. 1977.
Encyclopedia of Sociology. 1974.
Facts on File. 1940– .
Larousse World Mythology. 1965.
Mythology of All Races. 13 vols. 1916–1932.
Funk and Wagnalls Standard Dictionary of Folklore, Mythology, and Legend. 2 vols. 1949–1950.
The Golden Bough: A Study in Magic and Religion. 12 vols. 1907–1915.
International Encyclopedia of Statistics. 2 vols. 1978.
Encyclopedia of American Economic History: Studies of the Principal Movements and Ideas. 3 vols. 1980.
McGraw-Hill Dictionary of Modern Economics. 1984.
Encyclopedia of Advertising. 2nd ed. 1969.
A Dictionary of Business and Finance. 1957.
Encyclopedia of American Foreign Policy. 3 vols. 1978.
Black's Law Dictionary. 5th ed. 1979.
Encyclopedia of Psychology. 3 vols. 1972.
A Dictionary of Basic Geography. 1970.
Larousse Encyclopedia of Modern History. 1962.
Encyclopedia of American History. 1982.

The Humanities

Cambridge History of American Literature. 1943.
Cambridge History of English Literature. 15 vols. 1907–.
Encyclopedia of Philosophy. 8 vols. 1967–1973.
The Encyclopedia of Religion and Ethics. 13 vols. 1908–1927.
Encyclopedia Judaica. 16 vols. 1972.
Encyclopedia of World Art. 15 vols. 1959–1968.
Focal Encyclopedia of Photography. 2 vols. 1965.
The Film Encyclopedia. 1979.
Literary History of the United States. 4th ed. 2 vols. 1974.
Literary History of England. 1967–.
New Catholic Encyclopedia. 1979.
Oxford English Dictionary. 13 vols. 1933.
New Oxford History of Music. 1986–.

53e Indexes and bibliographies

Although the subject headings of the computer or card catalog and articles in encyclopedias and other such reference
works will enable you to compile a partial bibliography of
books on your topic, you will have to look elsewhere for bibliographical information about books that are not mentioned
in these sources and for articles and reviews published in
popular magazines, scholarly journals, and newspapers.

Indexes to Articles and Reviews in Popular Magazines

Book Review Digest. 1905–.
Nineteenth Century Readers' Guide to Periodical Literature.
   1890–1899.
Poole's Index to Periodical Literature. 1802–1906.
Readers' Guide to Periodical Literature. 1990–.

Specialized Indexes and Bibliographies

Art Index. 1929–.

Biological and Agricultural Index. 1964. Supersedes *Agricultural Index*, 1916–1964.

Business Periodicals Index. 1958–.

General Science Index. 1976–.

Current Index to Journals in Education. 1964–.

Education Index. 1929–.

Essay and General Literature Index. 1900–.

Humanities Index. 1974–. Formerly part of *Social Sciences and Humanities Index,* 1965–1974.

International Index. 1907–1965. Superseded by *Social Sciences and Humanities Index,* 1965–1974.

Index to Legal Periodicals. 1906–.

Music Index. 1949–.

MLA International Bibliography of Books and Articles on Modern Languages and Literature. 1919–.

New Film Index.

New York Times Index. 1851–.

Public Affairs Information Service Bulletin. 1915–.

Social Sciences Index. 1974–. Formerly part of *Social Sciences and Humanities Index,* 1965–1974.

Monthly Catalog of United States Government Publications. 1895–.

Books in Print. 1948–.

World Bibliography of Bibliographies. 1964–.

53f Microfilm resources and computerized information services

Much of the information in written reference works is now stored also on microfilm or in computers. Microfilm indexes such as *Magazine Index,* which lists articles in over 300 popular magazines, are useful because the researcher can easily

Press Enter J to view   Esc   Return to start
the citation(s) for the
highlighted subject   F1 Help   F2 Start over   F3 Print   F4 Mark

InfoTrac EF   General Periodicals Index-A   Brief Citations

Subject: flag desecration

_____ 12 of 115 _____

12   First amendment wrongs. (argument that flag burning is not free speech) (editorial) John O'Sullivan.
      National Review, July 9, 1990 v42 n13 p6 (1). Mag. Coll.: 5SM0525.

      Press Enter J for full record.

13   Burning issue. (argument that law prohibiting flag burning should be removed from jurisdiction of Supreme
      Court using Article III, Section 2 of the Constitution) National Review, July 9, 1990 v42 n13 p12 (1). Mag.
      Coll.: 5SM0531

14   Stars and snipes. ("embarrassing" anti-flag-burning constitutional amendment) (column) Michael Kinsley.
      The New Republic, July 9, 1990 v203 n2-3 p4 (1). Mag. Coll.: 5SL0429.

15   Get serious. (flag burning and other trivial issues distract George Bush and Congress) (editorial) The New
      Republic, July 9, 1990 v203 n2-3 p7 (2). Mag. Coll.: 5SL0432.

Sample screen from a computerized index

53
f

scan hundreds of items in a few minutes. Even faster are computerized research systems such as InfoTrac or Dialog Information Services, which can search thousands of entries for material pertinent to the researcher's interest. Computer searches are a convenient and reliable means of gathering bibliographical data on subjects in all academic areas.

Sample Screen from a Computerized Index

To gain the screen on page 406, the researcher began a trac search by entering the term "flag desecration" at InfoTrac's opening prompt.

54 · Selecting and Limiting the Subject

Unless you are assigned a specific research topic, your first task will be to choose a subject and limit it to manageable proportions.

54a Choose a subject.

Consider, first of all, the requirements of the assignment. Does it limit you to a general subject area such as literature, rhetorical mode (e.g., analysis, comparison/contrast, argu-history, or politics? Does it specify a particular approach or mentation, etc.)? Does it require the use of certain kinds of sources (e.g., scholarly books and articles, newspapers and general periodicals, media productions, unpublished materials, interview or survey data)? Or does it allow you to make these decisions for yourself?

Once you have answered these questions, make a list of issues or ideas that not only satisfy the requirements of the research assignment but also reflect your own interests or concerns. These might include subjects related to your academic field (e.g., genetic engineering, teacher tenure laws, etc.); ideas derived from the study of poems, plays, novels, or other forms of writing; social and political issues such as abortion, gun control, capital punishment, job discrimination, defense spending, nuclear energy; areas of special knowledge or expertise such as painting, photography, music; and any other promising subjects.

If this self-exploration fails to yield a suitable subject, skim through some of the general reference works discussed in Chapter **53,** or look over recent issues of a general periodical or professional journal to see what kinds of research and documented writing other people are engaged in. You might also generate ideas by talking informally with friends or faculty members.

54b Narrow the subject.

Once you have selected a subject, you will need to narrow it to the point that you can investigate it thoroughly and write about it effectively in the amount of time available to you.

Suppose, for example, that you were interested in doing research on nuclear energy. Although this subject is far too broad to work with, it can be restricted in several ways.

One approach is to begin with the general subject and make a list of words or phrases in which each term is more specific than the one before it. Eventually, you should arrive at a researchable topic, such as the final item in the example below:

Nuclear energy—hazards of nuclear energy production—accidents at nuclear plants—the Chernobyl accident—causes of the Chernobyl accident.

A second tactic is to compose an unstructured list of ideas related to the main subject and then look for patterns or relationships. The result might look something like this:

1. origins of nuclear power
2. safety record of nuclear plants
3. economic benefits of nuclear power
4. thermal pollution
5. radiation leaks
6. how nuclear power is produced
7. hazardous waste problems
8. reliability of nuclear power plants
9. history of the anti-nuclear movement

Background: 1, 6, 9
Advantages: 2, 3, 8
Disadvantages: 4, 5, 7

A third option is to generate ideas by asking questions about the subject:

How do nuclear power plants affect the environment?
What can be done to prevent accidents at nuclear power plants?
Is nuclear energy worth the risks?
Should there be a moratorium on the construction of new nuclear power plants?

Other techniques for generating ideas are given in Chapter **3.** Whatever method you use to find ideas, the topic you select should be one that sets reasonable limits for research and writing and leads you to sources of information that will help you refine your topic, develop a unifying thesis, and organize your first draft.

54c Choose a documentation style appropriate for your subject and audience.

Whenever you draw ideas or information from sources, you are obligated to acknowledge that indebtedness. The format you use for that purpose will depend, however, on the specifications of the style manual appropriate for the discipline in which you are writing.

In the sciences, there are many such manuals and handbooks, including both general reference works and those specific to a particular field, such as chemistry, physics, or mathematics. Below is a selected list of some of the most widely used books.

American National Standard for the Preparation of Scientific Papers for Written or Oral Presentation

Robert Barrass's *Scientists Must Write: A Guide to Better Writing for Scientists, Engineers and Students*

Robert Day's *How to Write and Publish a Scientific Paper*

American Chemical Society's *Handbook for Authors of Papers in American Chemistry Society Publications*

American Mathematical Society's *A Manual for Authors of Mathematical Papers*

In the social sciences, the most popular documentation guide is the *Publication Manual of the American Psychological Association (APA)*. And in the humanities, the standard reference work is the *MLA Handbook for Writers of Research Papers*.

Because the MLA style is the one used almost exclusively in composition classes, we have followed its recommendations throughout this section. Chapter **59** reviews APA conventions.

55 · Compiling the Preliminary Bibliography

As you find references to books and articles that seem pertinent to your topic, record each citation on a separate index card or piece of paper (most researchers use 3 × 5 inch cards for this purpose because cards are easier to file and rearrange).

Each of the cards in this **preliminary bibliography** should include a call number (see **53b**), which will enable you to find the book or periodical (if your library has it), plus all the bibliographical information you need to document the work in your research paper.

MLA style, like most others, requires three types of information for each bibliographical citation: the name(s) of the author(s), the title of the book or essay, and details of publication.

Author Information

1. Put the author's last name before the first name so that you can conveniently alphabetize entries when preparing the final bibliography. If there is more than one author, reverse only the name of the first one.

2. Write out the author's first name and include the middle initial as well, if that information is given in your source.

3. If a work has an editor or translator, indicate that fact by citing the name and the abbreviation **ed.** or **trans.**

Title Information

1. Include the subtitle as well as the title of a book, and separate them with a colon, even if a different punctuation mark is used in the source.

2. Underline the title of a book or periodical with an unbroken line.

3. Put quotation marks around the title of an essay or of a chapter in a book, the title of an article in a periodical, and the title of a short literary work (a poem, a one-act play, a short story, etc.).

Publication Information

1. If the work cited is a book, give the place of publication (the city alone is sufficient); a shortened form of the publisher's name (e.g., Heath, Holt, Random, Yale UP, U of Toronto P); and the date of publication. If the book is published in more than one volume or is part of a series, indicate that fact as well.

2. If the work cited is a scholarly journal, record the title, the volume number (or the volume and issue number if each issue numbers its pages starting with 1), the date, and the page numbers. If the periodical is a weekly or monthly magazine, include the title, the full date, and the page numbers. Use the same format for a daily newspaper, but indicate the section after the page numbers. Abbreviate months except for May, June, and July.

3. If the work does not fit either of these two categories (if, for example, it is a government document), consult the specific entries in examples that follow.

The most efficient method of recording this information is to use the appropriate form for each citation in the preliminary bibliography so that you can later prepare the final bibliography simply by alphabetizing the cards and typing them as a single list.

Listed below are sample bibliographical entries for the kinds of sources you are most likely to use in your research paper. To determine the format for a reference, first identify the type of source you are citing (e.g., a book by a single author, an article in a journal, etc.) and find the matching heading. Then use the sample reference as a model for your own entry.

Books

A book by one author

Schlesinger, Arthur M. <u>A Thousand Days: John F. Kennedy in the White House</u>. Boston: Houghton, 1965.

An anthology

List the name of the editor, followed by a comma, a space, and "ed."

Gunn, Giles, ed. <u>New World Metaphysics</u>. New York: Oxford UP, 1981.

Two or more books by the same author

In the preliminary bibliography, record information for each book on a separate card and cite the author's name both times. When incorporating such entries into the list of works cited, follow these procedures: Give the name in the first entry; in successive entries, substitute three hyphens for exactly the same name; alphabetize the works by title.

Walker, Alice. <u>The Color Purple: A Novel</u>. New York: Harcourt, 1982.

---. <u>Meridian</u>. New York: Harcourt, 1976.

A book by two or more authors

To cite a book with two or three authors, list them in the sequence they appear on the title page, giving the first author's name in reverse order. If there are more than three authors, cite only the name of the person listed first on the title page and use the abbreviation *et al.* ("and others") in place of the other authors' names.

Berry, Mary Frances, and John W. Blassingame. Long Memory:
    the Black Experience in America. New York: Oxford UP,
    1981.

Berg, Sanford, Jerome Duncan, and Philip Friedman. Joint
    Venture Strategies and Corporate Innovation. Cambridge:
    Oelgeschlager, 1982.

Danziger, James N., et al. Computers and Politics: High
    Technology in American Local Governments. New York:
    Columbia UP, 1982.

In the list of works cited, if an author of one entry is also the
first of multiple authors in another entry, give the full name
again. Repeat the full name whenever that same author is
part of a different authorship. Use the three hyphens in the
works cited only to stand for exactly the same name(s) as in
the preceding entry.

Howard, James H. Shawnee! The Ceremonialism of a Native
    Indian Tribe and Its Cultural Background. Athens: Ohio UP,
    1981.

Howard, James H., and Willie Lena. Oklahoma Seminoles:
    Medicines, Magic, and Religion. Norman: U of Oklahoma P,
    1984.

A book with a corporate author

Carnegie Commission on Higher Education. The Academic
    System in American Society. New York: McGraw, 1974.

A book with no author listed

Begin the entry with the title and in the list of works cited alphabetize by the first word that is not an article.

The Illustrated Heritage Dictionary and Information Book.
    Boston: Houghton, 1977.

A work in an anthology

Give the author and title of the work you are citing. Then cite
the title of the anthology. After the title, give the name of the

editor or translator, preceded by the abbreviation "Ed." or "Trans." Follow with city, publisher, and date. Skip two spaces and cite the inclusive page numbers. If the work has been published elsewhere before its inclusion in the anthology, give full information for the original publication and for the anthology. Use the abbreviation "Rpt. in" before the citation for the anthology.

Booth, Wayne C. "The Scholar in Society." Introduction to Scholarship in Modern Languages and Literatures. Ed. Joseph Gibaldi. New York: MLA, 1981. 116–43.

Tolkien, J. R. R. "Children and fairy stories." Tree and Leaf. By Tolkien. London: Allen, 1964. 102–110. Rpt. in Only Connect: Readings on Children's Literature. Ed. Sheila Egoff, G. T. Stubbs, and L. F. Ashley. 2nd. ed. Toronto: Oxford UP, 1980. 111–120.

An introduction, preface, foreword, or afterword

Hill, Robert W., Jr. Preface. Tennyson's Poetry. By Alfred Tennyson. New York: Norton, 1971. xi–xiii.

Penman, Bruce. Foreword. The Betrothed. By Alessandro Manzoni. Trans. Penman. New York: Penguin, 1972.

Cross-references in the list of works cited

To avoid needless repetition, when you are citing two or more works from the same collection, list the collection itself as an entry. List individual pieces separately, and cross-reference them to the main entry by following the author's name and title of the piece with the last name of the editor of the collection and the page numbers.

Frye, Northrop. "The Argument of Comedy." Kernan 165–73.

Kernan, Alvin B., ed. Modern Shakespearean Criticism. New York: Harcourt, 1970.

Knights, L. C. "How Many Children Had Lady Macbeth?" Kernan 45–76.

55

A multivolume book

Davis, Richard Beale. <u>Intellectual Life in the Colonial South,
1585–1763.</u> 3 vols. Knoxville: U of Tennessee P, 1978.

A book in a series

Robe, Stanley, L., ed. <u>Hispanic Legends from New Mexico:
Narratives from the R. D. Jameson Collection.</u> Folklore and
Mythology Studies 31. Berkeley: U of California P, 1980.

A book with an author and an editor

If you are referring primarily to the text itself, begin the citation with the name of the author.

Chopin, Kate. <u>The Complete Works of Kate Chopin.</u> Ed. Per
Seyersted. 2 vols. Baton Rouge: Lousiana State UP, 1969.

If you are referring to the work of the editor or translator, cite that person's name first.

Seyersted, Per, ed. <u>The Complete Works of Kate Chopin.</u> By Kate
Chopin. 2 vols. Baton Rouge: Louisiana State UP, 1969.

A book in translation

Schweitzer, Albert. <u>Out of My Life and Thought: An
Autobiography.</u> Trans. A. B. Lemke. New York: Holt, 1990.

A republished book

To cite a republished book, such as a paperback version of a hardbound book, give the original publication date before the publication information for the book you are using.

Anderson, Sherwood. <u>Winesburg, Ohio.</u> 1919. New York:
Penguin, 1976.

A book in more than one edition

Gurr, Andrew. <u>The Shakespearean Stage 1574–1642.</u> 3rd ed
Cambridge: Cambridge UP, 1992.

A book not written in English

Cite publication information as it appears on the title or copyright page. If desired, you may provide an English translation, in brackets, of the title, and you may substitute the English name of a foreign city.

Colet, Louise. <u>Lui: Roman Contemporain</u>. Geneva: Slatkine, 1973.

A book with a title within its title

If the title contains a title which normally carries quotation marks, keep the quotation marks and underline the entire title of the work you are citing. If the short title is usually underlined, do not underline it in the longer title; underline the rest of the title you are citing.

Barnet, Sylvan, ed. <u>Twentieth Century Interpretations of</u> The Merchant of Venice. Englewood Cliffs, N. J.: Prentice, 1978.

A book published before 1900

You may omit the name of the publisher.

Boswell, James. <u>The Life of Samuel Johnson, LLD.</u> Edinburgh, 1884.

A dissertation

Treat a published dissertation as a book, but add the name of the institution where it was written. If it has been published by University Microfilms International (UMI), include the order number.

Harrington, Robert Dickens. <u>Forecasting Corporate Performance</u>. Diss. Virginia Polytechnic Inst. and State U, 1985. Ann Arbor: UMI, 1986. DA8605442.

Citing Articles in Periodicals

In MLA style, the usual pattern for citing articles in periodicals is as follows: author's name followed by a period and two spaces; title of article followed by a period and two spaces; name of periodical, volume number, date, and inclusive page numbers separated by a single space. If no author is given, cite the title first and alphabetize by the title.

An article in a scholarly journal

References to scholarly journals (e.g., *American Literature, Journal of Marketing, Journal of the American Chemical Society*) follow one of these patterns:

Quirk, Tom. "Fitzgerald and Cather: The Great Gatsby."
    American Literature 54 (1982): 576–91.

Henderson, Bruce. "The Anatomy of Competition." Journal of
    Marketing 47.2 (1983): 7–11.

In the first entry, the volume number alone (54) is sufficient because this journal is continuously paginated; the page numbering of each issue begins where the previous issue stopped. In the second entry, the number 47.2 indicates that this journal is separately paginated and that this article is in volume 47, issue number 2.

Article in a weekly or biweekly magazine

"Teenagers and AIDS." Newsweek 3 Aug. 1992: 44–50.

Article in a monthly or bimonthly magazine

Wiltse, Gordon. "Journey to the Bottom of the
    World—Antarctica, The Last Wild Continent, Faces the
    Future." National Parks May/June 1990: 18–25.

Newspaper article

Haverman, Joel. "Time Running Out for Congress to Act on
    Deficit." Los Angeles Times 7 Nov. 1983: 1A.

If the city of publication is not part of the name of the newspaper, include it in brackets after the name. If the city is part of the newspaper's name but is not widely known, include the state in brackets.

Editorial

"The President's Failure." Editorial. Charlotte [NC] Observer 20
  Nov. 1987: 14A.

Nilsen, Alleen Pace. "On Computers and Related After-Shocks."
  Editorial. English Journal 76.3 (1987): 11.

Letter to the editor

Waller, Buddy. Letter. Atlanta Constitution 27 Nov. 1987: 26A.

A review

If it is known, the reviewer's name is cited first, followed by the title, if any, of the review. Next come the words "Rev. of," the title of the work reviewed, and the author.

Cowley, Malcolm. Rev. of The Grapes of Wrath, by John
  Steinbeck. New Republic 3 May 1939: 382.

An abstract of a dissertation

Follow the author and title with the *DA (Dissertation Abstracts)* or *DAI (Dissertation Abstracts International)* volume number, year, and page number. After a period and two spaces, give the name of the degree-granting institution.

Kline, John Lee. "An Examination of the Legal Rights of the
  Mentally Ill." DAI 47 (1986): 116A. Wayne State U.

Other Publications

A pamphlet

Unsigned

Marijuana: The National Impact on Education. Rockville:
  American Council on Marijuana, 1982.

Signed

Benedick, Richard E. Population Growth and the Policy of
    Nations. U.S. Department of State. Bureau of Public Affairs.
    Office of Public Communication. Washington: GPO, 1982.

An article in an encyclopedia

Treat an encyclopedia article or dictionary entry as a piece in
a collection. For familiar reference books, do not cite the editor's name or give publication information other than the
year. If the articles are arranged alphabetically, omit the page
numbers.

Schmitt, Barton D., and C. Henry Kempe. "Child Abuse." The
    Encyclopedia Americana. International ed. 1980.

Government publications

Usually the writer of a government publication is not named,
so treat the issuing govenment agency as the author. Abbreviations are acceptable if they are clear. Most federal publications come from the Government Printing Office (GPO) in
Washington, DC.

United States. Dept. of Transportation. National Highway
    Traffic Safety Admin. Driver Licensing Laws Annotated
    1980. Washington: GPO, 1980.

Citations from the *Congressional Record* require only a date
and page number.

Congressional Record. 11 Sept. 1987: 12019–24.

Published proceedings of a conference

Proceedings of the 34th Annual International Technical
    Communication Conference. Denver, 10–13 May 1987. San
    Diego: Univelt, 1987.

Treat particular presentations in the proceedings as you
would pieces in a collection.

Wise, Mary R. "The Main Event Is Desktop Publishing."
    Proceedings of the 34th International Technical
    Communication Conference. Denver, 10–13 May 1987. San
    Diego: Univelt, 1987.

Other Sources

Computer software

For commercially produced software, include the author of
the program, if known; the title; the version of the program,
preceded by the abbreviation "Vers."; the words "Computer
software"; the distributor; the year of publication; and the
computer for which the program is designed.

DisplayWrite 3. Computer software. IBM, 1984. IBM PC.

Guy, Charles, and Bruce Artwick. The Jet. Computer software.
    Sublogic, 1985. IBM PC.

Material from an information service

Treat material from an information service such as ERIC or
NTIS as you would a book, but refer to the service at the end
of the entry. If the information was published previously,
give full details of the original publication.

Beil, Cheryl, and Susan K. Green. "Influence of Living Habits on
    Roommate Compatibility." Journal of College and
    University Student Housing 16.2 (1986): 14–17. ERIC EJ
    348 875.

A television or radio program

The Day After. ABC. WRAL, Raleigh, NC. 20 Nov. 1983.

A film

When citing a film, give the title first and then the name of
the director, preceded by the abbreviation "Dir." Immediately
following the title, cite the main actors' names, the name of
the studio, and the date.

55

Terms of Endearment. Dir. James L. Brooks. With Shirley
    MacLaine, Debra Winger, and Jack Nicholson. Paramount,
    1983.

A performance

A Child's Christmas in Wales. By Dylan Thomas. Dir. Christian
    Angermann. PlayMakers Repertory Company. Paul Green
    Theater, Chapel Hill, NC. 9 Dec. 1987.

56 · Locating Sources and Taking Notes

When you have finished the preliminary bibliography, the
next step is to locate sources and take notes on them. As you
gather information, keep in mind that you are under no obligation to use everything you record in your notes. Some of
the sources that first seem most promising may later prove to
be irrelevant or unreliable, whereas references that initially
appear to have little value may furnish exactly the evidence
you need to explain a key point or clinch an argument in
your research paper.

56a Locate sources listed in the preliminary bibliography.

If you have not already checked the card catalog or computer
catalog to find out which of the sources listed in your bibliography are in the library and what their call numbers are, you
will need to do so now. Once you know the call number, you
can find the work by consulting the maps or other location
guides posted in the library or by filling out a book request
form, depending on whether your library has open or closed
stacks.

56
a

Under ideal circumstances, all the sources in your bibliography would be listed in the catalog and shelved exactly where the call number indicates they should be. In reality, however, conditions may be different. You may discover, for example, that some of the books and journals you have found in bibliographies or other reference works are not in your library's collection or that the particular volume or issue you need is missing. If any of these sources seem essential to your research, you may be able to obtain them through interlibrary loan. This is usually a slow process, however, so you should file interlibrary loan requests well in advance of your deadline for completing your note taking. If you have only a limited time in which to conduct research and write your research paper or if most of the sources in your preliminary bibliography are available only from other libraries, you may need to search for additional sources or even consider changing your topic.

56b Take accurate notes.

First, skim over each source to determine whether it is relevant to your topic and—if so—how extensively it should be cited in the research paper. Obviously, a book is more difficult to assess quickly than an article or chapter, but you can learn a good deal just by reading the introduction and by studying the table of contents and the index.

When you have identified the most promising sources, reread them carefully and take notes, following these procedures:

1. Record information on index cards (4 × 6 inch cards are more suitable for note taking than the smaller bibliography cards) or on sheets of paper.

2. Use a separate card or page for each piece of information and write only on one side so that you can conveniently arrange sources when you write your research paper.

3. At the top of each note, sum up the author's main point in a word or phrase. Later, when you are ready to write, these topical headings will let you quickly identify the contents of each note, decide whether the material should be cited, and—if so—determine when it should be introduced.

4. Just below the topic heading, write the author's name (or the name and a short title if you intend to cite more than one work by the same person) and the page number. This information will refer you to the complete entry for the source in your bibliography.

5. For each note, record information in one of the following ways.

(a) Photocopy the page on which the information appears and mark the relevant passage, or write down the exact language and punctuation of the original and enclose the passage in quotation marks, as in the example below:

Permanent effects of physical abuse

Elmer   p. 44

"Multiple fractures of the extremities, if not properly treated, may result in some permanent disability, such as a limp or limitation of motion, while subdural hematomas, suffered by a number of the children, may prevent the brain from growing normally and thereby cause permanent mental retardation."

(b) Paraphrase the desired information by completely rewriting it in your own language and sentence structure, using approximately the same number of words as the source:

> Permanent effects of child abuse
>
> Elmer   p. 44
>
> In one study group of abused children, many of the victims had suffered serious physical injuries, including fractured limbs and head injuries severe enough to cause blood clots. Unless these children receive the medical care they need, some of them may never walk or move normally again, and others will suffer permanent brain damage.

(c) Summarize information by shortening as well as rewriting the original:

> Permanent effects of child abuse
>
> Elmer   p. 44
>
> Abused children in one study group showed signs of serious, permanently debilitating injuries, some of which may prevent normal body movement or cause irreversible brain damage.

56
b

(d) Combine a quotation with a paraphrase or a summary:

Permanent effects of physical abuse

Elmer   p. 44

In one study group of abused children, many
of the victims had suffered severe, long-term
injuries. Some of these children had
"multiple fractures of the extremities,"
which could cause a permanent "limp or
limitation of motion." Others had been
struck on the head so forcefully that
blood clots or "subdural hematomas" had
formed, causing "permanent mental retardation."

Notice that the information at the top of each note card is
keyed to the bibliography card for this source:

HV
741
E 48c
1977

Elmer, Elizabeth. Children in Jeopardy:
    A Study of Abused Minors and Their
    Parents. Pittsburgh: U. of Pittsburgh
    Press, 1977.

Of these note-taking strategies, the first two are the most widely used. Some researchers prefer to quote all or most of their information when they take notes so that they can evaluate all the data and arrive at a definite thesis before deciding specifically how to incorporate each piece of evidence into the research paper. Others choose to paraphrase most of their sources in the note-taking stage so that when they begin writing, they can transfer the notes directly into their papers.

56c Avoid plagiarism.

Plagiarism is *the unacknowledged use of someone else's words or ideas*. It occurs when a writer omits quotation marks when citing the exact language of a source, fails to revise completely a paraphrased source, or gives no documentation for a quotation or paraphrase. The best way to avoid this problem is to be attentive to the following details:

1. When you copy a quotation directly into your notes, check to be sure that you have put quotation marks around it. If you forget to include them when you copy, you may omit them in the paper as well.

2. When you paraphrase, keep in mind that it is not sufficient to change just a few words or rearrange sentence structure. You must completely rewrite the passage. One of the best ways to accomplish this is to read the material you want to paraphrase, then cover the page so that you cannot see it and write down the information as you remember it. Then, compare your version with the original and make any necessary changes in the note. If, after several attempts, you cannot successfully rewrite the passage, quote it instead.

56
c

The difference between legitimate and unacceptable paraphrases can be seen in the following examples:

Source

"What is unmistakably convincing and makes Miller's theatre writing hold is its authenticity in respect to the minutiae of American life. He is a first-rate reporter; he makes the details of his observation palpable."

From Harold Clurman's introduction to *The Portable Arthur Miller*

Unacceptable paraphrase

What is truly convincing and makes Arthur Miller's theatrical writing effective is its authenticity. He is an excellent reporter and makes his observation palpable.

Legitimate paraphrase

The strength of Arthur Miller's dramatic art lies in its faithfulness to the details of the American scene and in its power to bring to life the reality of ordinary experience.

The differences between these two versions of Clurman's statement are striking. The first writer has made some token changes, substituting a few synonyms (**truly** for **unmistakably, excellent** for **first-rate**), deleting part of the first sentence, and combining the two parts of the second sentence into a single clause. Otherwise, this is a word-for-word copy of the original, and if the note were copied into the paper in this form, the writer would be guilty of plagiarism. The second writer, on the other hand, has changed the vocabulary of the original passage and completely restructured the sentence so that the only similarity between the note and the source is the idea.

3. Check to see that each note has the correct name and page number so that when you use this information in your paper, you will be able to credit it to the right source.

4. If you have any doubts about the way in which you have handled material from printed sources, confer with your teacher before you submit your paper.

Exercise

1. Read the following passage. Write a paraphrase of it; then, write a summary of it.

If you go through the daily papers and listen attentively to the radio and watch television carefully, you should have no trouble perceiving that our political and social lives are conducted, to a very considerable extent, by people whose behaviors are almost precisely the behaviors their school environments demanded of them. We do not need to document for you the pervasiveness of dogmatism and intellectual timidity, the fear of change, the rut and rots caused by the inability to ask new or basic questions and to work intelligently toward verifiable answers.

Postman and Weingartner, *Teaching as a Subversive Activity*

2. Read the following passage taken from Appletree Rodden's "Why Small Refrigerators Can Preserve the Human Race."

Once, long ago, people had special little boxes called refrigerators in which milk, meat, and eggs could be kept cool. The grandchildren of these simple devices are large enough to store whole cows, and they reach temperatures comparable to those at the South Pole. Their operating costs increase each year, and they are so complicated that few home handymen attempt to repair them on their own.

Explain whether each of the following passages based on this selection is plagiarized. If so, why? If not, why not?

Passage 1: A long time ago, people had boxes which kept certain food products from rotting. Now this particular family of cooling devices has grown so large entire animals can be held in them at temperatures far colder than those reached during winters in most parts of the world. They have become increasingly expensive, and they are so complicated that few home handymen attempt to repair them.

Passage 2: The size of refrigerators has increased so much in recent years that they are large enough to store a whole cow. In fact, they are so complicated to repair that few people try to repair them on their own.

Passage 3: Our notion of refrigerator has changed over the years. Once little boxes were used to cool milk, meat, and eggs. Now the refrigerators people use are large enough to store entire animals and are expensive to operate and repair.

Passage 4: The forefathers of the modern refrigerator were much more efficient to run for the simple purpose of cooling food. New refrigerators, however, because of their size and cooling abilities, are costlier to operate and more difficult to repair.

57 · Planning and Writing the Research Paper

If you have limited your subject adequately and researched it thoroughly, your reading and note taking should eventually provide you with the information needed to formulate a tentative thesis, organize your material, and compose a preliminary draft.

57a Formulate a thesis statement.

The thesis should be a single declarative sentence that sums up what you have learned about the topic through your research and what you want your readers to learn from your research paper. A precise, clearly phrased thesis sentence will guide your selection and arrangement of information and, at the same time, alert the reader to the design and direction of the essay as a whole. Notice how the thesis statements below combine these functions.

Anorexia nervosa, a condition that affects thousands of young women every year, has both psychological and social origins.

In The Grapes of Wrath, John Steinbeck affirms the universal values of unity, sacrifice, courage, and faith through his portrayal of the Joad family.

Contrary to the popular belief that food additives are unnatural or harmful, these substances provide vital nutritional supplements, prevent spoilage, enhance appearance, and aid in food processing.

57b Prepare an outline.

Once you have formulated your thesis, carefully reread your notes, discarding any that do not pertain directly to this central idea or proposition. Then, using the thesis statement as a guide, list the main points of your explanation or argument in the order in which you plan to discuss them. If a formal outline is required, assign a Roman numeral heading to each, and group your remaining notes under these broad categories. Your headings will in turn suggest subgroupings of ideas and examples that help develop each main point.

The result should be a detailed outline such as the one below (for additional information about outline form, see **4b**).

```
                 The Value of Food Additives

Thesis Statement: Contrary to the popular belief that food
additives are unnatural or harmful, these substances provide
vital nutritional supplements, prevent spoilage, enhance
appearance, and aid in food processing.

Introduction
I.    Misconceptions about food additives
      A. Belief that additives are unnatural
      B. Belief that additives are harmful
II.   Value of food additives as nutritional supplements
      A. Vitamins
         1. Riboflavin (B2)
         2. Alpha tocopherol (E)
         3. Cobalmin (B12)
      B. Amino acids
         1. Tysine
         2. Tryptophan
```

```
      B. Colors
         1. Caramel
         2. Carotene
         3. Paprika
V.    Value of additives in food processing
      A. Emulsifiers
         1. Glycerides
         2. Sorbitan
      B. Leavening agents
         1. Sodium bicarbonate
         2. Potassium acid tartrate
Conclusion
```

57c Compose a rough draft.

When you have finished gathering information, begin working your notes into the first draft of your research paper. As you write, keep in mind this is not the version of the paper that you will submit for evaluation, but a working draft that can be expanded, reorganized, or changed in other significant ways as the paper develops. More specifically, this early draft will give you an opportunity to organize related notes into paragraphs, move sentences around within paragraphs to achieve coherence, and arrange paragraphs in the order indicated by the outline so that you can test the logic and coherence of your original organizational scheme.

As you compose your essay, you can copy from your notes material that you have already expressed in your own words or recorded by combining short quotations with original statements or paraphrases. Extended quotations, on the other hand, will require further evaluation, for they can be used in numerous ways.

Suppose, for example, that you were writing an expository essay on the nuclear arms race and that you had quoted in your notes the passage (top of page 434) from Fletcher Knebel and Charles Bailey's *No Higher Ground*.

One option would be to quote the passage in full (or condense it by using an ellipsis mark) and introduce it with a statement such as the following:

At a time when the threat of nuclear war seems greater than ever before, the nations of the world would do well to remember what happened on the morning of August 6, 1945, when a single atomic bomb devastated the city of Hiroshima:

> First came heat. It lasted only an instant but was so intense that it melted roof tiles, fused the quartz crystals in granite blocks, charred the exposed sides of telephone poles for almost two miles, and incinerated nearby humans so thor-

Heat — detrimental effects on Hiroshima

Knebel and Bailey   p. 181

" First came heat. It lasted only an instant but was so intense that it melted roof tiles, fused the quartz crystals in granite blocks, charred the exposed sides of telephone poles for almost two miles, and incinerated nearby humans so thoroughly that nothing remained except their shadows, burned into asphalt pavements or stone walls. Bare skin was burned up to two and a half miles away."

~~oughly that nothing remained except their shadows, burned into asphalt pavements or stone walls.~~ Bare skin was burned up to two and a half miles away. (Knebel and Bailey 181)

Another approach would be to select portions of the quotation and adapt them to the grammatical structure of your own sentence, as in the following paragraph:

First, the people of Hiroshima felt an intense heat which "lasted only an instant," yet generated enormously high temperatures that changed roof tiles into running lava, "fused the quartz crystals in granite blocks," burned the exposed sides of telephone poles, and vaporized nearby people, leaving only "their shadows, burned into asphalt pavement and stone walls" (Knebel and Bailey 181).

A third alternative would be to rewrite the passage, as in the following paraphrase:

Peter Knebel and Charles Bailey explain that the heat generated by the nuclear bomb dropped on Hiroshima lasted only a moment, but its effects were devastating. The heat was so intense that it liquified roof tiles and rock crystals, charred telephone poles two miles from the blast, vaporized anyone near the center of the blast, and burned the skin of people who were over two miles from ground zero (181).

All three of these passages represent an effective and legitimate use of sources. The words that have been taken verbatim from the notecard in the first and second examples have been enclosed in quotation marks, the borrowed ideas in the second and third examples have been expressed in a language completely different from that of Knebel and Bailey, and the source and location of the quoted or paraphrased material have been clearly identified (see the next chapter for specific suggestions on documentation).

Throughout this preliminary stage of the writing process, keep in mind that you have at least as much to contribute as any of the sources you cite. For example, the thesis statement and most or all of the introduction and conclusion should be in your own language and should reflect your own insights. You will also require original language and thought to write the topic sentences around which you organize your paragraphs, the transitions that lead from one sentence or paragraph to the next, and the words or phrases that introduce and identify quotations and paraphrases. Furthermore, as you write you should not be reluctant either to revise your previous work or to alter your plans for the paper.

57d Document sources fully and accurately.

Although you need not acknowledge a source for generally known information such as the dates of the Civil War or the names of the ships that carried Columbus and his followers to the New World, you must identify the exact source and location of each statement, fact, or idea you borrow from another person or work.

One of the simplest and most efficient ways to acknowledge sources is the MLA documentation system, which requires only a brief parenthetical reference in the text of the paper keyed to a complete bibliographic entry in the list of works cited at the end of the essay.

For most parenthetical references, you will need to cite only the author's last name and the number of the page from which the statement or idea was taken, and if you mention the author's name in the text, the page number alone is sufficient. This format also allows you to include within the parentheses additional information, such as title or volume number, if it is needed for clarity. Documentation for some of the most common types of sources is discussed in the sections below, and additional examples of documentation in the context of a student research paper can be found in Ch. **58.**

References to Articles and Single-Volume Books

Articles and single-volume books are the two types of works you will be referring to most often in your research paper. When citing them, either mention the author's name in the text and note the appropriate page number in parentheses immediately after the citation, or acknowledge both name and page number in the parenthetical reference, leaving a space between the two. If punctuation is needed, insert the mark outside the final parenthesis.

Author's name cited in the text

Marya Mannes has defined euthanasia as "the chosen alternative to the prolongation of a steadily waning mind and spirit by machines that will withhold death or to an existence that mocks life" (61).

Author's name cited in parentheses

Euthanasia has been defined as "the chosen alternative to the prolongation of a steadily waning mind and spirit by machines that will withhold death or to an existence that mocks life" (Mannes 61).

Corresponding bibliographic entry

Mannes, Marya. Last Rights. New York: Morrow, 1973.

If the work you are citing has two or three authors, cite all their last names in parentheses and follow the conventions for spacing and punctuation noted above. If there are more than three authors, include the last name of the author listed first on the title page, plus the abbreviation *et al.*

Sample parenthetical references

(Berry and Blassingame 125)
(Berg, Duncan, and Friedman 85)
(Danziger et al. 28)

Corresponding bibliographic entries

Berry, Mary Frances, and John W. Blassingame. Long Memory: The Black Experience in America. New York: Oxford UP, 1981.

Berg, Sanford, Jerome Duncan, and Philip Friedman. Joint Venture Strategies and Corporate Innovation. Cambridge: Oelgeschlager, 1982.

Danzinger, James N., et al. Computers and Politics: High Technology in American Local Governments. New York: Columbia UP, 1982.

References to Works in an Anthology

When referring to a work in an anthology, either cite in the text the author's name and indicate in parentheses the page number in the anthology where the source is located, or acknowledge both name and page reference parenthetically.

Author's name cited in text

One of the most widely recognized facts about James Joyce, in

Lionel Trilling's view, "is his ambivalence toward Ireland, of which the hatred was as relentless as the love was unfailing" (153).

Author's name cited in parentheses

One of the most widely recognized facts about James Joyce "is his ambivalence toward Ireland, of which the hatred was as relentless as the love was unfailing" (Trilling 153).

Corresponding bibliographic entry

Trilling, Lionel. "James Joyce in His Letters." Joyce: A Collection of Critical Essays. Ed. William M. Chace. Englewood Cliffs: Prentice-Hall, 1974.

References to More Than One Work by an Author

When you paraphrase or quote from more than one work by an author, give the title as well as the name of the author and the page reference so that the reader will know which work is being cited.

If you mention the author's name in the text, you need not duplicate it in the parenthetical reference. Just cite the title (or a shortened version of it), skip a space, and insert the page number, as in the second example below. If you do not mention the author's name in the text, cite it first in the parenthetical reference, put a comma after it, skip a space, and insert the title. Then skip a space again and insert the page number (see the third example below).

Title cited in text

Stephen Gould asserts in his article "Singapore's Patrimony (and Matrimony)" that "some historical arguments are so intrinsically illogical or implausible that, following their fall from grace, we do not anticipate any subsequent resurrection in later times and contexts" (22).

Title cited in parentheses

Stephen Gould asserts that "some historical arguments are so intrinsically illogical or implausible that, following their fall from grace, we do not anticipate any subsequent resurrection in later times and contexts" ("Patrimony" 22).

or

In the words of one contemporary scientist, "Some historical arguments are so intrinsically illogical or implausible that, following their fall from grace, we do not anticipate any subsequent resurrection in later times and contexts" (Gould, "Patrimony" 22).

Corresponding bibliographic entries

Gould, Stephen Jay. *Ever Since Darwin: Reflections in Natural History.* New York: Norton, 1977.

---. "Singapore's Patrimony (and Matrimony)." *Natural History* May 1984: 22–29

References to Works of Unknown Authorship

If you borrow information or ideas from an article or book for which you cannot determine the name of the author, cite the title instead, either in the text of the paper or in parentheses, and include the page reference as well.

Title cited in the text

According to an article entitled "Going Back to Booze," surveys have shown that most adult alcoholics began drinking heavily as teenagers (42).

Title cited in parentheses

Surveys have shown that most adult alcoholics began drinking heavily as teenagers ("Going Back to Booze" 42).

Corresponding bibliographic entry

"Going Back to Booze." *Time* 31 Nov. 1979: 41–46.

References to Multivolume Works

When you borrow from one volume of a multivolume work, cite the volume of your source in parentheses as an arabic number *without* the abbreviation **Vol.,** and put a colon after it. Then skip a space and insert the page reference.

Sample references

Frazer points out that scapegoat rituals have been common throughout history, not only in primitive society but also "among the civilized nations of Europe" (9: 47).

Scapegoat rituals have been common throughout history, not only in primitive societies but also "among the civilized nations of Europe" (Frazer 9: 47).

Corresponding bibliographic entry

Frazer, Sir James G. The Golden Bough: A Study in Magic and Religion. 3rd ed. 12 vols. New York: Macmillan, 1935.

References to Information Gathered from Interviews

When citing an oral source, either mention the informant's name when you introduce the quotation or paraphrase, or give the name in a parenthetical reference.

Informant's name cited in text

When asked to comment on conditions in the dormitories, one of my informants, Sherry Stein, complained that the worst thing she could think of was the insect problem. "You just wouldn't believe how bad things are around here," she said. "I walked into the bathroom this morning and came face to face with the biggest roach on record."

Informant's name cited in parentheses

When asked to comment on conditions in the dormitories, one of my informants complained that the worst thing she could think of was the insect problem. "You just wouldn't believe how bad things are around here," she said. "I walked into the bathroom this morning and came face to face with the biggest roach on record" (Stein).

Corresponding bibliographic entry

Stein, Sherry. Personal Interview. 10 Apr. 1993.

References to Literary Works

When citing works of literature, observe the following guidelines for each genre.

Novels and other prose works subdivided into chapters or sections

Begin the parenthetical reference with the author's last name and page number (the author's name may be omitted if it is mentioned in the text of the paper or if the authorship is evident from the context) and insert a semicolon. Then skip a space and give the number of the chapter (with the abbreviation **ch.**) as well as the number of any other subdivisions.

Sample reference

At the beginning of The Great Gatsby, Nick Carraway characterizes himself as someone who has "a sense of the fundamental decencies" (Fitzgerald 1; ch. 1)—a trait that he displays throughout the novel.

Corresponding bibliographic entry

Fitzgerald, F. Scott. The Great Gatsby. New York: Scribner's, 1925.

Poems

When quoting or paraphrasing a poem that is divided into sections, cite the number of the book, part, or canto and put a period after it. Then give the line number(s). There is no need for abbreviations such as **bk.** (book) or **l.** (line). If the poem you are citing has no subdivisions, line numbers alone are sufficient—provided that the author and title are identified in the text of the paper. In such references, use the word **line** or **lines** before the numbers in the first citation so that the reader will not mistake line numbers for page numbers. Thereafter, cite only the number(s).

Sample reference to a poem with subdivisions

One of Byron's satiric techniques is to juxtapose the comical with the serious, as in this passage from Don Juan:

> But I am apt to grow too metaphysical:
>
> "The time is out of joint,"—and so am I;
>
> I quite forget this poem's merely quizzical,
>
> And deviate into matters rather dry

(9.321–24).

Sample reference to a poem without subdivisions

One of the questions that must be answered in any analysis of Jeffers's "Hurt Hawks" is whether the author's viewpoint is reflected in the narrator's statement "I'd sooner, except the penalties, kill a man than a hawk" (line 18).

Corresponding bibliographic entries

Byron, George Gordon, Lord. Don Juan. Lord Byron: Don Juan and Other Satirical Poems. Ed. Louis Bredvold. New York: Odyssey, 1935.

Jeffers, Robinson. "Hurt Hawks." Selected Poems. New York: Random, 1928.

Plays

When citing a play, give the act and scene number without abbreviations, plus the line numbers if the work is in verse. Use arabic numerals unless your teacher specifies Roman numerals, and separate numbers with periods.

Sample reference

Shakespeare repeatedly describes Denmark in images of unnaturalness as in Horatio's comparison of Denmark with Rome just before Caesar's murder, when "The graves stood tennantless and the sheeted dead / Did squeak and gibber in the Roman Streets" (1.1.115–16).

Corresponding bibliographic entry

Shakespeare, William. <u>Hamlet</u>. <u>Shakespeare: Twenty-Three Plays and the Sonnets</u>. Ed. Thomas Parrot. Rev. ed. New York: Scribner's, 1953.

References in Block Quotations

Quotations longer than four typewritten lines are indented ten spaces without quotation marks, and their references are put outside end punctuation.

> Implicit in the concept of Strange Loops is the concept of infinity, since what else is a loop but a way of representing an endless process in a finite way? And infinity plays a large role in many of Escher's drawings. Copies of one single theme often fit into each other, forming visual analogues to the canons of Bach. (Hofstadter 15)

Corresponding bibliographic entry

Hofstadter, Douglas. <u>Gödel, Escher, Bach: An Eternal Golden Braid</u>. New York: Vintage, 1980.

57e Revise and proofread your paper.

To identify potential problems as you develop your ideas and synthesize material from your sources, ask yourself questions such as these:

1. Have I expressed my ideas clearly and organized them coherently?

**57
e**

2. Have I included enough information from my sources to support the thesis?

3. Are all paragraphs relevant to the thesis and consistent with the intended arrangement?

4. Have I accurately quoted or paraphrased all ideas and information I have drawn from my sources?

5. Have I acknowledged each source in the text through parenthetical documentation as recommended earlier in this chapter?

6. Have I made my own judgments an integral part of the essay?

7. Do my conclusions follow logically from the evidence presented?

Don't be surprised if you have to answer *no* to some of these questions. The value of a rough draft is that it enables you to get ideas on paper without stopping to correct all mistakes. You can eliminate errors in subsequent drafts. If you discover any paragraphs that are irrelevant to the thesis, delete or revise them. If you find that your original plan of organization is flawed, rearrange those sentences and paragraphs whenever necessary to improve coherence. If you notice that more information is needed to support a particular point, go back to your notes for other examples or return to the library and do some additional reading. If you have strung together a series of quotations or paraphrases without transitions, add appropriate connectives or interpretive comments.

When you are able to answer affirmatively all the questions posed above, proofread and edit your paper. At this point, you should be concentrating on the smaller elements of the essay, searching for errors in grammar and punctuation, misspellings, inappropriate word choice, inconsistencies in point of view or verb tenses, and the other common problems discussed in Parts **IV–VI** of this text.

57f Prepare the final list of works cited.

After you have revised and edited the text of your paper, use your preliminary bibliography cards to prepare a list of all the works you have cited in your essay. (This list should be titled **Works Cited,** without quotation marks or underlining.) If you have recorded author, title, and publication information in the bibliographic format recommended in this chapter or followed the conventions prescribed by another style manual approved by your teacher, you will have all the information required for the works cited page. You need only alphabetize the cards for sources you used in the paper and type them as a single list. When you have finished, check to be sure that every source cited in the text appears in the works cited and that the entry for each source is complete and accurate.

57g Compose the final draft.

When you are satisfied that you have fulfilled all the requirements of the research assignment and that your paper is ready for submission, prepare the final draft. Consult your teacher to find out whether you need to submit an outline and what special guidelines you should observe. In addition, MLA style requires the following conventions:

1. Type the final draft neatly on only one side of $8\frac{1}{2}$-×-11-inch bond paper; do not use erasable bond, since it smudges easily. If your teacher allows handwritten papers, write legibly in blue or black ink.
2. Leave one-inch margins (excluding page numbers) on the top, bottom, and both sides of each page.
3. Double space throughout, including the works cited page. For a handwritten paper, skip a ruled line between each line of writing.

4. Do not make a separate title page. Instead, starting at the left margin, an inch from the top of the first page, type your name, your teacher's name, the name and number of the course, and the date on separate lines, double spacing between lines. Then double space and center the title of the paper. Double space between lines of the title and between the title and the first line of text.

5. Number all pages consecutively. Starting with page 1, type your last name before each page number (e.g., Jones 3) in the upper right corner, $\frac{1}{2}$ inch from the top of the page. Do not use the abbreviation "p." or add a period after the page number.

When you have completed the final copy, proofread it carefully, checking for transposed letters, omitted words or punctuation marks, and other typographical errors. If you note typographical errors and don't have time to type corrections, make the correction neatly in ink; draw a single line through the letters you want to delete.

58 · Sample Research Paper

The research paper that follows was written by Ashley Hinkle, a first-year student in an introductory political science class. Based on the conventions of the *MLA Handbook for Writers of Research Papers*, this essay—together with the introductory notes and page-by-page annotations that accompany it—provides a practical guide to parenthetical documentation style, techniques for using sources, methods of organization, revision strategies, and other important aspects of the research writing process.

Background

The research assignment

At the beginning of the course—Political Science 1010, National Government—the teacher distributed to each student the following description of the research assignment: "Each student will be expected to write a documented paper defending or challenging one of the attached statements. This argumentative paper must be typed, double spaced, at least five text pages in length, excluding notes and bibliography, and based on at least five substantive research sources other than the course text. Citations and bibliographic entries must conform to an accepted style manual. The grade assigned will be based on form as well as substance."

Ashley found several of the suggested topics interesting, and after thinking about them, she realized that she was most motivated to write about the following proposition: "Destruction of a US flag as a form of expression is, and should be, protected by the First Amendment."

Circumstances of composition

Having decided on this argumentative topic, Ashley reflected carefully on what she felt about flag burning. She then decided that she was most comfortable defending the proposition, but she reserved final judgment until she had completed her research. In an interview with the authors of this book, she said, "From the first, I knew which way I was going to argue, but as I read, I had to change my thinking about reasons for supporting the statement."

Because Ashley had some familiarity with her subject, she decided that she did not need to consult encyclopedias or other general reference works. She began by examining legal records and then moved to more general resources: "At first, I picked up several court cases such as Texas vs. Johnson.

Then I began to add book titles to my working bibliography by looking through the library's electronic catalog under the subject heading 'flag desecration.'"

For each source, she recorded the call number plus pertinent bibliographical information on a 3-×-5 inch card. Then she went to the reference room, scanned the files of the Info-Trac computer system for information about recently published articles on her subject, made additional bibliography cards for several studies that seemed especially promising, and looked up the call number of each periodical in another reference room resource—the serials catalog.

Below are several entries that Ashley made during her bibliographic research. Note that she has taken the time to convert the publication data for each book or article into the format appropriate for that source.

KF 4772
.S45
1990

Shiffrin, Steven H. _The First Amendment,_
Democracy, and Romance. Cambridge:
Harvard U P, 1990.

(Book by a single author—modeled on the sample entry on p. 413.)

AP
2
N6772

Jacoby, Jamar, et al. "A Fight for Old
Glory." <u>Newsweek</u> 3 July
1989: 18-20.

(Signed articles in a weekly magazine—modeled on the sample entry
on p. 418.)

PE 1431
. R33
1992

Ramage, John D., and John C. Bean,
eds. <u>Writing Arguments: A Rhetoric with
Readings</u>. New York: Macmillan, 1992.

(Essay collection—modeled on the "anthology" entry on p. 413.)

In the essay anthology edited by Ramage and Bean, Ashley found several articles on flag burning that seemed pertinent to her argument, so she made an additional bibliography card for each of them. She cited the information for the original publication before giving the publication information for the essay anthology in which the article was reprinted. The note card for one article looked like this:

"Waving the Flag Back." *The New Republic* 23 Jan. 1989. Rpt. in *Writing Arguments: A Rhetoric with Readings*. Ed. John D. Ramage and John C. Bean. 2nd ed. New York: Macmillan, 1992. 635-36.

(Essay in an anthology or an edited collection—modeled on the sample entry on p. 415.)

Next, Ashley used the call numbers and bibliographical information to find the books and periodicals in her preliminary bibliography and began reading. At first, she skimmed quickly over each work, noting major ideas and reflecting on how she might focus her argument. Through this process, she became familiar enough with the issues to formulate the thesis statement that appears at the top of the outline on page 452. She was then able to devise a plan of organization and develop a preliminary outline with the following subdivisions:

Introduction—statement of problem, issues involved (First
    Amendment, symbolic speech, etc.)
Arguments against flag burning
Defense of flag burning
Conclusion/Solution

At this point in the research process, Ashley knew the
kinds of information she needed to record in her notes: details about the history of the controversy, the exact wording
of the First Amendment, a definition of symbolic speech, and
data about court cases on flag burning and their outcomes.
With these considerations in mind, she began a process of intensive reading and note taking that continued for several
weeks. In her reading, she discovered references to additional relevant sources and entered the necessary bibliographic information on 3-×-5 cards. As she accumulated information, she grouped related notes under the outline
headings she had decided upon earlier. Later, after she had
finished her research, she rearranged material within each
section, discarded notes that seemed repetitious or irrelevant,
and prepared the more detailed outline shown on page 452.
When she was satisfied that she had adequately covered each
of the main points she had set out to discuss and that her organization was sound, Ashley wrote the first draft of her research paper.

As soon as she had finished this preliminary draft, which
consisted mainly of the quotations and paraphrases recorded
in her notes, she started revising. First, she concentrated on
the large elements of composition. She rearranged sentences
to achieve emphasis, inserted transitional words and phrases
to improve coherence within and between paragraphs, and
added her own comments to explain or interpret the information from her sources.

Turning next to smaller details, she varied her word
choice to eliminate unnecessary repetition, revised several
weak passive voice constructions, consulted a dictionary to

Outline

Thesis: This expression of political opinion (flag burning), though held in disgust by most patriotic Americans, should be protected as free speech by the First Amendment.

INTRODUCTION

    I. Historical context

        A. Early cases

           1. Red flag laws

           2. *West Virginia v. Barnette*

        B. Later test cases

           1. *Street v. New York*

           2. *Tinker v. Des Moines*

           3. *People v. Radich*

           4. *Texas v. Johnson*

    II. Opposing viewpoints

        A. Arguments against

           1. Difference between speech and action

           2. Danger of provocation

        B. Arguments for

           1. Potency of burning

           2. True patriotism

    III. Exceptions

        A. Criminal action

           1. Vandalism

           2. Trespassing

         B. Clear and present danger

CONCLUSION

confirm the spelling of several words that were not part of her usual vocabulary, and checked for possible errors in grammar and punctuation. When she finished, she compiled a list of works cited from her preliminary bibliography, made a few minor adjustments in her outline, and typed the final copy of the manuscript. Then, she proofread the paper once more to ensure that it was free of typographical errors and submitted it to her political science professor for evaluation.

Use and Documentation of Sources

The first paragraph of Ashley Hinkle's research paper exemplifies several characteristics of effective research writing:

1. Quotations and paraphrases are skillfully intermixed with original statements.

2. Passages quoted verbatim are varied in length and unobtrusively imbedded in the writer's own sentences.

3. Quotations are transcribed exactly as they appear in their sources and enclosed by quotation marks.

4. Each source is clearly identified by a parenthetical reference in the format recommended in **57d.** The idea from Jacoby, for example, is acknowledged by name and page number because his name is not mentioned in the text. Note that there is no parenthetical citation for Voltaire's statement because these words are so widely known and quoted that they are common knowledge.

Content and Organization

The first paragraph accomplishes several related purposes: it sets the argument in a historical context, it introduces the controversy, and it states the author's position on the issue.

Professor Smith

Political Science 1010

14 April 1993

                        Burning Issue

¶1   French writer and philosopher Voltaire spoke

for democratic-minded people everywhere when he

exclaimed, "I disapprove of what you say, but I

will defend to the death your right to say it."

Less than thirty years after Voltaire's death,

citizens of the new United States of America rati-

fied the First Amendment to their Constitution, an

amendment that reaffirms his sentiments:

            Congress shall make no law respecting an

            establishment of religion, or prohibit-

            ing the free exercise thereof, or

            abridging the freedom of speech, or of

            the press; or the right of the people

            peaceably to assemble, and to petition

            the government for a redress of

            grievances.   (*Constitution* 45)

"Freedom of speech" is not, however, as clear-cut

a concept as it might seem. Two hundred years af-

ter the Constitution was ratified, the United

States Supreme Court overturned a Texas law con-

victing Gregory L. Johnson of desecrating the

American flag. This decision ended decades of le-

Manuscript Form

The writer's name, the teacher's name, the course title, and the date are placed in the left corner of page 1, $\frac{1}{2}$ inch from the top and even with the left margin. On this page (as well as on the ones following) the author's last name and the page number have been placed in the upper right corner about $\frac{1}{2}$ inch from the top and one inch from the right edge of the paper.

The block quotation is indented ten spaces and double spaced, with double spacing also between the passage and the text above and below it. Note that the indentation eliminates the need for quotation marks unless they appear in the original.

Use and Documentation of Sources

Paragraphs 2 and 3 illustrate a range of techniques for using sources. We see a variation of parenthetical documentation in the way Ashley has cited the historical data reported by Haiman in paragraph 2. Usually the shortened title (*Freedom*) would be unnecessary, but it is essential here because the research paper cites two different works by this author. Note how in this paragraph the writer adapts information from four different sources in various ways. The third sentence paraphrases text from Haiman's book *Freedom of Speech*, while the second sentence from the end of the paragraph reduces content from Shiffrin's book to a brief summary. Direct quotation in paragraphs 2 and 3 sometimes includes an entire sentence or sometimes just a word or phrase.

Note, too, the use of the ellipsis mark to indicate omission of words in paragraph 2. In quoting the passage from Knaebel, the writer omits sixteen words to focus on the essential idea of symbolism as a "short cut from mind to mind."

gal controversy over the freedom of "symbolic speech" and the protection of a sacred national emblem. I believe with Justice Anthony Kennedy that this decision showed a "pure command of the Constitution" (Jacoby 18). Expressing political opinion through such an act, though held in disgust by most patriotic Americans, should be protected as free speech by the First Amendment.

¶2 As early as 1895, states had passed laws against the mutilation or misuse of the flag (Haiman, Freedom 47). The question of "symbolic speech" and whether it is implied in the First Amendment remains the most controversial issue over the constitutionality of these laws. Symbolic speech was first upheld in 1931, when the court found unconstitutional the Anti-Bolshevik "red flag" laws that forbade the display of a red flag or any other flag symbolizing opposition to organized government (47). Twelve years later in West Virginia v. Barnette, the Supreme Court majority struck down a law that required school children to salute the flag (Shiffrin 159). The court stated that "the case is made difficult not because the principles of its decision are obscure but because the flag involved is our own" (160). Justice Robert H. Jackson wrote, "the freedom to differ is not limited to things that do not matter much" (Jacoby 20). The court added that "sym-

Knaebel   632

"Symbolism is a primitive but effective
way of communicating ideas. The use of an
emblem or flag to symbolize some system, idea,
institution, or personality, is a short cut
from mind to mind."

(The middle part of this quotation is deleted in the text of the paper.)

Content and Organization

Paragraph 2 treats points I.A.1. and I.A.2. in the outline. The paragraph traces the early history of litigation involving flag burning and symbolic speech. Note how Ashley weaves the significance of each court decision into a historical narrative. Observe also how the paragraph culminates in a philosophical quotation that reinforces Ashley's position on symbolic speech.

Paragraph 3 treats point I.B.1. in Ashley's outline. Note that the first sentence of this paragraph prepares the reader for a review of a series of decisions in which "the Supreme Court often skirted the issue of flag burning." The rest of the paragraph discusses *Street v. New York,* the first of these decisions.

bolism is a primitive but effective way of communicating ideas . . . a short cut from mind to
mind" (Knaebel 632). Furthermore, "a person gets
from a symbol the meaning he puts into it, and
what is one man's comfort and inspiration is another's jest and scorn" (632-33). To support
this position, the court involved the Emersonian
interpretation of the First Amendment--to protect
the unorthodox, the dissenter, and the romantic
(Shiffrin 5). The Emersonian message is to "trust
your own intuitions, to speak out in favor of your
own ideals, and to oppose the 'straight prison-
like limits of the Actual,' to resist the convention of the 'old, halt, numb, bed rid world'"
(Shiffrin 1-2).

¶3   Since then, the Supreme Court often skirted
the issue of flag burning. In 1969, Sidney Street,
after finding out about the shooting of black activist James Meredith, publicly burned a U.S. flag
while saying, "We don't need no damn flag. If they
let that happen to Meredith, we don't need an
American flag" (Haiman, Freedom 48). Street was
convicted of violating the New York desecration
law which made it a crime "to mutilate, deface,
defile or defy, trample upon, or cast contempt
upon either by words or act" the American flag (48).
The Civil Liberties Union argued that while non-

Use and Documentation of Sources

All the information about the court cases discussed in paragraphs 4 and 5 comes from Haiman's two books, *Freedom of Speech* and *Speech and Law in a Free Society*, but notice the various ways in which Ashley integrates this material into her essay. She begins paragraph 4 with a brief statement about the court's finding in the *Tinker v. Des Moines* case, then follows with a block quotation giving Haiman's evaluation of that decision. In paragraph 5 she uses her own language to describe additional findings from Haiman's second book, citing within parentheses the title and page number of her source.

Content and Organization

Paragraphs 4 and 5 (corresponding to outline sections I.B.2. and I.B.3.) examine two other important cases: *Tinker v. Des Moines* and *People v. Radich*. Note that in both paragraphs the author includes only those details of the two cases that demonstrate the court's inability to reach a consensus about the constitutionality of flag burning.

verbal speech is conduct and not afforded the protection of verbal speech, "to distinguish between
symbolic and nonsymbolic communication is to erect
a wholly arbitrary boundary." They added that
"all communication is basically symbolic. Language, the medium of traditional communication, is
nothing more than a highly developed set of abstract symbols . . . " (49). A decision on the issue of symbolism was avoided, though, when a majority of five threw out the New York law because
it explicitly forbids using words to show contempt
(50). Nevertheless, Street v. New York gave an
insight into symbolic speech that would be applied
in years to come.

¶4   In the 1969 case of Tinker v. Des Moines Community School District, the Supreme Court called
the wearing of armbands to protest the Vietnam War
akin to "pure speech" (Haiman, Freedom 81-82). On
the 7-2 decision, Haiman commented

> The U.S. Supreme Court has had little
> trouble recognizing a black armband or
> the refusal to salute an American flag
> as First Amendment behavior, but it has
> had a great deal more difficulty extend-
> ing the concepts of speech to protect
> the public burning of a draft card or

Use and Documentation of Sources

As in previous paragraphs, Ashley skillfully integrates source material into the grammatical structure of her sentences. The first sentence in paragraph 6, for example, is based on the short quotation taken from the passage on the note card below:

Jacoby   18

"In a 5-4 ruling that shuffled the justices' usual ideological alliances, the Court established that First Amendment guarantees of free speech protect those who burn the flag in political protest."

In the next four sentences, the writer uses a similar strategy, departing from it only in the final sentence of the paragraph to use an indented quotation to present Justice Brennan's philosophical defense of flag burning as a "reaffirmation of the principles of freedom."

> alleged misuses and "desecrations" of
> the flag. (<u>Speech</u> 26)

But is there a difference between wearing an arm-
band and burning a flag? That question was left
to be answered later.

¶5   A decision was avoided once more in the 4-4
split in <u>People v. Radich</u> (1971). In this case, a
store owner displayed in his window a gun caisson
wrapped in a U.S. flag along with anti-war sculp-
tures (Haiman, <u>Freedom</u> 51). The right to this
form of symbolic speech was supported in the <u>Co-
lumbia Law Review</u> with the argument that when we
allow inadequate protection to symbolic conduct,
we place restraints on expression and in some
small way impede the channels of communication
(<u>Freedom</u> 51). Moreover, denial of First Amendment
protection for communicative conduct unnecessarily
alienates those who do not possess verbal skills,
and perhaps Radich had not the eloquence to put
into words his disgust and revulsion with America
and its involvement in what he believed to be an
unjustified war.

¶6   The case of free speech and the flag was finally resolved in the 5-4 ruling of <u>Johnson v.
Texas</u>, which "shuffled the justices' usual ideological alliances" (Jacoby 18) while establishing
"that First Amendment guarantees of free speech

Content and Organization

In paragraphs 6 and 7 (I.B.4. in the outline), Ashley culminates her review of court cases addressing the constitutionality of flag burning. In paragraph 6 she focuses on *Johnson v. Texas*, examining both the defendant's rationale for flag burning and the principle on which the Supreme Court based its decision of the case. At the end of paragraph 7, she prepares readers for the ensuing discussion of opposing viewpoints by demonstrating how the conflicting attitudes of Supreme Court justices reflect the divisions within the general population.

protect those who burn the flag in political protest" (18). Explaining his reasons for burning the flag, Johnson stated, "The American Flag was burned as Ronald Reagan was being renominated as President. And a more powerful statement of symbolic speech, whether you agree with it or not, couldn't have been made at that time" ("Texas" 2540). The court stated that, in this circumstance, the symbolic burning of the flag was conduct "sufficiently imbued with elements of communication" (2540). Justice Brennan explained, "We decline to create for the flag an exception to the joust of principles protected by the First Amendment" (Isaacson 14). Shiffrin described this decision as "Emersonian free speech" quoting Brennan for support:

> Our decision is a reaffirmation of the
> principles of freedom and inclusiveness
> that the flag best reflects, and of the
> conviction that our toleration of criti-
> cism . . . is a sign and source of our
> strength. . . . It is the Nation's re-
> silience, not its rigidity . . . that we
> reassert today. The way to preserve the
> flag's special role is not to punish
> those people who feel differently about

Use and Documentation of Sources

Throughout paragraphs 8, 9, and 10, Ashley uses summary and paraphrase to advance her argument. At the end of paragraph 9, she quotes from "Waving the Flag Back." When she found a reference to the McCarthy hearings of the 1950s in one of her sources, she decided to use this historical event in paragraph 10. Because the information is general knowledge, she did not need to document it.

Content and Organization

In paragraph 8 (II.A.) Ashley combines personal observations with interview data to explain the beliefs of people who disagree with the Supreme Court ruling in the Johnson case. Then in paragraphs 9 and 10 (II.B.1. and II.B.2.) she refutes those arguments while at the same time building support for her own position by extending the logic of the jurists in the court cases to reach her own conclusions. Note how Ashley links the arguments in paragraphs 9 and 10 by using the word "Furthermore" to indicate that additional information follows.

these matters. It is to persuade them
that they are wrong. (274)

¶7   On the <u>Johnson</u> decision, David O'Brien, a
professor of political science at the University
of Virginia, said, "James Madison, who wrote the
First Amendment, would have his heart warmed by
the decision, but he would have been appalled by
the 5-4 vote" (Isaacson 15). Divisions within the
Supreme Court, however, reflect the conflicting
attitudes of the American public. In fact, a
<u>Newsweek</u> poll found that 65 percent of Americans
disagreed with the decision while only 35 percent
supported it (Jacoby 18).

¶8   Opponents of the decision usually offer two
arguments in support of their position. As East
Carolina University philosophy professor James
Smith pointed out in a recent interview, the most
compelling argument against flag burning is that
such actions, however symbolic they might be, do
not constitute actual speech and therefore do not
fall under the protection of the First Amendment.
Another persistent argument against the act is
that some people view the flag not as a symbol but
as a treasured artifact possessing intrinsic
merit, so they feel compelled to react violently
in its defense. To such people, desecrating the

Use and Documentation of Sources

Ashley uses paraphrase in paragraph 11. For her concluding paragraph, she expresses her own view about the information she has presented. Therefore, she needs no quotation marks or parenthetical references.

flag may be an act equivalent to shouting "Fire!"
in a crowded theater.

¶9   It is precisely this veneration, however,
that makes burning the flag such a potent form of
speech. And for the flag to truly stand for freedom, the Supreme Court held, it must stand for its
most potent forms (14). Justice Brennan, who led
the majority, argued that constitutional protection is all the more imperative for speech that is
repellent (Jacoby 19). The editors of The New
Republic agreed, noting that in the Johnson case,
"the entire point of the prosecution was that
Johnson had conveyed an offensive idea, contempt
for the United States" ("Waving" 636).

¶10 Furthermore, punishing people for expressing
their views is not what patriotism in America is
really all about. Ask any of the hundreds of
loyal but dissident Americans who were persecuted
by Senator Joseph McCarthy and the House Committee
on Un-American Activities during the 1940s and
1950s. True patriotism in a democracy requires
the citizen not only to tolerate dissent but to
value it. Justice Kennedy wrote, "The hard fact
is that sometimes we must make decisions we do not
like. It is poignant but fundamental that the flag
protects those who hold it in contempt" (Jacoby 19).

¶11 Of course, there are some cases where burning

Content and Organization

In paragraph 11 Ashley has addressed the points she entered in her outline under III.A. and III.B. In an early draft she had included a paragraph on criminal action and another paragraph on clear and present danger. She decided, however, that such extensive treatment gave too much emphasis to minor exceptions to the general principles her paper had explained, so she condensed these two paragraphs into one.

Ashley concludes her paper in paragraph 12 by stating her central idea in her own words.

the flag is not acceptable. A person who burns someone else's flag on someone else's property invites charges of vandalism and trespassing (Isaacson 15). Also, there is the "clear and present danger" test. Oliver Wendell Holmes might have said that freedom of speech does not give a person the right to set a flag on fire in a crowded theater (15). It may also be hazardous to burn a flag at an American Legion meeting, in a crowd of Desert Storm veterans, or inside the Republican National Convention.

¶12 Flag burning in any form has been and will continue to be provocative and unpopular. A majority of Americans will never desire to engage in this form of symbolic speech, and most will feel defensive when dissenters do this drastic act. What we should all realize, however, is that the flag stands for the country's most important principles, the principles that define the United States of America. One of these principles is that no law should abridge our freedom to express ideas, whether in words or deeds. Surely the most convincing way to demonstrate respect for the flag is to exercise the tolerance for which it stands.

Works Cited

The format for the works cited list on pages 473–474 follows the conventions discussed in Chapter **55.**

1. Pages are numbered consecutively with the text, and the number of each page, preceded by the author's last name, is placed in the upper right corner.
2. The title **Works Cited** is centered one inch from the top of the page, with a double space between the title and the first entry.
3. Each entry starts at the left margin. If more than one line is necessary, the second line and any additional lines are indented five spaces.
4. Double spacing is used between entries and within entries of two or more lines.
5. Works are alphabetized by the author's last name except under the following circumstances;
   a. If more than one work by the same author is cited, the author's name is given only in the first entry. In subsequent entries, three unspaced hyphens take the place of the name (see the references to Haiman's *Freedom of Speech* and *Speech and Law in a Free Society* on the opposite page). Note, too, that such works are listed in alphabetical sequence by title.
   b. If the author's name is not given, the entry is alphabetized by title.
6. Note that when only one work in a collection is cited, full publication data for both the work cited and the collection are included in the same entry (see the citation for "Waving the Flag Back" on the opposite page).

Works Cited

Constitution of the United States. Washington: Library of Congress in assoc. with Arion Press, San Francisco, 1987.

Haiman, Franklin S. Freedom of Speech. Lincolnwood, Illinois: National Textbook, 1984.

---. Speech and Law in a Free Society. Chicago: U of Chicago P, 1981.

Isaacson, Walter. "O'er the Land of the Free." Time 3 July 1989: 14-15.

Jacoby, Jamar, et al. "A Fight for Old Glory." Newsweek 3 July 1989: 18-20.

Knaebel, Ernest. "West Virginia State Board of Education v. Barnette." United States Reports. Vol. 319. Washington: GPO, 1943, 625-45.

Shiffrin, Steven H. The First Amendment, Democracy, and Romance. Cambridge: Harvard U P, 1990.

Smith, James. Personal interview. 10 April 1992.

Stevens, John D. Shaping the First Amendment. Beverly Hills: Sage, 1982.

"Texas, Petitioner v. Gregory Lee Johnson." West's Supreme Court Reporter--Interim Edition. Vol. 109B. St. Paul, Minn.: West, 1989, 2533-47.

'Waving the Flag Back." <u>The New Republic</u> 23 Jan.
　　　　1989. Rpt. in <u>Writing Arguments: A
　　　　Rhetoric with Readings</u>. Ed. John D. Ramage
　　　　and John C. Bean. 2nd ed. New York:
　　　　Macmillan, 1992: 635-36.

59 · The APA Format

Scholars publishing in the social sciences usually follow the conventions prescribed in the *Publication Manual of the American Psychological Association, Third Edition.* Professors in the social sciences, therefore, often require papers written in their courses to conform to the APA style of documentation.

APA Reference Citations

In APA style, a manuscript's bibliography is titled "References." The format of APA references is illustrated below. Format includes where names, titles, and dates are placed; how words are abbreviated; how many spaces are indented from the left side of the page; how many spaces are left between parts of the bibliographic entry; how the parts are punctuated; and which words are capitalized.

Book by one author

Gordon, R. (1980). Interviewing: Strategy, techniques, and tactics. Homewood, IL: Dorsey.

Note that the author's first name is initialed, the date of publication comes after the initial of the author's first name, and only first letters of the article title and subtitle are capitalized.

Book by two authors

Resnick, L. & Weaver, P. (1979). Theory and practice of early reading. Hillsdale, NJ: Erlbaum.

59
a

Note that all authors' names are cited with the last name first; only the initials of authors' first and middle names are given.

Journal article

Thorndyke, P. W. (1977). Cognitive structure in comprehension and memory of narrative discourse. <u>Cognitive Psychology</u>, <u>9</u>, 77–110.

Journal article by multiple authors

Keon, F., Becker, A., & Young, R. (1969). The psychological reality of the paragraph. <u>Journal of Verbal Learning and Verbal Behavior</u>, <u>8</u>, 49–53.

Article in journal that paginates each issue beginning with page 1

Thompson, N. S. (1988). Media and mind: Imaging as an active process. <u>English Journal</u>, <u>77</u>(7), 47–49.

Note that issue number "(7)" is given for journals that begin each issue with page 1. This is not necessary for journals that number their pages consecutively throughout the year of the volume number. Note also that the volume number (77) is underlined.

Article in magazine

Steele, B. F. (1975, June). Working with abusive parents: A psychiatrist's view. <u>Children Today</u>, p. 3.

Note that the month of the magazine article is given after the date and that "p." or "pp." is used to indicate page numbers.

Article in newspaper (unsigned)

Trying to get men to sparkle like women. (1989, December). <u>New York Times</u>, p. 15.

Article in newspaper (signed)

Carmody, D. (1989, January 1). Increasing rapes on campus
    spur colleges to fight back. New York Times, pp. 1, 10.

Note that when the author's name is given, the day of the issue is cited. Note also that all pages on which a newspaper
article appears are cited.

APA In-text Reference

Like the MLA style, APA requires works to be cited in the
text by giving the author's last name. Unlike MLA, APA requires the date of publication to be included after the author's
name. In the social sciences, such documentation permits in-
text reference to serve two functions at once: 1) citing for the
reader the source of an idea and 2) using the author of the
idea as the subject of the sentence. Three variations in usage
and format are illustrated in the paragraph below:

The use of mental imagery as a conceptual peg has long
been established (Paivio 1966). Bartlett (1970) demonstrated
four specific means by which mental imagery may foster
abstract as well as concrete thinking. In 1971 Fischer
demonstrated how mental images can serve as symbols and
can be strung together to represent abstract propositions.

As the example above illustrates, APA in-text citations do
not include page numbers when information is paraphrased
or summarized. When a direct quotation occurs, in-text citations include "p." or "pp." and the page numbers:

Smith and White (1968) found that in paired associate
learning, "a concrete first term paired with a concrete second
term was the most powerful paradigm" (p. 47).

59b An article using APA reference format

Guiding Students Through Research Papers

Bruce Tone

In an article entitled "The Resource Paper, Again," Campbell (1984) contends that assigning the research paper to students who cannot write well and who cannot paraphrase and incorporate quotations from sources into their personal styles is a pedagogical mistake. Discussions of the research paper often begin apologetically, calling the assignment "the dreaded research paper," a sure route to "depressingly common horror stories," and the writing assignment "with the worst reputation of all." Yet such reports almost invariably refer also to some of the instructional attractions of the research paper and recommend methodologies that follow a limited approach to gathering, digesting, reacting to, and reporting information.

Peacock (1987) proposes such an approach under a title that begins "Research Revisited," implying that the research paper resurfaces periodically as a prevalent classroom assignment. A search of the ERIC [Educational Resources Information Center] database, however, suggests that some form of the research paper has continuously been assigned by many teachers.

A microcosm

The appeal of the research paper is understandable. It is, after all, a kind of microcosm of so many of the interrelated communication skills we want to teach to students: It commonly ties reading to writing. As a writing project, it usually involves the organizing and outlining of numerous facts and details. It develops comprehension that arises from synthesis and organization of information.

It can, with the direction of good teachers, promote critical thinking as evaluation of sources and experiences. In many classrooms, it incorporates listening thoughtfully to sources interviewed and giving oral reports to classmates. And certainly, the research paper is a valid reason to introduce and exercise a host of good study skills, including notetaking and use of library sources.

In subsuming many or all of these goals, however, the research paper appears to place too heavy a load on many students and teachers. How can all of these skills be taught, monitored and directed, and evaluated in one assignment?

Drudgery vs. motivation

The potential drudgery that the research paper can promote is evident in numerous curriculum outlines, which *begin* a student's preparation with extensive lists of study skills to be taught or reinforced. Equally prevalent, however, are numerous recommendations to begin with (and stress throughout the development of research papers) the nature of research as a question-asking process and to be sure that students are allowed to pursue questions of interest and importance to them. With such a purpose, the learning and application of the skills needed to complete the quest is reasonably motivated.

Larson (1982) argues that "by acting as if there is a generic concept defensibly entitled the 'research paper'—we mislead students about the activities of both research and writing" (p. 811). As do many who stress the word *research* and question emphasis on *paper*, Larson suggests that a "well-planned investigation of data" can treat student experience gathered outside of books—in interviews and observations, for example, which are highly regarded research techniques in a majority of fields and disciplines.

Schwegler and Shamoon (1982) do not disagree with Larson's solution, but they argue that having students write interpretive statements about some aspect of reality that they have researched is a valid assignment. The "strategies appropriate for these papers are easy enough to recognize—and to make part of research paper instruction in composition courses," (p. 818) they contend.

Instructional time

This kind of commonsense approach needs to take into account the amount of instructional time involved in making the research paper—even a limited approach to it—a meaningful experience for students. Perrin (1987) depicts the attitude that ignores this fact as teachers announcing "Research a topic of your choice and turn in a paper in three weeks. Don't plagiarize!"

An unwillingness to teach and guide the analytic and other writing skills that must be taught and practiced is also masked, he suggests, by "teachers who are so obsessed with mechanical form that the content of students' research papers is secondary" (p. 50).

Benson (1987) would agree. As do several writers, she advises teachers to offer students a variety of notetaking, footnoting, and bibliographic techniques to choose from and follow. Making choices related to the mechanics of a research project is highly compatible with an emphasis that stresses the value and enjoyment of seeking answers to questions that are meaningful to the young researcher.

Numerous reports in the recent literature acknowledge the need to guide students sequentially—over a period of weeks, months, or even years. However, these fall into two general and very different perspectives. One of these—most often represented by formal curriculum guides—usually begins with a highly subdivided set of the most basic of skills, such as learning how to use the card catalogue or practicing the paraphrasing of paragraphs as an exercise.

The other general perspective puts emphasis on guiding students to the selection of appropriately narrowed topics that promote questions they are interested in answering. Polanski's (1984) prescription for "Real-World Research" is one example and enumerates steps in such a process.

A sequence of instruction

Kelly (1985) offers steps or assignments in a highly sensible and sequenced process that clearly implies the teacher's involvement in guiding and critiquing each step. "Directed brainstorming to choose a topic" leads to framing a thesis question to guide the research; next, a "retrospective" essay assimilates and evaluates information found after initial searching. Then the student writes a report that summarizes, evaluates, and acknowledges source materials; and before the full-length paper is attempted, the student writes a kind of "buffer" essay which allows him or her to practice and get feedback on the combined skills that have been applied to a small body of information.

Eldred (1985) suggests a similar process approach.

Practical approaches

Many teachers who have long since abandoned the research paper may justifiably ask, "How do I work all those subassignments and my evaluation of them into a curriculum with many other goals?" The literature suggests numerous answers.

One is to limit the assignment and its goals in one or more of a variety of ways. A common approach is to use what is called "a casebook," a collection of essays or other materials on one general topic, as the source material for a research paper. Often such casebooks are single volumes in print, but Heaberlin (1986) explains how one can be created by the teacher and made up of articles and materials gathered from a variety of sources.

As with all limited approaches to the research paper, the use of the casebook sacrifices some of the potential benefits of the assignment—in this case, practice with the skills of finding and selecting sources. It is also apt to place some limits on the selection of topics, as do many focused approaches.

Demerly (1986) describes an assignment that most teachers would find a reasonable challenge for them and their students, and it is representative of approaches that target topics, designate types of source materials, and/or limit the product in terms of the number of sources selected and the total number of words.

Beatty (1987) reported on a research paper project that maintains key elements and benefits and proves to be a satisfying experience for remedial high school students. The students follow the key steps of choosing and narrowing a topic, posing "how" and "why" questions, taking notes, outlining, writing a rough draft, and revising as a response to the teacher's critique. Only four or five sources are identified by using the *Readers' Guide,* and notecards are tagged with questions the students have previously determined they want to answer so as to direct their focus when reading the sources. Footnotes are omitted. An oral report to the class is the final step.

The practice of targeting and paring research paper assignments to fit the time and attention a teacher is willing and able to give them is a highly responsible decision. The word *able* is a deliberate choice here. No teacher should attempt to teach research and reporting techniques that s/he does not fully understand—preferably through experience.

That admonition needs to be coupled to the related recommendation that adequate time be given to whatever assignment is designed so that students have time to find, digest, analyze, and respond to the accruing information and so that the teacher has time to mentor the process and teach and reinforce the skills essential to completing the assignment.

If that happens, one of the key pitfalls and concerns of many who write about the research paper is almost assuredly avoided. As George (1984) points out, plagiarism usually results from a student's not knowing how to synthesize, to think critically, and to report information with his or her own reaction or "voice." Any tendency to plagiarize is not apt to survive the guidance a qualified teacher gives a student through the posing of a question, the assimilation and organization of material, and the preparation of drafts or "buffer" segments.

References

Beatty, J. N. (1987). The research paper in a remedial curriculum. *Journal of Reading, 30,* 550–551.

Benson, L. K. (1987). How to pluck an albatross: The research paper without tears. *English Journal, 76*(7), 54–55.

Campbell, G. (1984). The resource paper, again. *English Journal, 73*(2), 72–74.

Demerly, E. (1986, March). Putting the past into the present through research papers. Paper presented at the meeting of the Mid-west Regional Conference on English in the Two-Year College, St. Louis, MO. [Note the format for citing lectures, speeches, and addresses.]

Eldred, J. M. (1985, April). A research project for the rhetoric/composition classroom. Paper presented at the meeting of the Midwest Writing Centers Association, Chicago, IL.

George, D. (1984). Creating contexts: Using the research paper to teach critical thinking. *English Journal, 73*(5), 27–32.

Heaberlin, H. (1986). Casebook approach to writing the research paper. *Language Arts Journal of Michigan, 2,* 26–28.

Kelly, R. (1985, March). Meandering roadways vs. super-highways: An approach to teaching the research paper. Paper presented at the meeting of the Conference on College Composition and Communication, Minneapolis, MN.

Larson, R. L. (1982). The "research paper" in the writing course: A non-form of writing. *College English, 44,* 811–816.

Peacock, J. W. (1987). Research revisited: Or how I learned to love the *Readers' Guide. English Journal, 76(7),* 57–60.

Perrin, R. (1987). Myths about research. *English Journal, 76(7),* 50–53.

Polanski, V. G. (1984, March). Real-world research for freshmen. Paper presented at the meeting of the Conference on College Composition and Communication, New York, NY.

Schwegler, R. A. & Shamoon, L. K. (1982). The aims and processes of the research paper. *College English, 44,* 817–824.

Glossary of Usage

a, an   Use **a** as an article before words beginning with consonant sounds, and use **an** before words beginning with vowel sounds.

a field
an opener

Note: **a** unit (**u** sounding as consonant **y**)
an honest person (**h** being silent)
a historian (**h** pronounced)

accept, except   The verb **accept** means "to receive"; the verb **except** means "to leave out." The preposition **except** means "other than."

The club **accepted** almost everyone who applied.
It **excepted** only people too young to purchase alcoholic beverages.
No one objected **except** a few young people.

affect, effect   The verb **affect** usually means "to influence"; the verb **effect** means "to cause" or "to bring about." The noun **effect** means "a result."

The drought has **affected** the corn crop.
The lobbyists could not **effect** a change in the administration's farm policy.
An **effect** of the drought has been increased prices for food.

aggravate, irritate   **Aggravate** means "to make worse," and **irritate** means "to make uncomfortable" or "to annoy." In informal use the two words are sometimes synonymous.

My poison ivy was **aggravated** by sunburn.
Poison ivy causes an **irritating** rash.

agree to, agree with, agree on   To **agree to** means "to consent to" something; to **agree with** means "to be in accord with" someone; to **agree on** means "to decide by mutual consent."

The club members **agreed to** a five dollar assessment.
I **agreed with** the majority of the members.
The committee **agreed on** a course of action.

all ready, already   **All ready** means "prepared." **Already** means "by this time" or "before now."

Fortunately the musicians were **all ready** to take their places, for the audience was **already** restless.

all right   In formal writing, use **all right** to mean "wholly correct" or "satisfactory," but not "acceptably."

FORMAL: The meal was **all right,** but the service was poor.
INFORMAL: Jerry may be sloppy but he can cook **all right.**

Alright is a misspelling.

all together, altogether   **All together** means "collectively" or "in a group." **Altogether** means "entirely."

The campers emerged **all together** from the woods; they were **altogether** tired and discouraged.

allusion, illusion   An **allusion** is "an indirect reference." An **illusion** is a "false impression."

Shelley's poem "Adonais" has many **allusions** to classical Greek culture.
The defeated team realized that their invincibility was an **illusion.**

almost, most   **Almost** means "nearly." **Most** means "the greatest part." The two are sometimes confused.

Insects have infested **almost** (not **most**) the entire supply of grain.
Insects have infested **most** of the grain.

among, between   **Among** refers to a relationship involving three or more, whereas **between** refers to a relationship of two.

We found great optimism **among** the President's economic advisers.
For dessert you may choose **between** pie and custard.

amount, number **Amount** usually refers to an uncountable quantity. **Number** refers to a countable quantity.

In a small **amount** of dirt you will find a great **number** of microorganisms.

and/or This construction can be appropriate in legal documents, but it is a needless complication in most other contexts.

anyone, any one **Anyone,** like **anybody** and **everyone,** is an indefinite pronoun. **Any one** is the pronoun **one** modified by the adjective **any.**

As **anyone** can tell, **any one** of these books would take a long time to read.

as, because To avoid confusion, do not use **as** to mean "because."

We used a spray painter **because** (not **as**) a brush would have taken too long.

as, like In formal usage **as** may be a conjunction, but **like** is not an appropriate conjunction.

You should do **as** (not **like**) the instructions direct.

assure, ensure, insure **Assure** means "to state confidently" or "to promise." **Ensure** means "to guarantee." **Insure** is sometimes used synonymously with **ensure,** but **insure** also means "to contract for protection" against loss.

The director of parks and recreation **assured** us the old playground would be popular again.
The renovations and new equipment **ensured** that children would enjoy themselves.
In the unlikely event that someone will get hurt, the city has **insured** the parks for $100,000 against liability.

awful, awfully   In formal usage **awful** means "awe inspiring" or "terrifying." Less formally it is used to mean "bad." **Awful** and **awfully** as substitutes for "very" are informal and trite.

She was **very** (not **awfully**) upset.

a while, awhile   The phrase **a while** is an article plus a noun naming "a short time." **Awhile** is an adverb meaning "for a short time."

They rested **awhile**. (**awhile** modifying **rested**)
They rested for **a while**. (**a while** object of preposition **for**)

bad, badly   **Bad** is an adjective; **badly** is an adverb. Avoid confusing their grammatical roles.

The patient felt **bad**. (**bad** a subject complement)
The patient had cut herself **badly**. (**badly** modifying **cut**)

being as, being that   Avoid these wordy, awkward substitutes for "because."

Because (not **being that**) Barry is claustrophobic, he would rather climb stairs than ride in an elevator.

beside, besides   Both words are prepositions; **beside** means "next to," and **besides** means "except for." **Besides** is also a conjunctive adverb meaning "moreover" or "in addition."

The young prodigy had few good traits **besides** musical ability.
Three old cars were rusting **beside** the shack.
We should leave the party now. Most of our friends have left, and **besides,** the band will stop playing in ten minutes.

burst, bust   **Burst** means "to come apart suddenly." Its past participle is **burst** (not **bursted**). **Bust** and **busted** are nonstandard.

can, may   In formal prose **can** denotes ability, and **may** denotes permission. In informal use, **can** denotes permission also.

The child **can** ride a bicycle, but he **may** not ride over two blocks from his home.

capital, capitol   **Capital** means "chief" or "primary," or the city that is the seat of a government. **Capitol** refers to a building that houses a legislature.

In our nation's **capital,** Washington, DC, the legislature meets in the **Capitol** building.

center around   This is an illogical phrase; use **center on** instead.

The speech **centered on** the theme of civic responsibility.

climactic, climatic   **Climactic** is the adjective for "climax" and refers to "a culminating moment" or "turning point." **Climatic** is the adjective for "climate" and refers to the weather.

The play's **climactic** moment came in the second act.
Some meteorologists specialize in studying the **climatic** conditions that give birth to tornadoes.

compare to, compare with   Use **compare to** to emphasize similarities (often of a figurative nature) and use **compare with** to emphasize differences or to discuss similarities and differences.

One critic **compared** the rock group's music **to** a cat fight.
Compared with professional tennis, our club's annual tournament is of little interest to the public.

complement, compliment   The verb **complement** means "to add to" or "to bring to perfection"; the noun **complement** means "that which brings to perfection" or "the quantity needed to complete or improve."

The model's manner **complemented** her appearance on the stage.
The architecture was a **complement** to the landscape.

The verb **compliment** means "to praise"; the noun **compliment** means "an act of praise."

The teacher **complimented** her students on their achievement.
We got many **compliments** on our successful performance.

comprise, compose **Comprise** means "to include" or "to consist of." **Compose** means "to form" or "to make up."

The trailer **comprises** two bedrooms, a kitchen, a living room, and two bathrooms.
The trailer is **composed of** (not **comprised of**) five rooms.

continual, continuous **Continual** means "happening again and again." **Continuous** means "occurring constantly without break."

In the British House of Commons, speakers are **continually** interrupted by the members.
The police siren sounded **continuously** for fifteen minutes.

criterion, criteria **Criterion** in singular; **criteria** is plural.

There are many **criteria** for success, but perhaps the simplest **criterion** is money in the bank.

datum, data In formal usages **datum** is singular, **data** is plural. "Result," "fact," or "piece of information" are commonly used instead of the singular **datum.**

The **data** from the public opinion poll **are** interesting but not surprising.
One fact from the survey stands out.

differ **Differ from** means "be unlike." **Differ with** means "disagree with."

Sue **differs from** most students because she continually **differs with** her professors.

different from, different than Generally use **different from** instead of **different than.**

Barry's reasons for liking Allison were **different from** mine.

Increasingly, however, writers are choosing **different than** as less wordy when a clause follows.

The outcome of the play was **different than** I remember.
The outcome of the play was **different from** the one I remembered.

discreet, discrete **Discreet** means "cautious," "tactful," or "unobstrusive." **Discrete** means "separate," "distinct."

At the divorce hearing neither spouse was **discreet** in describing the other's behavior.
The painting was composed of thousands of **discrete** colored dots.

disinterested, uninterested **Disinterested** means "unbiased." **Uninterested** means "not interested" or "feeling no concern."

In Olympic competition, gymnasts hope the judges will be **disinterested,** whatever the nationalities of the competitors.
Erwin remained **uninterested** throughout the irrelevant speech.

due to This phrase is most appropriate when used as as adjective meaning "attributable to" rather than as a preposition meaning "because of." **Due to,** therefore, most often follows a form of the verb "to be."

The team's losing streak is **due to** the coach's pending resignation.
The team is losing **because of** the coach's indifference.

each and every This is a wordy phrase that usually fails to achieve the emphasis a writer wishes. Use **each** or **every,** but not both.

The promoter counted **every** person who entered the stadium.

enthuse This verb is not as appropriate in formal usage as its corresponding noun, adjective, or adverb.

Marty was **enthusiastic** (not **enthused**) about her upcoming vacation.
She spoke **enthusiastically** (not **She enthused**) about her plans.

especially, specially **Especially** means "mainly" or "to an unusual degree." **Specially** means "for a particular reason."

The crew was **especially** pleased with the new sail, which had been **specially** made for their boat.

etc. **Etc.** is an abbreviation for the Latin phrase **et cetera,** meaning "and others" or "and so forth." Avoid using it in formal writing. In informal writing **etc.** can be appropriate at the end of a list to indicate that only unimportant items remain to be listed.

Like their predecessors, this year's incoming freshmen report that they have come to college to get an education, to find a spouse, to prepare for a lucrative vocation, **and so forth.**
Backpackers depend on lightweight provisions: dried meat, freeze-dried vegetables, dried cereal, nuts, **etc.**

every day, everyday **Every day** is an adverb phrase. **Everyday** is an adjective.

Every day the factory whistle blew at noon.
Dessert was not an **everyday** treat for our family.

every one, everyone In the phrase **every one, every** modifies the pronoun **one; every one** means "each individual" and usually precedes **of. Everyone** (like **everybody**) is an indefinite pronoun.

Every one of the musicians had dyed his hair an unnatural color.
Everyone was shocked at their appearance.

farther, further These words are sometimes used as synonyms, but in formal usage **farther** refers to distance in space, and **further** refers to other types of extent.

The cyclists had **farther** to go than they thought.
Her behavior got her **further** into trouble.

fewer, less **Fewer** refers to countable quantities. **Less** refers to degrees or amounts in general.

Frieda has **fewer** bad habits than Mark, but he has **less** conceit than she.

finalize Avoid this pretentious verb.

We will **finish** (not **finalize**) the plan as soon as we have all the information we need.

flaunt, flout To **flaunt** is "to show off." To **flout** is "to defy or scorn."

The peacock **flaunts** his exotic tail.
The drunk driver **flouted** every rule of the road.

formally, former, formerly **Formally** means "in a formal way." **Former** as a noun denotes the first of two persons or things named previously. **Formerly** means "at a previous time."

Although you have seen Sue before, I will **formally** introduce you at the party tonight.
Formerly we were close friends, but now we have little to do with each other.
The carpenter and the plumber both finished at the same time, but only the **former** remained to clean up the litter.

good, well **Good** is an adjective and should not serve in place of the adverb **well.**

The young violinist played very **well** (not **good**).

got Avoid using **have got** for "have" in formal prose.

I **have** (not I **have got**) no money at all.

great Avoid using the informal "great" instead of specific description.

Jack Nicholson was utterly convincing as a psychotic killer in *The Shining* (not Jack Nicholson was **great**).

hanged, hung As the past tense of **hang, hanged** means "executed" and **hung** means "suspended."

The war criminals were **hanged.**
Original paintings were **hung** in every room of the house.

have, of **Have** can be an auxiliary verb, but **of** should never be used as a verb.

We **should have** (not **should of**) left before now to avoid the crowd.

herself, himself, myself, ourselves, yourself These are reflexive pronouns and should not be substituted for **her, him, me, us,** and **you.** Intensive constructions use both the personal pronoun and the reflexive pronoun: **she, herself.**

You (not **Yourself**) can repair this car.
The only person who can repair this car is **you, yourself.**

hopefully In informal usage **hopefully** can mean "I (or we) hope that." Strict formal usage requires **hopefully** to modify a verb and to mean "in a hopeful manner."

The politician spoke **hopefully** about the future.
We hope (not **Hopefully**) it will not rain tomorrow.

imply, infer **Imply** means "to hint" or "to suggest." **Infer** means "to draw a conclusion."

In her welcoming speech, the club president **implied** that membership would be more expensive than the new members had been led to believe.
The new members **inferred** that belonging to the club would be more expensive than they had thought.

in, into **In** refers to position, condition, or direction. **Into** refers to movement or change. **Into** meaning "interested in" or "involved in" is not suitable for formal prose.

The dog is **in** his house.
He is **in** a bad mood.
Hastily the cook dumped dough **into** a baking pan and shoved the pan **into** the oven.
My parents are **interested in** (not **into**) meditation.

inside, outside Use **inside** and **outside** without the word **of.**

Our whole family was **outside** (not **outside of**) the house during the thunderstorm.

irregardless **Irregardless** is a double negative and is nonstandard. Use **regardless**.

Regardless of the weather, the workers will continue building the pipeline.

is when, is where Avoid using these inaccurate phrases in definitions.

Courage is the ability to control fear in the face of danger (not Courage **is when** a person controls fear in the face of danger.)

its, it's **Its** is the possessive form of **it**, just as **his** is the possessive form of **he**. **It's** is a contraction meaning **it is** or **it has**, just as **he's** is a contraction meaning **he is** or **he has.**

The dog broke **its** leash.
It's not the type of dog I want.

kind of, sort of **Kind of** and **sort of** are informal for "rather" and "somewhat."

She appeared to be **rather** (not **kind of**) interested in the play, but later she confessed that she had been thoroughly bored.

leave, let **Leave** means "depart" and **let** means "permit." They are synonymous when used with **alone.**

If this cold weather lasts, even the winter birds will **leave.**
Let (not **leave**) the child sit where he wants.
Leave (or **let**) her alone.

liable, likely In formal usage, **likely** refers to probability, and **liable** refers to legal obligation or to responsibility.

If you forget your raincoat, you're **likely** to get wet.
A law suit might establish that you are **liable** for damages.

lie, lay **Lie (lay, lain)** means "to recline." **Lay (laid, laid)**

means "to place." **Lie (lied, lied)** means "to say something untrue." To help your memory, think of the following sentence as meaning that the speaker is not going to recline but is going to put feathers (down) on the sofa: "I am going to **lay down** on the sofa."

Most of my friends **lie** (not **lay**) in the sun for hours at a time.
Only once have I **lain** (not **laid**) in the sun so long.
Lay your beach towel where our friends have **laid** theirs.

literally In formal usage, **literally** means "word for word" or "in actuality." Avoid using it as an intensifier to mean "virtually" or "extremely."

The marathon runners were **almost** (not **literally**) dying from the heat.

lots **Lots** and **lots of** are informal terms for **a great deal of, many,** and **much.**

He had **many** (not **lots of**) opportunities to win.

may be, maybe **May be** is a verb phrase. **Maybe** is an adverb meaning "perhaps."

The coach **may be** depressed after losing the game. **Maybe** we can cheer her up by taking her out to dinner.

neat In formal usage, avoid using **neat** to mean "pleasing" or "good."

Our treasurer had a **good** (not **neat**) idea for saving money.

nice **Nice** is an overworked adjective that is less informative than terms such as "appealing," "pleasant," and "polite."

Our waiter seemed **polite** (not **nice**) but shy.

nowhere near **Nowhere near** is informal for **not nearly.**

Although basketball is **not nearly** (not **nowhere near**) as violent as football, some people think it should, like football, be classified as a contact sport.

---

off of   Formal usage requires **off** or **from** rather than **off of.**

The police took several weapons **from** (not **off of**) the prisoners.

on account of   In formal usage, **because** is more appropriate.

They lost the contract **because** (not **on account of**) the competing firm promised to lower expenses.

ourselves   **Ourselves** refers to two or more persons. **Ourself** is used only in the special context of a king, queen, or Pope speaking in the first person singular.

Barry and I found **ourselves** suddenly in pitch dark.
"Let the traitors be brought before **ourself**," commanded Queen Elizabeth.

persecute, prosecute   **Persecute** means to "oppress" or "harass." **Prosecute** most commonly means to "carry out legal proceedings against."

Minorities are often **persecuted**.
The attorney general **prosecuted** everyone who had tried to bribe the police officers.

plus   The preposition **plus** means "in addition to" or "increased by." Avoid using it as a conjunction meaning "furthermore."

Reimbursement for travel includes the cost of an airline ticket **plus** the cost of transportation from the airport.
The consultants were late; **furthermore** (not **plus**), they were unprepared.

precede, proceed   **Precede** means "to come before." **Proceed** means "to go on" or "advance."

The senior class officers **preceded** their classmates into the auditorium.
The graduating class **proceeded** to their seats in single file.

principal, principle   The noun **principal** refers to a school's chief administrator or to an amount of money. The adjective **principal** means "first in importance." The noun **principle** means a "fundamental law" or "rule."

The **principal** disciplined those students who had participated in the food fight.
The **principal** reason for the committee's inaction was the indifference of its members.
The Magna Carta is founded on the **principle** that no individual is above the law.

prior to **Before** is less wordy.

We understood our minister's philosophy **before** (not **prior to**) her first sermon to us.

raise, rise **Raise** is a transitive verb meaning "to cause to be elevated." **Rise** is an intransitive verb meaning "to go up."

Many college students **raise** their grade point average in their junior and senior years.
Members of the press corps **rise** when the President enters a press conference.

real, really **Real** is an adjective meaning "actual" or "authentic." **Really** is an adverb meaning "in reality" or "actually." In formal usage, avoid using **real** as an adverb.

One thief brandished a **real** gun while the other held a toy pistol.
The customers were **really** (not **real**) afraid.

reason is that (because) Writing "the reason is because" is redundant. Write "the reason is that . . ." or "because" by itself.

The **reason** for the German failure to repulse the Allied invasion **was that** (not **because**) the Germans could not concentrate their forces.
The Germans failed to repulse the Allied invasion **because** they could not concentrate their forces.

in reference to, in regard to, relative to, with respect to

All these terms are wordy constructions for "about," "concerning," or "on."

We have corresponded **about** (not **relative to**) an advertising program.

sensual, sensuous   Both are adjectives meaning "pertaining to the senses," but **sensual** often suggests sexuality.

The dancer aroused the audience with suggestive, **sensual** movements.
The orchestra moved the audience with its **sensuous** music.

set, sit   **Set** is a transitive verb meaning "to place." **Sit** is an intransitive verb meaning "to take a seat."

Set your tray on the floor.
Yesterday we **set** all our house plants outside.
Sit down and relax.
Yesterday we **sat** by the stream.

shall, will   Modern usage requires little distinction between these two verbs. **Shall** is sometimes used to communicate determination. **Shall** is usually used in questions that serve as invitations.

Our foe **shall** not succeed.
Shall we try one more time?

so   Avoid using **so** to mean **very.**

The students' grades were **so** high, they all got **very** excited.

sometime, sometimes   The adverb **sometime** means "at an unknown time." The adverb **sometimes** means "occasionally."

The economists hope their prediction will come true **sometime** soon.
Sometimes the economy responds to government initiatives.

such a   To avoid vagueness, do not use **such a** as an intensifier unless it is followed by a subordinate clause beginning with **that.**

We had **such a** good time at the amusement park **that** we plan to return next year. (not We had **such a** good time!)

supposed to, used to   Always retain the **d.**

He use**d** to attend church regularly.
Mary was suppose**d** to bring the Frisbee.

sure   **Sure** is an adjective meaning "certain" or "reliable." It is nonstandard when it is used as an adverb.

To play shortstop you will need **sure** hands.
The laser **certainly** (not **sure**) has become a versatile device.

than, then   Do not confuse the conjunction **than** with the adverb **then.**

The brown bear is larger **than** (not **then**) the black bear.
First the male bear slouched into the clearing: **then** came the female followed by her cubs.

that, which, who   In strict formal usage, **that** serves in restrictive clauses, and **which** serves in non-restrictive clauses. Use **that** and **which** to refer to things and **who** to refer to humans.

Suicide is a response **that** only the most desperate people make.
Suicide, **which** is a desperate act, occurs most often during bad economic times.
The person **who** saved the mayor's life remained anonymous.

their, there, they're   **Their** is a possessive pronoun. **There** is an adverb or expletive. **They're** is a contraction of "they are."

We found a site where the ancient Indians had built **their** campfires.
It will be very expensive to go **there.**
They're unhappy because they don't have enough money.

try and   Formal usage requires **try to** rather than **try and.**

Often I **try to** imagine the future.

unique   **Unique** means "one and only" or "unlike any other." Avoid the informal meaning of "remarkable" or "strange." Avoid modifying it with "very" or "most" as if there were degrees of uniqueness.

Hammer's dancing style is **unique** (not **very unique**).
Our garden is **strikingly** (not **uniquely**) colorful in the spring.

utilize   **Utilize** is often a pretentious substitute for **use.**

Use (not **utilize**) your common sense.

very   This word is not needed as often as it is used. Omitting it lets an adjective or adverb speak for itself.

The dog was friendly and eager to please, but even its owners had to admit it was **ugly** (not **very ugly**).

wait for, wait on   To **wait for** is "to remain while expecting" something. To **wait on** is "to serve."

If you arrive before 7:00 a.m., you will have to **wait for** the store to open.
The short-order cook could **wait on** three people at the same time.

who's, whose   **Who's** is a contraction meaning **who is** or **who has; whose** is the possessive form of **who.**

She's a comedian **who's** funny and serious at the same time.
The voters will never approve of a candidate **whose** policies are so radical.

would of   Writing words as they are pronounced results in errors such as **would of** rather than **would have.**

your, you're   **Your** is the possessive pronoun and **you're** is the contraction of **you are.**

You're never going to learn Spanish if you try to do your homework while listening to rock music.

Glossary of Grammatical Terms

absolute phrase   A noun (or pronoun) and a participle that modify an entire clause.

The snow having melted, we found the landscape had lost all its charm.

active voice   See **voice.**

adjective   A word that modifies a noun or pronoun.

We sold that **rickety old** car.

Most adjectives can indicate degree:

COMPARATIVE DEGREE: old**er,** health**ier,** grand**er**
SUPERLATIVE DEGREE: old**est,** health**iest,** grand**est**

adjective clause   See **subordinate clause.**

adjective phrase   An infinitive phrase, a participial phrase, or a prepositional phrase that modifies a noun.

The plate **of spaghetti** lay untouched before the nervous child.

adverb   A word that modifies a verb, an adjective, or another adverb.

We dressed **quickly.**

adverb clause   See **subordinate clause.**

adverb phrase   A phrase (usually an infinitive or participial phrase) that modifies a verb, an adjective, or another adverb.

The assistant manager worked **behind the service counter.**

antecedent   The word or words to which a pronoun refers.

The **consultant** was so confident, **she** predicted that if **her** recommendations were followed, the company's profits would increase twenty percent. (**Consultant** is the *antecedent* of **she** and **her**.)

appositive   A noun or noun phrase that renames or further identifies the noun or pronoun it follows.

Dr. Wilson, **the superintendent of schools,** is an excellent golfer.

article   The noun-marking words **a** and **an,** which are *indefinite articles,* and **the,** which is the *definite article.* See **determiner.**

auxiliary verb   See **helping verb.**

case   The form nouns and pronouns take to help indicate a role in the sentence. Pronouns take a *subjective* form and an *objective* form, but nouns have the same form whether they are subjects or objects.

She (*subjective*) saw **him** (*objective*).

Nouns and pronouns take a *possessive* case form.

Mary's (*possessive noun*) pleasure is **your** (*possessive pronoun*) pain.

clause   A group of words comprising a subject and predicate. See **independent clause** and **subordinate clause.**

collective noun   A noun that names a group (**team, club, faculty**).

comparative degree   See **adjective.**

complement   A word or phrase that completes the predicate. *Subject complements* follow linking verbs and are also known as *predicate nouns* or *predicate adjectives.*

For several years, Norman was a **carpenter** (*predicate noun*).
The mayor was **tired** (*predicate adjective*).

Object complements are nouns or adjectives that follow and identify or modify a direct object.

We named our cat **Figaro.**
The jury found the defendant **guilty.**

See also **direct object** and **indirect object.**

complex sentence A sentence containing one independent clause and one or more subordinate clauses.

Although Stonehenge and other ancient stone structures may have been used as astronomical observatories (*subordinate clause*), no one can be sure (*independent clause*).

compound sentence A sentence composed of two or more independent clauses.

Thunder sounded faintly, so we turned the boat homeward. (two independent clauses joined by coordinating conjunction **so**)

compound-complex sentence A sentence containing two or more independent clauses and at least one subordinate clause.

While the customers fidgeted in their seats (*subordinate clause*), two violinists played their way through the restaurant (*independent clause*), and the manager went from table to table introducing himself (*independent clause*).

conjunction A word or word pair used to link elements within a sentence. See **coordinating conjunction, subordinating conjunction, conjunctive adverb,** and **correlative conjunction.**

conjunctive adverb An adverb that joins two independent clauses. Some conjunctive adverbs are **besides, consequently, however, nevertheless, therefore.**

There was a substantial amount of money in my account; **nevertheless,** the bank teller was reluctant to cash my check.

coordinating conjunction A word used to link words, phrases, and clauses of equivalent grammatical function. The coordinating conjunctions are **and, but, for, nor, or, so, yet.**

During the drought the crops wilted **and** died. (two verbs linked)
The book was a best seller, **but** the author did not want to make a movie of it. (two independent clauses linked)

correlative conjunction   A pair of words or phrases used to link words, phrases, and clauses of equivalent grammatical function. Common correlative conjunctions are **both . . . and, either . . . or, not only . . . but also.**

Both the puppy **and** its mother had to be wormed.
Either they go **or** I go.

demonstrative pronoun   A pronoun that points out. The demonstrative pronouns are **that, those, this, these.**

dependent clause   See **subordinate clause.**

determiner   A word that marks a noun. Determiners include articles, demonstrative pronouns, and possessive pronouns.

direct object   The word or words naming what a transitive verb acts upon.

The children invented **a new game.**

elliptical constructions   Clauses that omit words which can be understood from the context.

The retired pilot was convinced that he could still fly an airplane as well as any younger pilot (*could fly an airplane*).

expletive   A construction in which a clause begins with **it** or **there** and a form of **be.**

It was a mistake to leave the car's motor running.
There are few if any ways to succeed in business without taking risks.

gender   The classification of nouns and pronouns as *masculine* (**workman, he**), *feminine* (**actress, she**), and *neuter* (**theater, it**).

gerund The present participle (**-ing**) form of the verb used as a noun.

Sally believes that **reading** is more important than **sleeping.**

A *gerund phrase* is a gerund, its object, and any modifiers:

Losing the game so quickly bothered the players.

helping verb A verb used to complete a main verb: **be, can, do, has, have, may, must, ought,** etc.

My sister **has** kept over twenty nameless dogs.

idiom A customary expression that is figurative or that does not follow conventional patterns.

The customer **caught the waiter's eye.**
Bear in mind that we have only an hour of daylight left.

imperative See **mood.**

indefinite pronoun A pronoun that does not refer to a definite person or thing: **any, each, everyone, neither,** etc.

independent clause A group of words comprising a subject and a predicate that can be punctuated as a sentence or can be combined with other clauses.

The young comedian laughed uproariously, but **the audience remained impassive.** (two independent clauses joined by the coordinating conjunction **but**)

indicative See **mood.**

indirect object The word or words that name what indirectly receives the action of a transitive verb, usually a verb indicating a transfer.

Donna gave **her spouse** (*indirect object*) a **quick kiss** (*direct object*).

infinitive The uninflected form of the verb (listed first in the dictionary) that takes the infinitive marker **to: to be, to help, to propose.**

An *infinitive phrase* is an infinitive, an object, and any modifiers.

Infinitive phrases serve as nouns, adjectives, and adverbs.

Congress voted **to adjourn early.** (noun phrase as direct object)

inflection   An alteration to a word to communicate such ideas as time, case, or degree. The past tense inflection of **help** is **helped.** The objective case inflection of **he** is **him.** The comparative inflection of **happy** is **happier.**

intensifier   A modifier that indicates the degree of an adjective or adverb (**so** foolish, **rather** indignant, **very** quickly).

interjection   A grammatically independent word or phrase that expresses an exclamation or pure emotion: **Ah! Oh! Ouch! Please,** etc.

interrogative pronoun   A pronoun used in asking a question.

Whose coat is this?
What is the answer to our question?

irregular verb   See **verb.**

linking verb   See **verb.**

modifier   A word, phrase, or clause that describes another word, phrase, or clause. Adjectives, adverbs, and absolute phrases are modifiers, as are phrases and clauses used as adjectives and adverbs.

mood   A form taken by a verb to indicate the writer's perspective on the subject matter. The *indicative mood* is the most common form and is used in statements expressing actual or very probable circumstances.

Our school **uses** several means to identify gifted students.

The *imperative mood* is the form of commands.

Use the stairs in case of fire in a hotel.

The *subjunctive mood* is the form used to express conditions that are hypothetical, recommended, or contrary to fact.

I wish that I **were** a year older!
A state law mandates that every driver **use** seat belts.

nominal   A noun or any other word or word group that can serve as a noun.

To ask for help (*infinitive phrase*) is no disgrace.
Gaining the poet's permission (*gerund phrase*) to quote from her latest book was a long and frustrating task.
That he had bought a new suit did not mean **that he would dress up more often.** (two *subordinate clauses*)

nominative case   Another term for *subjective case;* see **case.**

nonrestrictive modifier   A word, phrase, or clause that does not limit the identity or meaning of what it modifies. Commas usually set off nonrestrictive modifiers. (Compare to **restrictive modifier**).

Germaine, **who has no talent for drawing,** was given the task of designing the decorations.

noun   A word that names. Most nouns can be made plural, usually by adding **-s** or **-es** (**parts, classes**). Nouns can also indicate possession, usually by adding **-'s** in the singular and **-s'** in the plural (the **day's** end, the **horses'** food). Nouns can serve as subjects, objects, and complements in sentences. A *proper noun* names a specific person or place: **Barry, Philadelphia.**

noun clause   A clause that, like a noun, serves as a subject, object, or complement. See **clause, nominal.**

The detective discovered **that the murderer was a relatively tall person.** (subordinate clause as direct object)
What remained after the tornado interested no one. (relative clause as subject)

noun phrase   A phrase that, like a noun, serves as a subject, object, or complement. See **phrase, nominal.**

Spending two weeks on duty in the Army Reserve (*gerund phrase as subject*) was not my idea of a vacation.

number   The forms taken by nouns, pronouns, and verbs to indicate singular or plural meaning: **a record, several records; a man, several men; she swims, they swim; he is, they are.**

object   A word or group of words naming what is affected by a verb, infinitive, or participle. See **direct object** and **indirect object.**

OBJECT OF VERB: Contractors built **these houses.**
OBJECT OF INFINITIVE: Allison wants to build **a house.**
OBJECT OF PARTICIPLE: I had never heard of one person building **a house.**

A word or word group directly following a preposition is called an *object of a preposition:*

We swam for **a while.**
The children hid in **the closet.**

participle   A word made from a verb, usually by adding **-ing, -d,** or **-ed** to the form which the verb takes in the infinitive. Irregular verbs use inflections other than **-d** or **-ed.** Participles may serve as adjectives, adverbs, and, with helping verbs, as part of a predicate. A **participial phrase** serves as a modifier and is composed of a participle plus its own objects and modifiers: The joggers returned, **dripping** (participle) **sweat** (object) **on the floor** (modifier).

PRESENT PARTICIPLE: **acting, living, thinking, running**
PAST PARTICIPLE: **acted, lived, thought, run**
PERFECT PARTICIPLE: **having acted, having lived, having thought, having run** (or **having been acted,** etc.)
PRESENT PARTICIPLE AS ADVERB: The runner slept, **dreaming** of success in the next day's race.

PAST PARTICIPLE AS ADJECTIVE: The night guard found three **unlocked** doors.

PARTICIPLES AS PART OF PREDICATE: Mike is **running** in the race.

passive voice See **voice.**

person The forms taken by pronouns and verbs to indicate someone speaking, someone spoken to, or someone or something spoken about.

	Singular	Plural
FIRST PERSON	**I am** ready.	**We are** ready.
SECOND PERSON	**You are** ready.	**You are** ready.
THIRD PERSON	**She, he, it is** ready.	**They are** ready.

phrase A group of words that serves as a unit, such as an object, a complement, or a modifier. A phrase lacks a subject, predicate, or both. See **absolute phrase, adjective phrase, noun phrase, gerund, infinitive, participle, preposition.**

predicate The verb, its auxiliaries and modifiers, plus any objects or complements.

The wind and hail **had completely destroyed our garden.**

predicate adjective See **complement.**

predicate nominative Also called the *predicate noun.* See **complement.**

preposition A word that indicates a relationship between a following noun, noun phrase, or pronoun (called the *object of the preposition*) and another part of the sentence. Prepositions include **at, behind, for, in, over, to, upon, with,** etc. The preposition and its object constitute a *prepositional phrase.* Prepositional phrases can serve as adjectives, adverbs, and nouns.

The fish **in this pond** (*adjective*) are not big enough to eat.
The moon shone **upon the fields** (*adverb*).
Toward the east (*noun*) was not the way we should have gone.

principal parts A verb's four basic forms: infinitive, present participle, past, past participle.

Infinitive	Present Participle	Past	Past Participle
(to) spill	spilling	spilled	spilled
(to) make	making	made	made
(to) see	seeing	saw	seen

pronoun A word that takes the place of a noun or noun phrase (the pronoun's antecedent). Pronouns are commonly classified in the following eight categories:

DEMONSTRATIVE: that, these
INDEFINITE: anybody, everyone
INTENSIVE: herself, yourself
INTERROGATIVE: what, which
PERSONAL: I, they
RECIPROCAL: each, other
REFLEXIVE: I myself, you yourself
RELATIVE: who, which, that

See **antecedent.**

proper noun See **noun.**

regular verb See **verb.**

relative clause A clause that has a relative pronoun as its subject. Relative clauses are a type of subordinate clause, and they usually serve as adjectives.

Houston is a city **that has no zoning codes.**

restrictive modifier A word, phrase, or clause that limits the identity or meaning of what it modifies. Restrictive modifiers are not set off by commas. (Compare to **nonrestrictive modifier.**)

A committee member **who has no talent for drawing** was given the task of designing the decorations.

sentence modifier A word or phrase that modifies the entire sentence.

Frankly, I am bored.

See **absolute phrase.**

simple sentence   A sentence composed of one clause.

We should make some plans.
The flock of geese returned.

subject   The noun or nominal about which the predicate makes a statement.

Horses canter.
The snow turned my car into a white hill.

The *simple subject* is the subject without its modifiers. The *complete subject* is the subject plus its modifiers.

The old broken broom leaning against the door is still useful. (**Broom** is the simple subject. **The old broken broom leaning against the door** is the complete subject.)

subordinate clause   A clause that serves as an adjective, adverb, or noun. A clause is subordinated by an introductory subordinating conjunction.

Shimmering under the sun were a dozen large puddles **that the storm had left behind.** (adjective clause)
If erosion continues at this rate, nothing will grow in this ground three years from now. (adverb clause)
The twins did not believe **that they would ever live apart from each other.** (noun clause)

subordinating conjunction   A conjunction that introduces a subordinate clause. Some subordinating conjunctions are **after, because, if, once, while.**

superlative degree   See **adjective.**

tense   The form of a verb that indicates the time of the verb's action or condition.

PRESENT	I think	PERFECT	I have thought
PAST	I thought	PAST PERFECT	I had thought

FUTURE I will think   FUTURE PERFECT I will have thought

transitive verb See **verb.**

verb A word or group of words indicating an action or condition. A *transitive verb* takes a direct object: Bees **spread** (verb) **pollen** (direct object). A *linking verb* connects a subject to a complement: She **became** (linking verb) **a star** (complement). An *intransitive verb* does not take an object or a complement: The professor **lectured** (intransitive verb). *Regular verbs* add **-d** or **-ed** to the infinitive form to make the past tense and the past participle. *Irregular verbs* form the past tense, the past participle, or both, in other ways.

	Present	Past	Past Participle
REGULAR VERBS	happen	happened	happened
	rule	ruled	ruled
	respond	responded	responded
IRREGULAR VERBS	fight	fought	fought
	make	made	made
	is	was	been

verb phrase A verb plus at least one helping verb.

The campers **will eat** three hearty means each day.
We **had been accustomed** to a raucous environment.

Some grammarians use *verb phrase* to mean the same as *predicate.*

verbal A form of a verb used as a noun, adjective, or adverb. Gerunds, infinitives, and participles are verbals.

Swimming (*gerund*) gives me an appetite.
To hope (*infinitive*) sometimes requires courage.

voice the function of a transitive verb that indicates whether the subject of the verb acts or is acted upon.

ACTIVE VOICE: As usual, Al caught only tiny fish.
PASSIVE VOICE: As usual, only tiny fish were caught by Al.

Index

Deity, references to, 269
Deliveryman, 170
Demonstrative pronouns, 104, 106, 322–323
Denotation, 160–161, 165
Dependent clauses, 134, 135
Descent, 362
Description, 47–48
Desért, 363
Désert, 363
Dessert, 363
Destiny, 166
Determiners, noun, 99
Dewey Decimal System, 398
Dialog Information Service, 407
Dictionaries, 161–163, 319, 356
  biographical, 401, 402
Direct address, 223
Direct object, 120
Discreet, 363
Discrete, 363
Dissent, 362
Dissertations, citing abstracts of, 419
Do, 94, 95
Draft, 160–161
  exploratory, 76
  final, 445–446
  rough, 433–435, 444
  sample essay, 376–378
Draft copy, print out, 85
Drama, writing about, 370–372

Each, 302
Editing, 5, 78–79
Editorials, citing, 419
Effect, 362
E.g., 275
Either . . . or, 112, 296, 303–304, 348–349
Element, 165
Elicit, 363

Ellipsis mark, 254–255, 433
Elliptical clauses, 136, 327–328
Emigrate, 363
Emphasis, 72, 128, 242, 267
  exclamation point for, 217–218
  writing with, 194–198
Empty phrases, 191–192
Enclosure list, for business letters, 388
Encyclopedias, 401
  forms for citing articles in, 420
Ensure, 363
Episode, 46
Essay, composing, 1–6. *See also* Writing
Essay examinations, 380–385
Essential, 165
Et al., 276
Etc., 276
Etymology
  dictionary conventions, 163
  and spelling, 356
Euphemisms, 184
Every, 302
Everybody, 302
Everyone, 294, 302
Evidence, 25
Except, 362
Exclamation point, 217–218, 251
Expect, 165
Expletive constructions, 124, 179, 189–190, 305
Expletives, 124
Exposition, 10, 11, 68
Expressive writing, 11–12

Factor, 165
Fallacies, avoiding, 32–35
False choice, 34
Famous, 165
Fate, 166

and colon use, 239
in quotations, 250
Persecute, 363
Persona, 15–16
Personal pronouns, 102–103,
    283–285, 323–324
Personification, 175–176
Persuasion, 9–10, 11, 50–51
Photocopying references, 424
Phrases as modifiers, 129–130.
    See also Absolute phrase;
    Infinitive phrase; Participial
    phrase; Prepositional phrase
    effects of words, and 131–132
Place holders, 124
Place names, 269
Plagiarism, avoiding, 251–252,
    427–429
Plan, 166
Planning, 4
Plays, citing, 442–443
Plot, in literature, 369–370
Plurals
    forming, 360–361
    of letters, punctuating, 259
    of nouns, punctuating, 258
    of pronouns, 102
Poetic conventions, 13
Poetic drama, 260
Poetry
    punctuation used with, 260
    quoting or paraphrasing,
        441–442
    writing about, 372–374
Policeman, 170
Possessive case, 103
    inflections, 287–288
    punctuation used with, 258,
        259
Possessive pronouns, 106, 259
Post-hoc fallacy, 32
Predicate, 118

Predicate adjective, 106
Preface, citing references from,
    415
Prefixes, 109, 356
    punctuation used with, 262
    and spelling, 357
Premise, 28
Prepositional phrases
    dangling modifiers in, 327–328
    defined, 110, 129
    nominal, 140, 179
Prepositions, 110, 129
    defined, 110
    object of, 110
Present participle, 92, 96, 129
Present subjunctive, 97
Present tense, 95, 122
Pretentious language, 183
Prewriting, 4
Primary sources, 397
Principal, 363
Principal parts, 91
Principle, 363
Procedure, specifying steps in,
    45
Programs, word-processing,
    81–85
Progressive tenses, 95
Pronoun(s), 101–105
    as adjectives, 106
    -antecedent disagreement,
        292–296
    antecedents, 321–324
    case forms of, 282–287
    defined, 101
    demonstrative, 104, 106
    first person, 102
    indefinite, 104
    intensive, 103–104
    interrogative, 105
    nonsexist, 167–169
    personal, 102–103